MONEY BY INTERN

HOW TO GET STARTED MAKING MONEY ONLINE

VOLUME 2 OF 2

By Burt Anderson

Amazon Paperback

ISBN: 978-1-893257-78-8   First Edition
Copyright 2012   Lions Pride Publishing Co., LLC

Every effort has been made to make this book as complete and accurate as possible. However, there may be mistakes in typography or content. Also, this book contains information on earning internet income only up to the publishing date. Therefore this document should be used as a guide only - - - not as a definitive source of internet income information.

This book is for information purposes only and does not impart legal, accounting, financial or any other form of business advice to readers who must consult their own

current or historical facts. Words used such as "anticipate", "expect", "project", "estimate", "plan", "believe", "intend" and other words and phrases of similar meaning might be used in conjunction with discussions of potential earnings or financial performance.

The use of our information, products and services should be based on your own due diligence. You agree that neither the Author nor Publisher is liable for any success or failure of your business that is directly or indirectly related to the purchase and use of our information, products and services.

To my beautiful wife Melanie, whose patience and understanding allows me endless hours writing on the computer while she works a demanding 9 to 5 and still keeps our household from falling apart!

To Napoleon Hill for writing *Think and Grow Rich,* the book that can change lives.

And to the late internet commerce genius and visionary Cory Rudl who paved the way in the '90s for the countless internet millionaires that followed. Without his wisdom and personal inspiration I would never have embarked on my successful personal cyber- journey.

INDEX – VOLUME 2 OF 2

You are about to embark on the adventure of a lifetime!

For the past month I worked on this book about eighteen hours a day, every day. When I began I had no idea how long it might end up being. As it turned out, it became a far too long to fit into a single book. I decided to split it into two Volumes, each designed to stand alone, each designed to contain key information of equal value to newbie and experienced internet marketer alike.

Each Volume is in itself a rather long book, 89,000 words give or take a few. To someone new to internet commerce, this must seem pretty overwhelming. I was torn between splitting this book up even further into a number of smaller books, a "series" if you will. From a commercial standpoint I could surely have made more money had I done so. (Believe it or not writers have to eat too!)   But I decided to make it a two volume compendium of everything I have learned over the past decade and a half, and to allow the reader to pick and choose to decide which path to internet wealth to follow. Either Volume can stand alone.

This necessitated putting some information into each Volume that exactly duplicates that same information in the other Volume. Chapters 1 through 3, and my Conclusions, along with the obligatory "About the Author", and a useful Glossary, needed to appear in each Volume. In this manner it is less important for anyone, especially a newbie, to purchase both Volumes to quickly establish an internet business. Either Volume will suffice.

Over the years I have purchased countless internet courses for anywhere from $197.00 to $2,500.00. I still have all of them in my library. **I am certain that either Volume of this book, which you have purchased at a very tiny fraction of the value of the information it contains, will prove to be the best purchase you have**

ever made! Please do not judge their **value** by their low price.

My associates believe I have lost my mind to sell these books so inexpensively. I disagree. It is my genuine intention to expose as many unemployed and under-employed individuals as possible to the incredible opportunity to earn a living offered to everyone by the internet. I'm 75, very comfortable, and well past the time when I need to earn a few extra bucks. I want this book to be my legacy. If I can help **one** individual to reach the American Dream that will be great. If I can help hundreds, or even thousands, I will consider my life to have found its true purpose.

With all that said, I believe I should list below the Chapters in this Volume 2 that are best suited for persons at various levels of internet experience. That is not to say that the best approach would not be for you to at least read through the entire book once, and then return to the Chapters that seemed most appealing. This can, however, serve as your guide.

<u>FOR EVERYONE:</u> Chapters 1, 2, 3, CONCLUSION. <u>*READ THESE FIRST!!!*</u>

<u>FOR A NEWBIE WANTING TO EARN MONEY QUICKLY:</u>

Chapters 44, 45, 46.

IF YOU, AS SOMEONE UNFAMILIAR WITH THE INTERNET AND NEEDING TO EARN MONEY AS QUICKLY AS POSSIBLE, FOCUS 100% OF YOUR EFFORTS ON THE ABOVE SEVEN CHAPTERS, YOU SHOULD BE ABLE TO BEGIN EARNING INTERNET CASH QUICKLY WITH AN ABSOLUTE MINIMUM OF INVESTMENT.

<u>FOR A NEWBIE WANTING TO WORK A TINY BIT HARDER AND MAKE A LOT MORE MONEY:</u>

Chapter 22, 23, 24, 26, 40.

FOR THE NEWBIE WHO REALLY ENJOYS SOCIAL SITE INTERACTION:

Chapters 35, 36, 37, 38.

FOR A NEWBIE OR ADVANCED READER WHO WANTS TO BE AN AUTHOR:

Chapters 28, 29, 30, 31, 32, 33, 34.

FOR THE NOT-SO-NEWBIE: Chapters 25, 39, 41, 42.

FOR ADVANCED READERS: Chapters 27, 48, 49.

FOR THE MOST ADVANCED READERS:

Chapters 43, 47, 50.

Do not lose site of the fact that most internet entrepreneurs (infopreneurs) engage in most or all of the above pursuits at the same time. It is the **combined** multiple streams of internet income that merge to become a mighty river of internet wealth.

It is my most sincere hope that you will take up the challenge of reading and learning this material. If you truly want the freedom of earning a very good, perhaps spectacular, income from the comfort of your home, you have before you the blueprint for that success.

GodSpeed!

WHAT IS NEW IN VOLUME 1 OF 2   [CHAPTER 4 – 21]:

MODULE TWO – NICHE MARKETING
CHAPTER 4: FINDING YOUR BIG-MONEY NICHE
CHAPTER 5.   KEYWORD SEARCH FOR TOP DOLLARS
CHAPTER 6: CREATING FAST-SELLING VIRTUAL PRODUCTS

MODULE ONE – INTRODUCTION

CHAPTER 1: YOUR SUCCESS BLUEPRINT

CHAPTER 2:   HOW TO MAKE A WONDERFUL LIVING FROM HOME

CHAPTER 3:   GET WEALTHY WHILE STAYING OUT OF TROUBLE

CHAPTER 1

YOUR SUCCESS BLUEPRINT

I wrote this Chapter in an effort to create a mind-set through which perhaps you can extract real life-changing value from the many pages of this "how-to" internet instruction manual.

In 1934 a brilliant author named Napoleon Hill published a book titled: "*Think and Grow Rich*". Every salesperson and marketer should own a copy, and should read it and re-read it frequently. It is as valid today as it was seventy-five years ago. If you do not already own a copy, get one. You can download it for free at Amazon last time I checked. If you do own a copy, even if you read it recently, reading this short Chapter will help reinforce Mr. Hill's life-changing philosophy.

I live an extremely comfortable life. My wife and I want for little. Almost everything we have achieved over the years we attribute largely to the words of wisdom penned by Mr. Hill. I first read his book in 1955. It changed my life, and it can change yours. **So can internet commerce.**

What I am writing in this Chapter is a brief summary of the ideas and concepts contained in Hill's book that I personally have found to be the most useful. Reflect deeply on each gem of wisdom. There's very little fluff offered here. They may not be exact quotes, and I have added a few ideas from other great minds, but I have lived by and applied this wisdom for decades with great success.

Mr. Hill had profound insight on higher education. He states that formal schooling does very little more than to put one in the mind set to learn how to **acquire** practical knowledge. Pleasantly drifting through an unspecified academic curriculum without purpose or without a definite future course of action (true of the vast majority of college students, especially the "BA" crowd) is a total waste of time and money. He states: "You do not get any **practical** knowledge in college....NONE."

Personally possessing a Bachelor of Science (BS), a Master of Business Administration (MBA), and a useless PhD, I could not agree more than I do with Mr. Hill's analysis. I truly never learned anything in college that could be directly applied to any real-world job. I wasted countless hours in night-school and more money than I care to calculate.
Hill points out that college professors specialize in teaching knowledge, but do not specialize in teaching the **USE** of knowledge. Knowledge itself is not power, it is **POTENTIAL** power. It becomes power only if and when it is organized into definite plans of action and directed to a definite worthy end. Knowledge has no value except that which can be gained from its application towards that end.

Any man is educated once he knows where to get knowledge when he needs it (for example this book) and how to organize that knowledge into definite plans of action. As knowledge is acquired it must be organized and put into use for some definite purpose.

A young Abraham Lincoln, arguably our greatest President, lived by one rule: "I will study and get ready and someday my chance will come". He recognized the need for practical knowledge. He studied, learned, and became a great President.

It pays to know how to <u>purchase</u> knowledge. There is no fixed price for sound ideas. Behind all sound ideas is **specialized** knowledge. This is why so many internet entrepreneurs have become wealthy. <u>This is why I wrote this book of specialized knowledge.</u>

Hill lists the six great fears of every human being. Understanding human fears can guide your internet marketing efforts, because addressing and in some way ameliorating these fears with your product offerings is your key to marketing success:

The Fear Of Poverty (The need to make money);

The Fear Of Criticism (The need for praise and envy by others);

The Fear Of Ill Health (The need for better health);

The Fear Of Loss Of Love (The need to find love);

The Fear Of Old Age (The need to extend one's life);

The Fear Of Death (The desire to live forever).

Some studies have suggested that The Fear Of Public Speaking is stronger than any of these, but Mr. Hill failed to mention that!

The fear of poverty manifests itself through indifference, indecision, doubt, worry, over-caution, and procrastination. Procrastination, the opposite of decision, is a common enemy that everyone must conquer. **Both** poverty and riches are the offspring of thought.

Hill states that ALL fears are nothing more than states of mind, and as such are subject to control and direction. The author Henley penned famously: "I am the master of my fate, I am the captain of my soul". Hill adds: "...because we all have the power to **control** our thoughts. Every human being has the ability to completely control his own mind".

Hill points out that even more powerful than the six human fears listed above is one's own **SUSCEPTABILITY TO NEGATIVE INFLUENCES.** Without a doubt the most common weakness of all human beings is the destructive habit of leaving their minds open to the negative influence of other people.

Strip such "low tone" (a Scientology expression) people from your life and you derive immense benefits. (Apparently Mr. Hill was a Scientologist before L. Ron Hubbard stole his ideas!).

Never forget: **SUCCESSFUL PEOPLE DO WHAT THEIR CRITICS SAY CAN'T BE DONE..........EVERY DAY**! Your critics greatest fear is that you, God forbid, might actually succeed.

Hill outlines six steps to personal riches. He credits Dale Carnegie for teaching these steps to him, and points out that the amazing inventor
Thomas Edison adhered religiously to this formula:

Fix in your mind the exact amount of riches you desire;

Determine what sacrifices you are willing to give in return for them;
Establish a definite date to possess them;

Create a definite plan and begin immediately (ready or not) to put this plan into action;

Write out the above steps **in longhand.**

That's the easy part! Hill then insists that twice a day you read aloud your written statement. Do this once before bedtime, and again once on rising in the morning. As you read, see and feel and believe yourself **already** in possession of the riches.

The key is to create in your mind a burning desire for a definite form of riches. Riches can be financial, spiritual, mental or material. Success comes to those who become **SUCCESS CONSCIOUS**. Failure comes to those who indifferently allow themselves to become **FAILURE CONSCIOUS.**

You must cultivate a persistence that does not even **recognize** failure as a possibility. The three most important roads to riches are **persistence, persistence and persistence!**

Every failure brings with it the seed of an equivalent success. Every adversity, every failure, and every heartache carries with it the seed of an equivalent or greater benefit. **No one is ever defeated until defeat is accepted as a reality. There are no limitations to the human mind except those we acknowledge.**

Forty years ago I attended an excellent motivational seminar run by a gentleman named Joel Weldon. He handed out to his audience a great marketing gimmick to get his point across. It was a tin can with a label that read: **"Success Comes In Cans And Not In Cannots".** I still have the can on my desk. I have never forgotten that profound wisdom. Neither should you. Truer words were never spoken.
Weldon added: "Forget the excuses. Accept responsibility. And take ACTION! **Whether you think you can or you can't, you're right!".**

Basketball great Michael Jordan is credited with saying: "Most people fail because they make up imaginary excuses (the "cannots") The only person that can stop you is yourself." Don't make up excuses. Don't focus on CANNOTS. You CAN do anything you make up your mind to do.

Will every plan you start succeed? Probably not. Mine certainly did not. Thomas Edison tried hundreds of filament materials for his light bulb before achieving success and changing the world! If the first plan you adopt does not work replace it with a new plan. If the new plan fails to work replace it with another. Lack of persistence is why most fail. **No man is ever whipped until he quits in his own mind.**

A quitter never wins and a winner never quits. The only "good break" anyone can afford to rely upon are those self-made breaks brought about through persistence. <u>Riches do not respond to wishes.</u> They respond only to definite plans backed by definite desires through constant persistence.

Definiteness of purpose is the starting point from which one MUST begin. Ideas can be transmuted into riches through the power of definite purpose plus definite plans.

And remember, the starting point of all achievement is **desire**. Anyone can <u>wish</u> for riches, and most people do, but only a few recognize that a definite plan plus a burning <u>desire</u> for riches are the only dependable means of accumulating wealth.

It is often said that "good things come to those who wait". In my experience **BETTER** things come to those who **REFUSE** to wait. Wait not for someone else to decide to make something happen. You can make it happen by yourself, **NOW**.

Desperation can be a very positive influence. Leaving oneself with no possible way of retreat you either win or perish. Hill points out historic examples of how this philosophy won military battles in the past. Winston Churchill is credited with saying: "The only sure way to accomplish something positive is to create a situation that is so untenable that you must solve it or perish".
Napoleon Hill stated one overriding truism: "**WHATEVER THE MIND OF MAN CAN CONCEIVE AND BELIEVE IT CAN ACHIEVE. Thoughts are things! And powerful things at that, when mixed with definiteness of purpose, and burning desire, can be translated into riches.**"

Earle Nightengale, a great motivational speaker, used the phrase: "You are what you think about". It was the keynote phrase of his "The Strangest Secret" seminar.

All achievement, all earned riches, have their beginning in an idea. More gold has been mined from the thoughts of man than has ever been taken from the earth. <u>One sound idea is all you need to achieve success.</u> One book, such as the one you are reading, can make all the difference in the world.

Hill is convinced that once riches begin to come they come so quickly, in such great abundance, that one wonders where they had been hiding during all those lean years. When one is truly ready for riches they magically put in their appearance. I know this was true in my life. It can be true in yours, through internet commerce, through this book.

Do not ever envy those who have become great. Success is to be envied, not reviled. Hill states that "Experience has taught me that the next best thing to being truly great is to emulate the great, by feeling and action, as nearly as possible". The great always have persistence and a determination to repel failure. They make definite plans and execute them <u>without hesitation.</u> Emulate, not envy, nor hate, these individuals. Don't fall into the trap of today's "class warfare" rhetoric as is being waged constantly by various political figures.

Remember: Life is like a checkerboard. The player opposite the board from you is TIME. You are playing against an opponent who will not tolerate indecision. If you hesitate to move, or fail to move quickly, your pieces will be wiped off the board by time. Take action NOW!

<u>Get involved in internet commerce today. Read this book, choose your path, and ACT ON IT.</u>

Good luck!

CHAPTER 2

HOW TO MAKE A WONDERFUL LIVING FROM HOME

UNEMPLOYED? UNDER EMPLOYED?
YOU HAVE NO EXCUSES WHATSOEVER!

I've often said: "I'd gladly participate in any experiment that would test the effects on me of sudden great wealth". Can money buy happiness? All I ask is the chance to prove it can't! **If you share these feelings, this book is for you.** What is the information in this book worth? Let me give you an idea of what it would cost you for at least one of the academic internet marketing college credentials you can actually earn on-line while sitting at home.

For a mere **$21,000.00** (!!!!!) one fully accredited on-line University will issue you seven different "Certificates of Achievement" for completion of online "eight-week or less" internet commerce courses they offer. I assume these are really super-great courses. They'd better be for that kind of money. **At that rate this 300+ page book would be a major bargain at $1,997.00!**

The irony is that all of the many internet millionaires I know invested at the most a few hundred dollars to get started. Others, the so-called "Bum Marketers", didn't even invest a dime! Some of these earned their first million dollars within two years. Their "Certificates of Achievement" are their bank statements!

At first glance this book might look overwhelming. I grant you that there is a lot of information you can eventually absorb, but taken in little bites (and bytes!) it really is not at all difficult. Warren Buffett is credited with saying: "There seems to be some perverse human characteristic that likes to make easy things difficult".   Just take it slow and **let it be easy**.

Making serious money marketing on the internet is NOT difficult, unless you decide to make it so. Don't. Many newbies starting with zero knowledge and few if any liquid assets have become very successful internet entrepreneurs. It just takes a bit of time and patience.

The more people you listen to, the more products you buy, the more confused you are likely to become! Many newbies buy lots of stuff from dozens of different "gurus", seeking the magic silver bullet to internet riches. What they end up with is lots of excellent information and not a clue what to do with it. It is called the "Paralysis of Analysis".

Are you perhaps gainfully employed but sick of the nine to five rat race? Or perhaps working two jobs to make ends meet? I recall seeing a cartoon years ago, probably in the *New Yorker*. There's a bum sitting on a bench in a large city watching masses of business-clad people racing to and fro. He asks the simple hypothetical question to no one in particular: "Who's Winning?" Profound. These days the answer apparently is: "No One". No one, that is, except internet entrepreneurs! <u>They are today's winners in a very difficult employment market.</u>

Being an internet entrepreneur is not just about making money. Working from home, far from the nine-to-five rat race, is all about **you** being able to do what **you** want, whenever **you** want, wherever **you** want, with whomever **you** want, for as <u>long</u> as **you** want. <u>Internet commerce is, in my opinion, about making the most money you can with the greatest possible freedom.</u> Nothing could be more American!

It is reported that unemployment in the United States, if one includes those who have simply "given up looking", today may top twenty percent. The "official" government figure is stated as being well under half of that, but still terribly high. The "safety net" created by various government stipends and food stamps has led some to simply adjust their lifestyles accordingly and survive as long as possible without working at all or even looking for a job.

I am absolutely dumbfounded by certain behavior I see all around me. There are countless unemployed people receiving decent monthly checks, and receiving food stamp cards, and making ends meet quite well. In theory I have absolutely no problem at all with a social safety net for the **truly** needy due to unforeseen negative circumstances not of their own doing.

What I do have a BIG problem with is that many, if not most of these on-the-dole people see themselves as sort of "temporarily-retired". They figure that if their benefits ever do give out they will eventually need to find work. Until then they choose to make zero effort to find employment. That is especially true if the employment they might find pays them even less than their "free" income.

They sit around and watch TV and smoke and drink beer and get fat, and love every minute of it. I know quite a few that have greatly lowered their golf handicap! What has happened to American initiative? What are we becoming? "To each according to his needs; from each according to his ability to pay." Isn't that Marxist? Very sad.

Many of these "poor and/or unemployed" folks of whom I speak have cell phones and iPads and iPods, and Kindles, and cable TV, and decent cars. They spend untold thousands on cigarettes and beer. They live as well as **aristocrats**, the very top few percent do, in most of the 200+ under-developed countries in the world. Yet they are counted as "poor" here in the USA. **They are not poor**. The truly poor starve to death. No one in America dies of starvation unless they choose to do so. Few if any make that choice.

I've tried to share with many of these folks the information in this book. The most common response I hear is: "I can't afford to do that".   This is followed closely by: "I don't know anything about computers". But when probed, the clear reason is: "I'm comfortable, leave me the hell alone". Remarkable.

I am certain that there are some unemployed individuals really trying as best they can to support their families. They wish they had a real full-time job. Many work multiple menial jobs to make ends meet. It has reportedly caused a large increase in the number of persons diagnosed as clinically depressed. **It is these people who are really trying to get out from under by working hard with whom I wish the most that I could share this how-to book of internet commerce knowledge.**

FACTS:

Computer knowledge? You need virtually none.

Up front money? You need virtually none.

Must one have money to start an internet business and earn a decent living income? NO. It <u>can</u> be done with virtually <u>zero dollars</u>, no money at all up front . Sure, it's harder and slower that way, but quite doable. And I share how this can be accomplished in the pages of this book.

For the annual cost of a daily pack of cigarettes or a few less brewskies one can buy everything ever needed to succeed on-line <u>big time</u>. A $500 investment spread out over a year, much of it one-time investments, can provide everything needed to quickly create and run a prosperous internet business that can provide income for the rest of your life.

The time the average person spends watching mindless TV programs and sending Tweets and interacting with "friends" on Facebook and watching moronic videos on YouTube and pinning nonsense on Pinterest is reported to be thousands of hours a year. Applying a portion of this time to developing an internet business would open up the opportunity to achieve the American Dream that most complain is unattainable because of our "bad economy". I say: "Hogwash".

Some will say they just don't have very good luck. To those I say that luck is where opportunity and creativity meet. You make your own luck, not wait for it to drop out of the heavens. Thomas Jefferson said: " I'm a great believer in luck, and I find the harder I work the more I have of it." **The American Dream is attainable, without luck, and I can show you how.**

I can say unequivocally that **THERE IS NO EXCUSE FOR ANY MENTALLY-CAPABLE REASONABLY-LITERATE PERSON EVER BEING UNEMPLOYED.** The reality of internet commerce has created the opportunity for almost anyone to earn a very good living working from home in front of a computer screen.

Being unable to read English at a high school level, being unable to understand and follow simple English-language instructions, and being unwilling to work hard are the only disqualifiers I can think of. **No one else *need* ever be unemployed or under-employed.**

It is absolutely true that in the present economy, and for the foreseeable future, conventional jobs in both the private and public sectors will continue to be difficult to find or keep. This is especially true for those with limited formal education or a lack of specific skill sets. **But EVERYONE has absolutely unlimited employment opportunities working from home using a computer.**   I am certain that after you read this book you will believe this to be true.

I once saw a cartoon where two guys are sitting at a bar and one says to the other: "Not only am I not on line, I don't even know what 'on line' means"! And to be sure there are many who know nothing about computers, or the power of the internet, or the unlimited opportunities offered by internet commerce.

Fortunately, very basic beginner's training (as in the "For Idiots" book series) is available for FREE from any public library. Any large bookstore has many books for sale that are written for individuals who are totally clueless about computers. If you fall into that "clueless" category, your first step is to learn how to use a computer. It is not rocket science. The average kid in kindergarten does it. So can you.

The good news is that the actual amount of computer knowledge needed to be successful making money from home is <u>very small</u>. Basically all you need to know is how to turn the computer on and learn how to access and "surf" (look around) the internet, **and** follow the basic information found in an internet commerce "how-to" book such as this one.

Once one reaches that small level of competence all that is needed is a set of step-by-step instructions on the many ways one can make money sitting in front of a computer screen. **<u>I share these many ways in this how-to internet commerce book.</u>**

If you are reading this Chapter and already possess basic computer skills so much the better. You are well on your way to making as much money as the effort you are willing to expend will allow. If you already have advanced computer skills you may find some of the material in this book a bit elementary, but you can easily skim through the basics.

If you are one of many who have tried in the past to earn money using your computer and failed to do so to the full extent you hoped, there are many reasons why this might be true. **Do not be discouraged.** Just pretend you know nothing at all, start from scratch applying the techniques shared in this book, and you just might be amazed!

As pointed out earlier, success with internet commerce requires three things**: PERSISTANCE, PERSISTANCE, and PERSISTANCE!** Most persons fail at almost anything new because they give up too easily.

There is no "free lunch*", **EVER**. It is not at all difficult to make money from home sitting at your kitchen table in front of a computer screen if you have a willingness to learn, a willingness to work hard, and have **persistence.** What I most like about internet marketing is that it is like pulling cash out of your head simply by knowing the right steps to take.

This how-to internet commerce book is the distillation of knowledge gained over the past sixteen years. I also bring a certain amount of additional background knowledge into the mix. Aside from an academic engineering and marketing background, I have been a real estate broker for over thirty years, securities principal for twenty, and licensed for ten years or more in insurance and mortgages. And I've been a prolific published author since 1970. All of this background helps me break down seemingly difficult and complicated material into easily handled step-by-step bites.

Every individual has a different set of life-skills. Some have almost none. Because of this, every individual will have a different experience learning how to make money with a computer working from home. Sadly, many will fail because they are simply not sufficiently motivated to even give it a try or to stick with it when initial progress may seem painfully slow.

Do not be misled by ads you might see on TV or hear on the radio or read in the media that would lead you to believe that riches await you for simply investing a few hours a week in some computer internet marketing program or other. **Nothing could be farther from the truth**. If there is a magic bullet to internet success I've yet to find it, and I have tried!

It **is** true that after some period of time, once you have learned many of the basics and set everything up so that it all virtually runs itself you can spend far less time than you must spend initially. Eventually you will be able to take many days or even weeks off at any time you want and it will have virtually no effect on your residual internet commerce income. You can sit on a beach in paradise somewhere with a laptop and watch the money coming in to your accounts and do little else. It took me years to reach that point. Was it worth it? Damn skippy!

There is no limit to the amount of money one can make in internet commerce of one kind or the other using a computer from the comfort of one's home. Thousands of individuals are reported to have proven that fact beyond a doubt. The purpose of this book is to share with you what my wife and I have learned over the past sixteen years. I hope to provide you with an awareness of the many creative ways that anyone, regardless of formal education, background, or prior computer knowledge, can make a wonderful living with a personal computer from the comfort of their home.

Many millionaires have been created in the past decade applying one or more of the techniques shared in this book. I personally <u>know</u> (not know OF) a number of them. I know <u>of</u> a great many more. Some are quite famous in internet commerce circles. Many more go about their profitable internet business entirely "under the radar". Personally I prefer the latter approach, which I why I publish under a number of different pen-names.

Aside from those who have made millions, many others have simply supplemented their incomes, or made their lives much easier. Some have paid off their bills. Others have bought the luxuries they only previously dreamed about. A few I know have been able to start charitable foundations to help those less fortunate than themselves. This latter pursuit is presently my personal goal, though for years non-altruistic "survival" topped the list!

Keep this in mind: **THIS BOOK IS ABSOLUTELY NOT INTENDED TO OFFER A "GET RICH QUICK" SCHEME.** If such a thing exists I have never found it, and believe me I have looked! Hard. It is, however, a very real potential vocation, the income from which can exceed anything you have ever earned in the past from a typical 9 to 5.

The reason this book isn't many thousands of pages long....and well it could be...is that I expect you, no matter how new to internet commerce, to be able to self-navigate the various websites I suggest that you visit. Remember to enter "http://www." before all of the website addresses that I suggest you visit (although most browsers today will enter the " http://www." for you). As you progress you will find a vast amount of valuable information on line. I especially find that periodically accessing *Website Magazine* at websitemagazine.com keeps me up to date on the rapidly changing world of internet commerce.

I did not feel the need to include computer "screen shots" in this book. These can fill up ten pages instead of ten lines of descriptive text. Any website worth visiting has excellent tutorials, often videos, and extensive FAQs (Frequently Asked Questions), and discussion forums. I do not need to add illustrations from these sites to make this book ten times longer than it already is or needs to be. I assume you can browse to a website and read it for yourself. (Please don't prove me wrong!)

I could spend thousands of extra pages describing to you everything that I can simply point you to online. There is no reason for you to pay me for including that information. I have seen 5,000+ page internet courses that contain far less real usable information than I am sharing with you in this much shorter book.

You will find, however, that certain information is repeated, often even within the same Chapter. This was not done to lengthen the book! If I believe it is particularly important information it will be repeated as often as I feel it is necessary for emphasis.

If you want an at-home internet business to be a full-time great paying job it will take your full-time commitment. Don't forget, a conventional nine-to-five job, including commute time, is a ten to twelve hour a day commitment, five days a week. Your internet commerce job will also require a serious time commitment for you to make comparable money. Can lots of money be made in your spare time? Yes. It will just take a lot longer to make it happen without a full-time effort.

At least at the beginning of your quest for internet riches you could well need to devote twelve or more hours a day seven days a week for a couple of months. The good news is that it gets MUCH easier as you gain some experience.

After six months to a year many successful internet commerce entrepreneurs find themselves earning far more money than they ever have or ever dreamed possible. They often find that they are devoting less time than the normal nine-to-five demands. **It is those first months of commitment that can make the difference.**

Remember: Every day millions of innocent people are forced from their homes by a disaster called "work". You need not be one of them. You are on the edge of a cliff standing on the brink of something called "the rest of your life". Don't ask: "Should I proceed?". And don't jump off! Just back off the cliff, get off your duff, and simply get in gear!

I'm a si-fi fan big time. I love Star Wars. The single most profound dialog occurs when Yoda explains to Luke that: "There is no try. There is either do or not do." This may have been inspired by Winston Churchill's WWII assertion that to get anything serious accomplished you need to set up a scenario wherein you have no choice but to succeed.

Unemployed? Underemployed? Hate your job? Need more money? Yoda's and Churchil's profound statements relate directly to you.

You do not even need to own a computer. Almost any library has computers connected to high-speed networks that can be used at no cost. They will even instruct you on how to use it! If you do not own a computer and want to do so, most computer stores sell excellent used computers at very reasonable prices, often well under a hundred dollars.

For a hundred dollars or less you should be able to find "last year's model", which is more than adequate for your purposes. In fact, most five-year-old computers will do just fine, at least until you have a thriving on-line business, at which time dropping a few hundred bucks on a hot current model with various bells and whistles will seem to be a non-event.

The fact of the matter is that at Walmarts today you can buy a top-quality laptop computer for under four-hundred dollars that has capabilities that,
if they were even available ten years ago, would have cost four-hundred-**thousand** dollars! Incredible computing power has become ridiculously inexpensive, and will continue to drop in the coming years.

Though the library high-speed internet connection is free, you should get a "high-speed" internet connection at your home if you can afford to do so. It is possible to connect to the internet over a standard telephone line at no added cost, but it is painfully slow. Time is money. High speed connectivity is least expensive where either your telephone company or electricity provider can directly connect you, often at very low additional cost, if any. Cable TV connectivity is another excellent option where available.

If you are unfortunate (from an internet connectivity-speed perspective, like me) enough to live in a **very** rural area where high-speed internet connectivity is not possible, there are satellite services (such as Hughes Net) that are available as long as a receiver placed on your roof has an unobstructed shot at the satellite. Unfortunately, this is the most expensive way to get high-speed service, but as a last resort it is a viable, and perhaps only, alternative.

I would not care to try to have an on-line business using a slow-speed telephone modem, but it is not impossible. There are many people doing it. I just do not personally have that much patience!

Many of the money-making techniques I will share with you in this how-to internet commerce book require zero money to implement once you have a computer and internet connection. This is known in the trade as "bum marketing", and it can be very profitable. In fact, at least one technique requires no computer at all! Other techniques require varying amounts of money to accomplish. None require a huge up-front investment as is the case with starting almost any other business or "brick and mortar" store or franchise.

On the internet the old adage: "it takes money to make money", is not strictly true. Making money with virtually no investment of money is an internet- reality that can be learned. I hope to teach you how in this book.

Please read the following statement more than once, because it expresses the reason why marketing on the internet is easier than one might imagine: **"MAKING MONEY FROM HOME ON THE INTERNET IS A PURE _NUMBERS GAME!_"**

The number of individuals using computers to find information, gain knowledge, and buy things is in the multiple-**billions**. The number who purchase everything from $0.99 reports to $100,000+ cars is in the many hundreds of millions.

The key fact to grasp is: **A VERY SMALL PERCENTAGE OF A LARGE POPULATION CAN STILL BE A HECK OF A LOT OF PEOPLE!** You don't even need a small <u>slice</u> of the internet commerce pie. **All you need to do is lick the knife!**

Your internet commerce job is actually very simple. **<u>You will be finding whatever a focused group (your "niche") of people want to buy and then selling it to them.</u>** That's the whole enchilada! I will share with you how to do both. There need be no cost involved to develop this information, and then provide it.

Let's discuss just what it is you will be "selling". It is important to understand that there is no "face-to-face" selling involved, and no "telephone selling". Everything is done on your computer. But what exactly will you <u>be</u> "selling"?

You have two basic choices: physical products (such as cameras, TV sets, books, clothing, etc.) and "virtual" products (items that can be delivered electronically). Most of the successful internet entrepreneurs I know have chosen NOT to sell physical products for a number of reasons.

It is true that one can find internet-based warehouses in the United States that will sell you virtually any product you can imagine at below-retail prices for you to re-sell on the internet for a profit. They will even ship directly to your customer without you ever touching the product. These programs **abound** in late-night TV commercials.

"You can charge your customer whatever you want and keep the difference between your cost and your selling price." Sounds easy, and the TV and radio commercials for companies that "teach" you how to do this would have you believe it is easy. It isn't, and here is why:

For starters, you find yourself in competition with the Walmarts and Costcos of the world who can buy almost anything in huge quantities at discounts that simply are not available to us regular folk.

But more important, you are competing directly with hundreds, if not thousands, who, just like you, responding to the **same** TV ad, and are trying to sell the same stuff. Consequently each marketer has to cut prices to the bone, ever and ever lower, to beat out everyone else.

What this leads to is you ending up with so little profit on each item that it becomes almost impossible to make a lot of money. I've heard of people selling $900.00 TVs for $5.00 net profit. That's just nuts.

I imagine that there are a few individuals who have found a way to actually make selling physical products profitable. Perhaps some specialize in a tiny market segment that is unattractive to the big retailers. But the percentage who fail at this sort of internet marketing is reportedly vastly higher. Very few succeed.

There are a few exceptions to the "no physical products" rule. Beyond a doubt many individuals make money selling physical items on eBay and Craigslist and similar sites.

Collectable items such as coins, stamps, antiques, old postcards and the like find a ready market there. So do CDs and DVDs that you can resell or create yourself. But the "warehouse drop-ship of expensive large items" business model is a very tough road to internet riches.

There is another "exception" involving physical products in a roundabout way. This involves you sending customers to the web addresses of companies of all sizes that sell their **own** physical products direct to consumers on their own websites. You can get paid just for sending them the customers! You personally offer no product, physical or virtual. This is called **"Affiliate Marketing"**, and it is one primary means of creating internet wealth that I share with you in this how-to book Volume..

Aside from the insanely profitable Affiliate Marketing, we will be focusing our attention on "virtual" products that you can create and sell. A virtual product is anything that can be sent to a customer electronically over the internet. It can be a book, a report, a "how-to" booklet, a course of instruction, or specialized information on almost anything imaginable.

It is important for you to understand that you do NOT have to actually write anything yourself. You can learn how to obtain all of the **free** written material you will ever need.

The following two lists are important summaries. The first represents the many ways to earn internet income that I will be sharing with you throughout this how-to book Volume 1. The second list summarizes the talents that you will acquire, over time, that will enable you to earn a very good income from the comfort of your home.

Both lists are alphabetical, not in order of importance. You will learn that many of the income streams can be achieved with little or no investment of your money up front. You will certainly not be learning it all at the same time!

Once you become aware of the possibilities open to you, and the specific talents you need to apply to each, you can choose your own internet marketing destiny.

Don't panic, but below is a long list of possible ways for you to profit from your new internet business. All will be discussed to the best of my ability within the pages of this Volume:

YOUR 20 POSSIBLE MULTIPLE STREAMS OF INTERNET INCOME

AdSense by Google
Amazon Kindle eBook Publishing (you should **start** here)
Amazon Printed-Book-On-Demand Platform
Articles
Classified Ads (free and paid)
Domain Name Flipping
Email Lists
Ezines
Forums
Google AdSense
Google AdWords
Local Merchants
Membership Sites
Newsletters
On-line Advertising
Off-line Advertising
Picks & Shovels
Publishing eBooks: Beyond Amazon
Social Site Marketing
Website Flipping

THE 15 KEY INTERNET MARKETING TALENTS YOU WILL LEARN

Advertising
Article Writing

Autoresponder Programming
Buying Google AdWords Traffic
Creating Ezines
Creating Podcasts
Creating Book Covers
Domaining
Email List Building
Forum Participation
Placing Google AdSense Ads
Social Site Domination
Writing For Publication
Writing Press Releases

Please do not be overwhelmed by the above. Your learning will be step-wise. Any one of these can be learned in a week or less, some in a day. You can focus on one limited means of creating internet income, become proficient at it, and then move on to another, and another, and another. You can even decide to focus on **just one**, such as Affiliate Marketing, and make a very fine income.

The key to your success in internet marketing is that many potential customers are just plain lazy. They want instant gratification with minimum effort. The main fact to understand here is: **PEOPLE WILL PAY FOR GOOD INFORMATION THAT THEY CANNOT FIND EASILY OR FIND COMPILED IN ONE PLACE.** Fortunes are being made on that one single principal by clever internet entrepreneurs (known as "**Infopreneurs**") all over the world.

JUST LEARN HOW, AND DO IT!

CHAPTER 3

GET WEALTHY WHILE STAYING OUT OF TROUBLE (LEGAL AND ETHICAL CONSIDERATIONS)

Let's get this "legal Chapter" out of the way early. Before I share with you the various techniques learned over a decade of trial and error, failures and successes, **you should read this Chapter**. After you have completed this book, read this chapter again. It will mean more to you then, after you have a fuller context within which to consider the legal implications of your new internet business.

I am not a lawyer, nor an accountant, and nothing I write in this book should be construed as legal or tax or investment advice. You should **ALWAYS** seek the advice of professionals, lawyers and accountants and financial pros, whenever you decide to start a business, or if you have any legal, tax, financial or estate issues once you begin to score internet profits.

Having a successful internet business is fun and profitable. It offers a freedom that few vocations offer. (Aside from being a golf pro I can't imagine a better money-making pursuit!) It offers the opportunity for considerable wealth. But it takes time and focus, care and persistence. The absolute last thing you need is any sort of legal or ethical problem. An awareness of possible pitfalls is a good start towards achieving a clean business profile. Consider the public's perceived value of a top Better Business Bureau rating. Point made?

Let's first look at Federal laws that regulate internet practices at this writing. Surely there will be more laws coming along down the road.

A big part of your marketing will of necessity be email based. Done correctly email is perhaps your best marketing tool available. Done incorrectly it can land you in jail!

The "Can-SPAM Act" was passed by both houses of Congress in 2003 and became law in January 2004. It is an acronym for: "Controlling the Assault of Non-Solicited Pornography And Marketing Act". From that date on all unsolicited email has been referred to as SPAM.

Back in the '70s there was a famous Monty Python skit about SPAM, the meat product. The final punch-line was: "I HATE SPAM". I suspect some government genius reverse-engineered the acronym to create the name of the Act to fit the universal hatred of unsolicited email.

Whether this notoriety has helped or hurt the marketing of Hormel and their ever-popular SPAM meat product (reportedly an acronym for Specially Processed Anonymous Meat) remains to be seen! (Obscure irrelevant fact: the SPAM meat product is incredibly popular in Hawaii and is even found there at McDonald's! Having lived in Hawaii for five years I developed a passion for eating SPAM to this day!)

For the ten or so years prior to enactment of the act, sending out unsolicited marketing emails was the primary source of income for most internet entrepreneurs! In fact, there were " How To SPAM " seminars galore, with names such as "Creative eMail Marketing", and "Email Your Way To Wealth". There were many serious written courses available for many hundreds of dollars. I still have many that I purchased in the '90s gathering dust in my library!

Back then you could even legally send pornography to a minor! There were simply no rules governing commercial emails. Obviously the government stepped in for the public's protection. It is your responsibility to study and abide by the Can-SPAM Act. Check out at the government

site: ftc.gov/bcp/conline/pubs/buspubs/canspam.shtm
This site has all of the relevant updates. Be **certain** to
check this out. It is your sole responsibility to learn the
letter of this law. Ignorance of the law is never an excuse.

The following list is far from complete, but it represents
areas that are most easily and often violated, many times
innocently and with no malice of forethought:

For starters, NEVER use a false or misleading header.
"From", "To" and routing information must be accurate to
allow the recipient to contact you.

Do not use deceptive subject lines. Make the subject line
relevant to the content.

You should clearly identify your email as an advertising
message.

You must include your current physical address.

Primary to this law is the requirement that if a recipient of
one of your emails asks to be removed from your list you
MUST do so. Neither you nor anyone affiliated with you
may ever send another email to that recipient. To facilitate
this you MUST have an opt-out link in your email (tied to
your autoresponder), and you have ten days after a
removal request in which to comply.

You are required to keep a list of everyone who has ever
unsubscribed. This is known as your "Suppression List".
And you may not sell, rent or give out this list to anyone.

Penalties for violation of the act are rather strict. EACH
violation can cost you $11,000.00.! The Federal Trade
Commission (FTC) can actually seize your property. And
should you involve minors, or do something particularly
egregious, or are a repeat offender, you can do hard time

in a Federal prison. You don't want to do that. Don't SPAM.

If and when you decide to join an Affiliate Program, be CERTAIN to take a long, hard look at their email-marketing policy. Perhaps the ugliest provision of the "Can SPAM Act" is that any company can be found in violation of the Act even if they themselves did not send the email message! Ouch!   Because of this, understandably nervous potential-affiliate merchants may stipulate:

No email marketing of any kind to market our products;

Prior approval of your email messages;

Prior approval of your entire list of email addresses;

The merchant may require you to "scrub" your email list against   suppression lists that they themselves keep. There are services you can hire yourself to do this. Check out unsubcentral.com, or do a Google search for "list scrubbing services".

Some merchants may even require you to add, <u>in addition</u> to your own signature, address and opt-out link, THEIR email signature and opt out link.

All of this might seem like a giant pain in the ass. It is not only for the better good of society as a whole but it is definitely in <u>your</u> best interest as well. "Trust" is a very critical issue in internet marketing, and showing clearly that you take the laws seriously goes a long way to instilling that trust in your visitors and customers.

Incidentally, these laws are in effect in the United States only. Massive amounts of SPAM still originates "legally" from foreign-based companies.

Now let's look at another important Federal Law, the "Unfair or Deceptive Acts or Practices Act". <u>Internet advertising is strictly governed by this act.</u>

As with Can-SPAM, you should access and print out the FTC publication at: ftc.gov/bcp/edu/pubs/business/ecommerce/bus41.pdf.

Some highlights of this law are:

You will find that the laws governing internet advertising are essentially the same as for off-line advertising. This is to the delight of every **legitimate** internet marketer who now can compete on a level playing field with the internet slime-balls that abound.

Ads should be clearly identified as such and should not be misleading in any way.

Disclaimers, disclosures and warnings must be conspicuous and clear. They must not be in "fine print", but must follow the general style of the website regarding size and color.

If your visitor will be receiving email from you they must be clearly told to expect your advertising email messages.

There can be no inflated claims about the value of your product.

You must disclose any dangers or limitations of your product.

If your website sales letter is very long, repeat your disclosures relative to your claims about your product.

Know the law. As I mentioned before, and it needs repeating, ignorance of the law is absolutely no defense whatsoever should you ever get caught in a violation.

There are many other activities that are closely regulated. The government has placed very strict restrictions on the installation of software on your visitor's computers. Prior to these regulations affiliates and advertisers were able to easily and remotely install software without visitors' consent. These are known as "black hat" techniques. Some are still practiced.

The three types of software (also collectively called "malware") in question are "Spyware", "Adware", and "Parasiteware".

Spyware transmits information about the internet activities of anyone using a computer on which this software is installed. Quality virus protection software can generally remove these programs.

Adware software is used to display advertising on a computer based upon their on-line behavior.

Parasiteware is your worst nightmare as an affiliate marketer. It allows a thief to steal your affiliate commissions by changing and redirecting your unique affiliate identification links.

If you have reason to believe that you are the victim of parasiteware (because your once-steady commissions have dropped off suddenly or dramatically) you should immediately contact your affiliate network's manager. They can often determine the origin of the problem. Unfortunately it is very unlikely that it would be economically feasible to attempt to sue the offending parasite-marketer once identified.

One reason to only use large and reputable pay-per-click advertisers such as Google is the documented fact that some of the smaller PPC networks (beware the penny-a-click crowd) are known to install Spyware and Adware on your computer.

There are also specific Federal regulations governing adult-content websites, and on-line gambling sites. As with all of our Federal laws, foreign-based companies are not obligated to adhere to them. This is why there is still a huge amount of spyware, adware, and parasiteware, as well as pornography, and gambling sites, found throughout the internet.

Until recently the U. S. Department of Justice held that online gambling in all forms was illegal under the Wire Act of 1961. This act bars bets via telecommunications across state lines or international borders. A new interpretation by the Office of Legal Counsel states that the Wire Act only applies to wagers on a "sporting event or contest". This opens up a considerable window of opportunity for such endeavors as online card games.

The matter of tracking cookies is coming under increasing scrutiny. The European union recently passed a set of privacy directives known affectionately as "The Cookie Law". It is well worth noting. You should look carefully at your own websites to avoid problems in the future regarding your use of tracking visitors. Your Privacy Policy should list the cookies on your site by name and purpose. For other-party cookies be certain to identify their source. You should also disclose any social-sharing buttons that might link to outside sites that gather data.

It is not only necessary to follow all of the Federal laws. You must also comply with Local, County and State laws as well.

Local Home Owner Association or zoning codes can be found at most City Halls. There may be rules that could apply to your affiliate marketing business-from- home. Your County may have its own business regulations, usually available at the County Courthouse offices. Permits are a wonderful way for all government entities to scrape up additional revenues.

Equally important to you are your State laws regarding businesses. These relate to incorporation, taxes, unemployment insurance, workers compensation, minimum wage, and business licenses. These can usually be checked out on-line at your State government websites.

Aside from strict adherence to all Federal and local laws, there is also the area of ethical behavior that all serious internet marketers must address. To run a truly ethical web business you must:

Keep your visitors private information private;

Not spread false rumors about your competitors;

Comply with your merchant's advertising rules;

Not make false or misleading claims about your products; Not make any promises that you or your affiliated merchant cannot keep;

Deal with visitor's complaints promptly and fairly;

Not lie about your internet income.

One of the "gray" areas of internet commerce law is in regard to collecting sales taxes from every buyer and remitting them to each buyer's state. This would be a daunting if not almost-impossible task for any internet marketer, but with States all looking for new revenue sources it is an obvious potential pain.

My tax accountant shrugs his shoulders on this one. It is also unclear whether sales to buyers even in my home state should includeaState sales tax. One problem is often my not even knowing the physical location of buyers of my virtual products. Be certain to check this matter thoroughly with your tax advisor.

Of course you have to pay Federal personal or Corporate income taxes on all of your net internet profits. Up until 2011 there was apparently no way for the IRS to accurately monitor your internet income. You were obligated by law to report this income, but it is said that many did not voluntarily comply. Enter the shiny new IRS 1099K form.

As I understand it, effective for 2011 payment-collection middlemen such as PayPal are required by law to send you and the IRS 1099Ks documenting your internet income. Not reporting all of your internet income will now open you up to a tax fraud audit. You do not want that. It is a very compelling reason for you to keep very detailed records of your expenses spent in generating your 1099K income.

One almost inevitable change that is coming is a universal internet sales tax designed by Uncle Sam as one route to reducing the Federal deficit (or more likely providing them with more money to find some creative way to waste). What impact this might have on overall internet sales is impossible to assess, but no-one in the industry is looking forward to its implementation. It is quite likely to happen in 2013.

Laws change, and as internet marketers it is our duty to keep up with the changes. For example, recent court rulings have redefined the gambling laws and actually made certain formerly-illegal practices absolutely legitimate. The new interpretation is that the law only applies to "sporting events or contests". (Theory: permit and regulate everything else to raise tax revenues.) This has opened up a whole new area of internet marketing opportunities.

One very important thing to remember is to NEVER exaggerate the merits of a product. The Federal Trade Commission (FTC) actually monitors this sort of fraud rather closely. It is also a VERY bad idea to "fake" endorsements and testimonials. The FTC has hit one website owner with a $250,000 fine for doing just that. Not exactly a cost-effective website.

It is a fact that sex and gambling are extremely profitable ventures on-line. Legal involvement in certain of these areas of commerce are more governed by one's personal moral code than by law. There is so much money to be made in other areas of internet commerce it just isn't necessary to participate in these "adult" endeavors. Then again, perhaps, I'm just an old prude.   If that shoe fits you, wear it.

Knowing the various laws and ethical expectations governing internet commerce is essential to your marketing success.   Once you get in the habit of doing things correctly, staying out of trouble becomes second-nature. Always err on the side of caution.

In the long run nothing is more important to you than your reputation as an ethical and law-abiding internet businessperson.

<u>Do everything you can to establish and maintain that reputation.</u>

MODULE FIVE
ADVERTISE FOR HOT TRAFFIC

CHAPTER 22

KNOWING INSIDER ADVERTISING KEYS

There is no more important Chapter to study and learn than this one. Advertising can cost nothing. Advertising can cost a fortune. Advertising can be very cost effective. Advertising can be very cost _ineffective_. Advertising can be your downfall or your windfall. **Advertising is the key to the vault!**

Unlike in the movie *"Field Of Dreams"* if you build a website (and you are the only one who knows of its existence) they definitely will NOT come. A very few visitors might accidentally stumble upon your site, mostly because they happen to enter a Google search term that precisely matches your domain name, but for all intents and purposes you will make no money at all by simply creating a website.

I never cease to be amazed at the many TV ads promoted by certain major domain hosting companies that proclaim: "Buy a domain name, build a business website here, and customers will find you and come flocking to your door!"

Big lie. Bad misrepresentation aimed at the unknowing masses. Nothing could be further from the truth.

So what's an internet marketer to do? Fortunately there are many alternatives, some free, some costly, but taken together it is absolutely possible to drive massive amounts of traffic to your offers and generate huge sums of money. **The key is creating great ads and understanding different advertising options.**

"Advertising" is a very general term. It is necessary to understand all of the different ways you can "advertise" to drive visitors to your website. Let's start with the obvious.

Ever since newspapers and magazines were invented, publishers realized that they could greatly increase their revenue by accepting advertising from merchants. Indeed, there are many free publications that forego subscription revenue entirely and derive all of their revenue from ads. There are also thousands of websites that employ this same revenue model.

You have two basic off-line media choices. You can advertise in general interest media that have massive readership (such as *Popular Mechanics*) or you can advertise in niche publications in your area of interest that have smaller readership (such as *Golf* magazine).

You will want to create the shortest ad possible that contains your keyword-rich link, whether it be to your website or directly to one of your affiliates. Creating short ads is an art form but it can be learned. "Want free money guaranteed? Click on.....". Get the idea?

When one thinks of "running ads" the first things that come to mind for most business persons are the Yellow Pages, and classified ads in newspapers and magazines. The Yellow Pages have been virtually buried by the internet, and in my opinion any merchant with a brick-and-mortar store who spends money on YP ads is wasting most if not all of it.

Running conventional classified ads in newspapers and magazines can be a cost-effective way to advertise your presence on the internet. A well-crafted ad will pull in visitors if it is promoted in some media that focuses only on your niche. If you have a gardening product your ad belongs in a gardening magazine. Duh.

You might have success with running such ads in a general audience magazine's classified section under a classified-ad sub-heading that matches your niche. These ads can be expensive, but can show a profit. Check out magazines.com for ad ideas. Because magazines in general have "coffee table life" your ads might be seen for years!

You can prove this to yourself for free by referring to the past year's issues of any publication carrying classified ads. Look for ads that have run in most or all of the past twelve issues. These are ads that must be making money or they probably would stop running them (although wishful thinking sometimes trumps sanity).

I'm sure you are familiar with Einstein's classic definition of stupidity: "Insanity: **doing the same thing over and over again and expecting different results."** Don't do that. You will go broke that way.

Try to emulate the general style of those ads you find that run continuously and are probably making money. When seeking ideas check out magazines.com. You should still go to a magazine store to see what sort of classified ads are running. Remember, magazines have "coffee table life". Your ad may produce results for years!

Some internet entrepreneurs spend vast sums of money on television infomercials. These are generally run on cable or satellite TV during late night hours. I believe at any given time between 11PM and 3AM on any given day you can surf your TV listings and find at least three internet-related infomercials. Some have run for years, so they obviously must produce a positive return on investment.

Many of these TV ads offer an inexpensive hard-cover book, usually $19.95 plus shipping and handling. How many hard copy books can one possibly sell at this price to make a profit? The answer is, not enough! You can't turn a profit paying for TV ads selling a single twenty dollar book. The book is the pre-sell.

Once the author has your name and address (and usually during the ordering process you are asked for your telephone number and email address as well ("to send you your confirmation and paid receipt") he or she has something that, over time, has considerable value and more than covers the cost of the TV ads.

The author of the book being offered knows the "lifetime value of a book buyer". He or she knows how many follow up products, from other books to CDs and courses and ultimately expensive personal training, have been sold in the past to any given customer.

It might take years for you to reach the level where the value of a single visitor can be calculated with some degree of certainty, and where you have developed a sufficient number of products to make a TV commercial pay off, but it is not impossible. And it can make you a multi-millionaire. I personally know three individuals who have done so. Just look at it as a possible long-term goal.

But you may be a beginner, so let's talk about things a beginner can do at little or no cost.

The real key to inexpensive internet advertising success is focusing on running ads in newsletters and ezines (on-line magazines) of other internet marketers, that is, by placing free and paid ads <u>online.</u> There are thousands of sites on which you can place advertising for FREE.

This basically falls into the category: "If you toss enough poop against a wall some of it figures to stick". Don't expect great FREE results, but you sure can't beat the price. FREE is good. A Google search for "free online classified ads" turns up a huge number of possible sites. Some I have used are: salesspider.com; usfreeads.com; classifiedads.com and global-free-classified-ads.com

Some places to consider for placing your classified ads are: eBay classifieds; Yahoo! classifieds; Craigslist; Nationwide Newspapers at naationwideadvertising.com; inetgiant.com; homebusinessmag.com; classifiedads.com; usfreeads.com; adlandpro.com; internetbasedmoms.com; and Mike Filsame's free ad blog (you can post daily)..

Good off-line publications in which to advertise money making opportunities are: *Sparetime Opportunities; Entrepreneur; Moneymaking Opportunities; Money N Profits; Opportunity World; Start Your Own Business.*

It might also be a good idea to consider advertising in a "Card Deck". A Google search for "Direct Mail Card Deck Advertising" should find many opportunities.
Paid internet ads are a different story. If you can find a website that relates to your topic, but where your specific item does not compete with that website's products, approach the owner about paying to advertise on the site. You can also buy ads on internet newsletters and ezines that relate to your topic. Here again, do a Google search: "internet newsletters and ezines". A good site to check out is listopt.com.

Incidentally, any advertising you do on websites, your own or one you pay for the privilege, **DO NOT USE BANNERS,** those little rectangles with a short message that a visitor is expected to click on.   Banner ads worked well in the early days of internet marketing. They were a novelty at that time.

As people became more accustomed to surfing the internet they have seen so many banners, and clicked on so many that provided useless information, that virtually no one clicks on them anymore. Actual physical retinal studies have shown that web surfers actually look away from banners!   The key is to use in-"contextual links", links imbedded directly within your written text.

In order to pinpoint your most productive ads quickly and automatically check out hypertracker.com. It's $20/month, but used judiciously it could be well worth it.

PRESS RELEASE MAGIC

The single best FREE ADVERTISING is by posting Press Releases. It can lead to lots of clicks if you do it right. As with ads, writing press releases is an art that can be learned.

Just do a Google search for "how to write a press release" and lo and behold there are 700million+ results from which to choose! (This insanely large figure is why getting top-three positioning on the first page of a Google search is so critical.)

There are very specific rules to follow, and surprisingly few marketers actually follow them. A single error in a press release is a guaranteed route to the circular file. Here are the rules you MUST follow:

Always double space your press release. Editors like lots of room between the lines to make notes.

Never send more than one single page. Editors prefer brevity.

Use san-serif fonts (without the tips on letters like **"T"** in Times New Roman), black type, on 8 ½ x 11 white quality bond paper. Not all capitals.

In the upper left hand corner put: For Immediate Release. If the release is time-sensitive, replace this with: For release after.........; or For release the week of.......; or whatever fits your situation.
In the upper right corner put: (Your name, email address, phone number and FAX number).

The headline MUST be newsworthy. Writing: "I Just Wrote An Exciting Book" will elicit the editor's thought: "Then why the hell don't you take out a paid ad in my publication". Guaranteed circular file. . For this ebook my headline for a local news release might be: "Internet Expert Has Solution To Unemployment in Arizona".

The body of the release is best answered by asking yourself the question: "What makes my ebook or report newsworthy?" You must present yourself as the expert in the headline or body of the release. I don't care what niche topic you have chosen you can creatively write (or have ghostwritten) copy that the reader of some publication would be excited to read. And be sure you have some way for the reader to contact you, preferably your website address.

And exactly how do you get your press release out to a universe of editors? Email is the logical choice. Fast and cheap. Also by far the **worst**. Editors get hundreds of emails a day. If it doesn't end up in the automatic spam file it is highly unlikely that it will get noticed at all anyway.

FAXing is not a terrible choice. (Radio stations actually prefer it.) But it is not the best choice. If you are sending out to a thousand or so editors it is an inexpensive and acceptable way to go.

What method is best to use? Plain old-fashioned snail mail, addressed to the Editor by name (infinitely better than "To Editor"). The fact that this is the most expensive way to send out a release and is more labor intensive means that fewer people use it and your news release will stand out and almost certainly get read.

You can always hire outside help with press releases: Check out wireworld.com; merchantwire.com; and xpresspress.com (or do a Google search for such help and prepare to be overwhelmed with the number of results!) As I suggested often earlier, be certain to check out fiverr.com and see how many individuals will offer press release help for five bucks!

There is another way to obtain valuable free advertising, but it takes a lot of skill. This is by getting free public relations (PR) in both the online and offline worlds. This is actually far easier than it sounds. Almost every publication needs "filler material".   If you can make your product "exciting" you can frequently find eager outlets for your reports.

Even radio and TV shows have dead space that needs filling. You need to come up with some sort of newsworthy angle that an editor or station manager would see fit to put before its audience.

Young internet guru Anthony Morrison (anthonymorrison.com) seems to have mastered getting his message across in media interviews. It is a vastly more effective than any other advertising, but it is also far more difficult to generate. There is an excellent book on the subject by Dr. Jeffrey Lant titled: "The Unabashed Self-Promoters Guide". It is the Bible of free-self-promotion ideas. I believe it is out of print, but if you can find a copy on eBay or in a used book store or even your Public Library you would do well to buy it.

Always welcome, because it is free, is word of mouth (or word of "mouse"!) through newsgroups, chat rooms, bulletin boards, forums and "expert" sites. This is one of your long-term strategies, and need not be your highest priority. Long-term this is probably the best way to become known and develop lifetime customers.

Go to livinginternet.com and click on "Usenet". Find as many newsgroups related to your subject as you can and post messages in appropriate places. Go to epinions.com and sign up to become an opinionated expert in your niche.

Establish a presence in your niche at: yahoo.com/features/chatrooms. Participate in Bulletin Board and Forum discussions. Check out: findchatrooms.com.

It is even possible for you to start your own bulletin board and forum community. Check out hoop.la (not .com) for their version of the process for doing this.

Often overlooked, but very important, is creating your "signature" for absolutely everything you send out or hand out, every eMail, every business card, every report. It should include a short message, your name, web address, and email address. Remember, **EVERY CLICK COUNTS**.

Within the signature most place a simple URL link, their actual website address. This is well and good, but it can be improved upon. To optimize the value of your links you want to create keyword rich kinks. This requires messing a bit with HTML code, but if you can fill in your information in the following code you will be fine (omit the brackets):
<a href=http://www.[your exact URL]>[your keywords]</a>

Use this enhanced link wherever you can.

Another free advertising method is exchanging links between your website and a complimentary site, which can help you both, a win - win. (It's even better if you can create and own both sites yourself!). For example, a site that sells pianos might be happy to link with a site that sells piano sheet music.

Each site owner benefits from the traffic of the other. It is also worthy of note that links to your site from relevant-content sites adds to your ranking in the search engines.

Incidentally, if you do link between your **own** sites it is important that each website has a different hosting company. Google will not give you credit for links between your own sites, but if they originate at different hosts this will not be a visible problem. The number of incoming links is important in Search Engine Optimization as discussed in Chapter 14.

Utilizing lists of email addresses, your own or rented ones, to promote your ads is another very popular way to place your ads in front of potential buyers.

Advertising can be in any form you can imagine. A billboard on a major highway with your domain name on it might work (HostGator, a domain hosting company, uses one in my area). Skywriting? Notes on bulletin boards in post offices? Whatever works.

Anyplace you can imagine to get your message out can result in clicks, and any click can be cash in your pocket. To pinpoint your most productive ads quickly and automatically check out: hypertracker.com, for $20/month.

Somewhere down the road if you want to do serious (read "expensive") ad campaigns check out the following site: valueclick.com

Write ezines and articles. Focus your attention on creative advertising and you unlock the vault to a continuous stream of internet income for the rest of your life.

If you are ever asked: "How many 'Buy It Now' buttons do you have in cyberspace today?", you do **not** want your answer to be "None!". Internet marketing is a pure numbers game. Only by getting involved, getting lots of those "Buy" buttons out there, can you hope to make a living sitting at your computer.

<u>JUST DO IT!</u>

CHAPTER 23
WRITING KILLER ADS FOR BIG BUCKS

If you don't know squat about writing ads, you can search Google for "how to write an advertisement". I just checked that out and it returned a mere 33.8 million choices! There ought to be something useful to you in there somewhere.

Ad writing is a learnable skill. There are certain guidelines that have been true since print advertising dawned in the 1800s. The basic formula is **"A I D A"**. This stands for **A**ttention, **I**nterest, **D**esire, **A**ction. Memorize this and keep it in your mind every time you write any advertisement.

You create the initial **attention** with certain universal key words: FREE, SAVE, EXCLUSIVE, DISCOUNTED, WHOLESALE.

The **interest** is the sizzle. Use emotion. Use passion. "Dominate...........". State the benefits of what your headline claims. Let them know with clarity what it is you are offering.

You create **desire** with words like EXCLUSIVE, PRIVATE. Answer the "Station WIIFM" question: "**W**hat's **I**n **I**t **F**or **M**e".

The **action** part is the key. This is the cliffhanger, the call to action. Use terms like: "WHILE SUPPLIES LAST", "EXCLUSIVE OFFER", "LIMITED TIME OFFER", "CLICK NOW", "HURRY BEFORE IT'S TOO LATE", "SIGN UP NOW!", "CLICK ON THE LINK BELOW", "DON'T MISS YOUR CHANCE TO....". **Always** be certain to TELL THEM WHAT TO DO. People WANT to be told what to do.

The secret to a successful ad **is the *HEADLINE.*** It is reported that studies show you have three seconds maximum to keep a visitor sufficiently interested to your ad to read it! If the headline fails to get attention, no matter how well-crafted your ad might be it is useless unless they actually read it. Your headlines must dominate at least one of four competitive aspects: PRICE, QUALITY, SERVICE or EXCLUSIVITY. Buying **your** product is their best bet to get what they want.   Promising quick results in the headline is a very good idea.

An effective headline <u>forces</u> your potential customer to read more of your ad. It must instantly ignite an emotion that fascinates them into reading the entire ad. It must address one of five very basic human needs. It has to make it difficult for the prospect to ignore what follows. If the headline fails to get attention, you are wasting your time and money.

The five basic human needs are listed below in order of importance are:

PSYCHOLOGICAL NEEDS: These are the very basics of thirst, hunger, shelter, clothing and sex.
SAFETY & SECURITY NEEDS: The need for physical, emotional and financial security.

SOCIAL NEEDS: The need for affiliation, love, affection, companionship and acceptance.

ESTEEM NEEDS: Self-esteem, recognition, attention, respect and achievement.

"SELF" NEEDS: Known as self-actualization, it is the need of an individual to reach their full potential as they perceive it.

Two additional needs are:

SALVATION: Need to feel closer to heaven.

INSIDER NEED: The need to know things others do not know.

Your job is to "feel" your customer's needs, wants and desires and write your headlines accordingly, with as much passion and emotion as you can.

Here are some emotional triggers that successful internet marketing entrepreneurs address in their advertising headlines:

People want to live as long as possible;
People want to make and save money;
People want to save time;
People want comfort;
People want to learn new things;
People want to give and receive love;
People want to be popular;
People want to look their best, physically & clothing-wise;
People want to eliminate the negative things in life.

Remember, "Accentuate The Positive, Eliminate The Negative, Latch On To The Affirmative, Don't Mess With Mister In-Between". This applies to advertising copy as well as headlines. In your advertising copy include wording that will:

Eliminate/Reduce: hard work;
Eliminate/Relieve: stress;
Eliminate/Reduce: risk;
Eliminate/Prevent: embarrassment;
Eliminate/Relieve: pain;
Eliminate/Ease: doubts;
Eliminate/Free: from worry;
Eliminate/Free: from fear;
Eliminate/Free: from anxiety;
Eliminate/Reduce: guilt.

Always remember that people want to be thought of as smart; successful; attractive; expert; influential; creative; important; knowledgeable; efficient and sociable. And they want the personal freedom to be

independent, to travel, to resist being dominated and pushed around, to control others, and to have their own business. Address these issues in your advertising for certain success.

Advertising copy addressing wealth, love, health and beauty, and safety have proven over time to be the best for generating positive responses and making sales.

There are at least ten different and distinct "types" of headlines with which to open your advertisements. These are:

Headlines beginning with "How To" (e.g. "How To Train A Doberman");

Headlines that pose a question (e.g., "Are You Sick And Tired Of The 9 -5");

Headlines that make a command, and focus solely on the your offer's most important benefit (e.g., "Triple Your Income Next Year");

News Headlines, written as an announcement (e.g. "Announcing A New Breakthrough In Dog Training");

The Headline Offering A Solution: (e.g., If You Have Trouble Training Your Puppy This Report Will Make You An Expert".);

Headlines offering a benefit: (e.g., "Make More Money With My System";

The Personalized Headline: (e.g., "Here's How **You** [if possible insert actual name from a mail-merge program] Can Earn More Money");

The Testimonial Headline: (e.g., "[recognized name who has liked the product] says that [product] is the best"; OR signing your own name at the end: (e.g., "I found this report to be the best! [signed]").The Guarantee Headline:

(e.g., "Announcing a report guaranteed to help you train your dog!");

The Discount Sale Headline: (e.g., "Get up to 70% Off Our Widget If You Act Today").

Keep in mind that people do not want to be "sold", but they love to buy. First and foremost they buy on emotion, and justify their buying decision later with logic. You must be sure to back up your emotional pitch with the logic that will reinforce that justification.

Your Sub-Headline follows exactly the same rules for keywords and power words, fonts and colors as the headline. It is often a bit longer, with more keywords. Do not use words you used in the headline. Explain nothing here. That follows in the body of the ad. Try to create a sense of mystery or secrecy so they read on to the body of the ad.

Keep the ad body as simple as possible, but make it stand out. The buyer only wants to know specifically how they are going to benefit from the purchase of your product. The body of your ads needs to be keyword rich and state benefit after benefit after benefit. In his famous book *TESTED SENTENCES THAT SELL,* written decades ago, Elmer Wheeler counseled: **"Sell the sizzle, not the steak**". This is as true in internet marketing today as it was decades ago when Wheeler coined the phrase.

And ALWAYS conclude with a call to action. This single seemingly obvious item is frequently overlooked to the great peril of the advertiser. People need, WANT, to be told what to do! **Tell them what to do.** *"**BUY NOW, FROM ME!**"*

For help with contextual ads I suggest you visit kontera.com and study what they have to offer..

Note that if you are doing affiliate marketing, your affiliates will often provide ad copy for you to use. Unfortunately a lot of it is not crafted as well as it might be. Do not hesitate to modify their ads. Consider adding your personal endorsement to the affiliate ad.

If you have a product that might appeal to individuals in different niches be certain to run your ads directed towards those different niches. For example, this book could be offered to "people looking to work from home", or to "people who want to learn how to market on the internet".

Here is a technique used by some top pros. You can also take advantage of some phrases that are permanently burned into the public consciousness. Insert your product or product benefit for the underlined words:
"I Did Not Have Sex With That Woman";

"Houston, We Have A Problem";

"Show Me The Money";

"I Made Him An Offer He Couldn't Refuse";

"Beam Me Up (a xxxxx) Scotty";

"Play It Again, Sam" (phrase actually never uttered in Casablanca);

"Go Ahead, Make My Day (with a xxxxxx)";

"I Will Fundamentally Reshape America";

"Tear Down That Wall".

Just think of any such lines that have stuck in your head over the years and use them effectively in your advertising. Also note that virtually anything that is really funny, really gross, or somehow intriguing has the potential to go viral, rapidly spreading across the internet social sites.

Do not hesitate to invoke the names of famous people in your ads: "Start Hitting Sale Home Runs Like Babe Ruth"; "Slam-Dunk The Competition Like LeBron James"; "Get Noticed Like Lady GaGa". These make attention grabbing headlines and subheadlines.

Another technique is to use heavily advertised phrases: "We Try Harder";
"Just Do It"; "Reach Out And Touch Someone"; "Like A Rock"; "Good To The Last Drop". Jot some down some while watching ads on TV, or reading media ads. Piggybacking on the millions of dollars spent to burn these phrases into the public consciousness is what you are trying to accomplish. (Watch out for using copyrighted trademarks.)

Once you find ads that work well for you, keep them as a template to just fill in the name of each different product in that niche. Also keep copies of any ads you see on line that you like. Eventually you will create a very valuable file for future use.

Without properly crafted advertisements your multiple streams of internet income would become a dry wash! Take this Chapter, as well as Chapter 12, very seriously, and do not try to reinvent the wheel. The information contained herein has been proven over time by countless successful advertisers to produce the highest possible returns on investment.

JUST DO IT!

CHAPTER 24
PAY PER CLICK ADVERTISING SOLUTIONS

Google pay-per-click AdWords advertising is acknowledged by all experienced internet marketers as the single best way to drive traffic to your website. What very few marketers, even those with some experience, fail to realize that there are MANY nuances to AdWords.

Unless these are fully understood, and the entire AdWords platform mastered, you are guaranteed to fail. The only place I know of where you can go broke faster than you can on AdWords is in Vegas or Monte Carlo!

Casinos are a "never win" scenario. If you stay there long enough, and keep re-wagering your "winnings", you will leave penniless. Regardless of the many "How to win at......" gambling books are out there you cannot "learn" how to be a long-term winner in a casino

AdWords is exactly the opposite. You CAN learn to be a consistent winner! Thousands of internet fortunes have been made, and continue to be made, by internet marketers who have taken the time to learn how. It isn't rocket science, but it does take time and serious study. It also requires discipline.

Before actually learning the mechanics of AdWords, you must do a great deal of preliminary work so that when you do use it properly your results will be as close to optimum as possible. Getting the most out of your AdWords dollars is hard enough. Paying for that advertising to drive traffic to a poorly executed website is a total waste of money.

You may get some sort of perverse satisfaction over driving thousands of visitors to your website for traffic's sake. If these visitors do not take a sufficient number of actions to generate sufficient revenue to cover your advertising costs you will get very discouraged very fast. Or very broke.

So let's see what we have to accomplish before we dive into AdSense.

Once you have everything in place, found your niche full of crazed individuals, identified whatever it is they want to buy, created the product, and set up a website with a keyword-rich domain name and a reputable host, **NOW** the fun starts. And the profits.

As I have said often in this book, the sad truism of internet websites is: "If you build it they **won't** come". Our job as internet entrepreneurs is to give them a damn good reason **TO** come. It does absolutely no good to have a great website of which you are really proud if you are the only one on earth who knows it exists! It is not very likely that someone will stumble upon your website entirely by accident.
There are many ways to drive traffic to a website at zero cost. Article writing, blogging, news releases, social site interaction and many others are the best way to go for a newbie or for someone with limited resources.

But in addition there are many places where you can **pay for visitors**. We will now look at ways you can directly **BUY** traffic, and truly achieve **almost instant results** if you choose to go that route.   If you choose to risk some money, in reasonably-controllable amounts, it is **the fastest way to generate revenue**. You just have to be careful that you generate more money than you spend buying the traffic!

The most common approach to buying traffic is "Pay Per Click" marketing (PPC in the trade, also often referred to as "CPC" or "Cost Per Click"). It is extremely powerful

What is amazing about PPC advertising is that you can:

Pin-point target your potential customers;

Tailor what your visitor sees to their exact interests;

Drop the visitor off exactly where you have placed the offer that matches their interest;

Pay only when they get to your offer;
Accurately measure your results;

Set a "do not exceed" budget;

Run ads 24/7/365 with zero supervision on your part!

Overall, PPC marketing does all the things more "traditional" advertising does, but does it faster and in general more cost effectively, plus it adds the benefit of easily measurable results. **In effect, it sends you "perfect traffic".**

You must become familiar with the key PPC resource links. This is where you buy your paid advertising. Go to, and search through, the following major pay-per-click search engines:

Google Adwords site at: google.com/adwords;

Yahoo Search Marketing site at: searchmarketing.yahoo.com;

Microsoft Ad Center at: adcenter.microsoft.com.

GOOGLE ADWORDS IS KING

Google AdWords is **classified-advertising nirvana!** Compared to off-line advertising it is far more focused, and a lot less expensive. For a lower cost your promotions are targeted to the very people who are interested in your product. This contrasts with off-line ads where only a few readers might even notice your ads at all, let alone care.

In 2000 Google decided to take full advantage of its strong brand and created the automated self-serve advertising program they named "AdWords". (The idea of paid search engine advertising had been pioneered a few years earlier by a company called "GoTo", later named "Overture" and ultimately acquired by Yahoo!.)

It is far easier to set up an AdWords campaign than any offline advertising because everything takes place at a single focused location. And there is virtually no time delay to wait for results. I have seen an AdWords ads score hits **within minutes** of publication! Pay to play.

AdWords started out as a strictly cost-per-thousand-impressions platform. Overture's platform was based on click-throughs, not just eyeball views, and was preferred by advertisers. In 2002 Google got the message and turned to a bid-for-position platform based on keywords that remains a bit modified in that form today.

There are many hundreds of millions of Google search visitors every day. Google-searching has become habitual for many (such as me), and it is reported that the average United States user performs over three Google searches daily.

Google complicates your AdWords experience with various algorithms used to evaluate the relevancy of your website vis a vis your ad wording. They also factor in the percentage of people who actually click through to your website, and will even disable ads that show very low clickthrough rates.

So, even though it is essentially an auction-for-position platform, you cannot be 100% certain that a given bid will provide the expected placement.

Your AdWords account has three components, your "Account", "Campaigns" and "Ad Groups". Your **account** is associated with your unique email address, password, and billing information. Your **campaign** is where you choose your daily budget, geo-targeting, and any ending date. The **ad group**, which can contain multiple ads, is where the ads are created and your keywords chosen.

WHAT GOOGLE WANTS

Google wants people who click on your ads to be taken to a relevant site and have a valuable experience. They want their visitor to find what they are looking for. And they do not want different ads going to the exact same landing page. If Google sees a tight relevancy between the keywords in an ad group and the copy of your ad you will be rewarded with a lower cost per click.

If you set up your campaigns, as described above, with a single keyword in an ad group AND that keyword in the headline you will have a happy Google. That's a good thing! You will also be rewarded by Google for high click-through rates, and also for the length of time you run a particular ad.

Your ad position will rise and your cost per click will decrease as your ad ages and your click through rate is high or rising. These are compelling reasons for taking a great deal of time setting everything up optimally to begin with, and why many who fail to do so have disappointing AdWords results.

In summary, there are four basic considerations for minimizing your costs per click and keeping Google happy: Your ad relevancy, the quality of your landing page, your click-through rate, and your AdWords history.

GOOGLE TOOLS

One thing I can say about Google is that they want you to do things right and give you lots of FREE help along the way. Here are over a dozen really useful FREE Google tools:

"Mass Keyword Search" allows you to find out how your website ranks for up to ten keywords at once. You can also study the top hundred sites for your specific keyword. Access this at: googlerankings.com/mkindex.php.

A great "Guide To Google-Friendly Design" can be found at:
googlerankings.com/googlefriendly.php.

"Google Trends" at google.com/trends will allow you to analyze trends over time.

"Google Insights" at: google.com/insights/search/ enables you to compare search volume patterns across various categories and time frames.

"AdSense Preview Tool" at:
googleadspreview.blogspot.com/ allows you to see what ads Google is most likely to place on your website.

The "Ultimate SEO Tool" when presented with your URL will give you a list of the most frequently used keywords and the number of times they appear, as well as the keyword density. Access this at:
googlerankings.com/ultimate_seo_tool.php.

The "Position Report" button will tell you how your website ranks for each search term.

The "Website Optimizer" tool at:
google.com/websiteoptimizer can help you compare optimization strategies.

Probably the best known and most useful Google tool can be found at: adwords.google.com/select/KeywordToolExternal. By typing in keywords in "Keyword Tool External" you can see how many people searched using that term in the past month. It is generally believed that the ACTUAL number is as much as six times what is stated.

The general Google learning center can be found at: google.com/adwords/learningcenter/.

You can find website tutorials , compliments of Google, at: google.com/intl/en/websiteoptimizer/tutorials.html.

At google.com/reader you can learn all about RSS feeds and how to take advantage of them on your website.

To find the "Page Rank" (a   0 – 10 Google ranking of popularity) of any website install the toolbar found at toolbar.google.com.

STARTING YOUR AWORDS CAMPAIGN - KEYWORDS SEARCH

If you are unable to determine whether any affiliate is scoring big with pay-per-click in a particular vendor offer, you are really left with the alternative of doing some very cautious testing on AdWords.

An important consideration when contemplating launching any AdWords campaign is closely following Google's written policies regarding website content and advertising copy content. Google clearly states all content which they will not accept. Read it, and abide by it. Google's decisions are black and white. There is no gray area. There is no negotiation. If you get restricted, or banned completely, that's it. Game over.

Next comes the fun part. At least I think it is fun. It is VERY time consuming to do it correctly, but correctly is the ONLY way to do it. Your next task is keyword research. **Your success is 100% dependent on it.**

There are two kinds of keyword research, "deep" and "broad". Your success depends upon your full understanding of the difference. In deep keyword research, every keyword you search for will have the exact same "root" keyword. For example, if your niche is "golf", a deep keyword search would be every possible keyword phrase starting with the word "golf":
"golf for beginners"; "golf courses" "golf (whatever)".

Someone conducting a golf search might well type in something without using the word "golf" at all. The point is, going "wide" takes a heck of a lot more thought than just searching the most "obvious" keywords. Every niche has a massive number of sub-niche keywords that often convert much better than the obvious ones, and at a much lower cost.

You may need a lot more of these more-obscure terms, but combined they will provide you with far more revenue overall. You want to cast the widest net possible with the broadest keyword list you can find!

There are many tools available for doing your keyword search. The most often used, because it is arguably the best, is Google's own FREE keyword tool. Two excellent tools that are not free are KeywordElite (my personal favorite) and KeywordSpy. Also check out Microsoft's available tools at:
advertising.microsoft.com/search-advertising/adcenter.

You want to find the most extensive list possible, which may be a list containing thousands of keywords. You want to know how many searches per month each keyword gets.

Further, you want to see exactly on which keywords your competitors are bidding.

Look at the keyword list for search terms that have nothing whatsoever to do with your specific product. You will enter these terms in your AdWords control panel as "negative keywords". Any time one of these show up in a search your ad will **not** be shown. For example, if you are trying to sell something, "free" is a very important negative key word!

The fact is, your negative keyword list is at least as important as your primary keyword list. **This is very often overlooked by many internet marketers.** Excluding these irrelevant terms will greatly increase your click-through rate. Your traffic is better targeted, and you will get more conversions for your ad revenue. Having a strong negative keyword list will give you a significant competitive advantage.

Believe it or not the internet marketing pros can have lists of 50,000 or more keywords on which they offer bids. This can be a bit overwhelming for a newbie. My suggestion is to start by narrowing-down your list to the top few-hundred with the highest search volume.

If possible you may want to break your keyword list down into logical segments. Each segment will be a separate campaign with a slightly different website landing page. One way to do this is to separate into groups those keyword phrases that have a word in common.

This allows you to create separate landing pages optimized for that common keyword. This is a major plus for your overall campaign. Google allows up to 100 ad groups when you are first starting out.

An ad group can have a single keyword in it, up to a 2,000 limit. You want one different unique keyword in each ad group, and you should create two ads for each ad group as

well. Google prefers to see between twenty and fifty keywords in each ad group.
To summarize:

Each keyword group should go into a separate campaign;
Each campaign should go to an appropriate landing page;
Each campaign should have ONE unique keyword per ad group;
Each ad group should have two ads;
Every ad must contain the relevant key word;
The tighter you can target your keywords to your ads and landing page the better.

SETTING YOUR BID PRICE

After you have completed all of the above you are faced with the final task of setting your bid prices. This is make or break time.

As a generality, you want to set your bids high enough so that 75% of your ads end up on the first page of search results. If you can achieve a higher percentage that's great.

The key is having a good idea of your conversion rate. In some cases your affiliate manager will be able to provide this information. If not, there are universally-accepted guideline minimums. If you are asking the visitor to actually buy something, figure a 1% conversion rate. If all the visitor has to do is fill out a form a 10% conversion rate is reasonable. With these figures in mind apply a simple arithmetic formula:

Your Bid Price = Conversion Rate x Commission = Earnings Per Click

For example, a ClickBank product offering a $40.00 commission relates to a bid of $0.40. Strategically you want to set your bid high enough to land on page one of the search results but not so high that you burn through your daily budget in fifteen minutes!

Here is where your risk tolerance might be the determining factor in how many keywords you actually use. It is conventional wisdom that if you do not spend $5.00/day/every 50 keywords. If you have a list of 1,000 you want to use, you need to budget $100.00/day. If you are uncomfortable with that amount, then start with 100 keywords at $10.00/day, or even the minimum suggested 50 minimum keywords at $5.00/day.

Incidentally, Google in its infinite wisdom, might exceed your daily minimum on a given day, but will average it out over a month of ads so as not to exceed your daily minimum on average.

No matter how small a keyword list you use, be certain to have as complete as possible a list of NEGATIVE keywords as you can generate. You could well be working with 50 keywords and 100 negative keywords. The key is to start small, and build as you get positive returns on investment from certain keywords.

This brings up a very important point. **Many potentially-successful affiliate ppc marketers give up much too soon**. They run a campaign, have a negative return on investment, and quit that program. Then they repeat with another program, and get the same results. After a few more tries they decide that AdWords marketing is a fraud. These people have made a fundamental error.

If they are losing 100% of their ad revenue there is clearly something very wrong with their ad or their landing page. But that is seldom the case. They might be getting 30% to 60% of their ad revenue returned as commissions. Those commissions _must_ have come from some of the keywords. They weren't an accident of fate!

Generally only 10% or fewer of your keywords will be found to have converted. The trick is to find out precisely which keywords converted, toss out all of the others, and run a second campaign only using the keywords that converted. That seems like a no brainer, but very few newbies think to do it.

In the "good old days" of Google AdWords, one could bid on any keyword for a nickel, write any crappy ad, and send traffic anywhere. Fortunes were made this way, but over time Google realized that their advertisers were not getting their money's worth. Potential buyers were being sent to non-relevant websites. PPC ads were misleading. Google search **users** were having a bad experience. What's a Google to do?

Enter the "Google Quality Score", "QS", algorithm. A set of quality and relevancy guidelines were put in place to help provide the best possible user experience. No one outside of Google knows exactly how the score is determined, but there are certain parameters that can be deduced logically.

Of primary importance is how relevant the keywords on which you are bidding within your AdWords AdGroup to the content of the ads you are writing. Your CPC (Cost Per Click) will be determined by Google based on how targeted your keywords are compared to your ad and headline.

Another important part of Google's algorithm relates to your landing page, to which they assign a "Quality Score", "QS". For starters, your PPC ad keywords must tie-in exactly with the landing page keywords. To obtain a high QS you must follow the guidelines below. There are "keyword hot-spots" that must be optimized:

Domain: Best choice is: (your primary keyword).com
Next best: (your primary keyword).any relevant URL.com
Least useful: any relevant URL.com/(your keyword)

Title tag: This is a simple piece of HTML code located at the very top of your webpage. The code looks like this: <title>(keyword-rich description)</title>. Google allows 70 characters, Yahoo 115. If possible, put the keywords in alphabetical order which actually has a small effect on rankings.

Headline & Subheadline ; You need to put a bit of HTML code around your headline and subheadline. <h1> is for the headline, <h2> for the subheadline. Thus: <h1>(keyword rich headline)</h1> , and for the sub-headline: <h2>(keyword-rich subheadline)</h2>. You can use <h3> tags around any other less critical subheads used throughout the body text.

Content : You need keywords specifically in the first and last paragraphs, and a bit between, By actual count of words vs keywords you should be shooting for between 4% and 6% keyword density. More than that and Google will penalize you for keyword-spamming. And it is best to stick to only two or three of your optimum keywords.

Behind images: I'm not particulatly fond of having any images at all, because they slow your download time. If you choose to use one or two, note that many webmasters overlook doing this. When you do, it gives the spider-bots even more keywords to help your rankings. Normally, your image would show:
 <img src= "image .jpg" height="120" width="476">. This gives position and size, but nothing for a bot to index. You need to add an <alt> tag within this code. Your final code should read:
<img src= "image .jpg" **alt= "your keywords"** height="120"width="476">.

Description meta tags & keyword meta tags: Meta tags are background HTML that tells the indexing spider-bots what your page is all about. They should be

positioned just below the title tag. They look like this:
<meta name ="description" content="**your full description">.** "Your full description" is the text included in your search results listing.
Directly below that is your keyword meta tag. This would look like:
<meta name="keyword" content="**your primary three keywords**">.
Separate your keywords with a comma.

There is no solid agreement that meta tags are any help in rankings. Search engines change their ranking algorithms so moften that trying to out-guess them is futile. You certainly will not be penalized for using them.

Sitemap: You simply must have an "xml code" sitemap. Without one the indexing spider-bots may never see all of your pages. Bots need a trail to follow, and the site map provides it. At the bottom of every page of your website every page will be just two clicks away from each other. It makes the search engines happy.

Google even helps you to build an XML sitemap. Enter your URL at: google.com/webmasters/sitemaps. Google will create a sitemap for you that you can simply paste into your website. You can also use snapsitemap.com.

Your visitors also need to have links from every page on your site to every other page. These are links created when you build your website, not the special XML sitemap created by Google.

It also helps to put in links to .org and .edu authority sites related to your niche. Announce these on a link to "Other Resources". Google loves links to non-profit sites.

Your QS has the greatest effect on your minimum allowable bids. Google wants to see a "real content" website not just a landing page set up entirely to send the visitor to your affiliate merchant. The latter is known as an "affiliate bridge page" and can result in Google shutting you down completely. You don't want that. Ever.

Five to ten pages of unique content will suffice.   Have an "Additional Useful Information" section at the bottom of your landing page with links to various relevant articles. Be certain to put a **call to action** at the end of EVERY article. Also have an "Articles" link at the bottom going to a separate page that lists hyperlinked titles to every article.

If your site is a comparison or review site have a "Read Full Review" link for each product. This link takes the visitor to a separate page with the detailed review.

You want to set up your campaign with ONE keyword per AdGroup and that one keyword in your ad and headline. Each AdGroup must be pointed towards a different landing page. This single keyword technique is based on my own past experiences and that of a number of very successful AdWords users with whom I have discussed this.

However, my Google AdWords manager (yes, they do assign you a manager whose job it is to see that you get off to a good start.) suggests four to five closely related keywords be put in each AdGroup. I have no problem with that except that it just requires more work trying to decide a group of keywords that are VERY similar to each other.

Remember, your ad must tie in with the keywords in the AdGroup and having more than one keyword in an AdGrouipo makes this rather tricky.

It is also worthy of note that your CTR (click-through-rate) not only affects how much you pay per click but **also** the minimum allowable bid. You need to optimize your ads for the highest possible CTR. Google also factors in your bidding history. You are rewarded the longer you run ads in AdWords. This is unfortunate for newbies. This relates to your account history, ad history, and campaign history. As you build more and more history you will find that over a period of weeks either your ad position will rise, your PPC will drop, or both.

NOTE: If you delete an ad or even a keyword you wipe out your history. If you decide to replace an ad or keyword always keep the old ad running and place the new ad as an additional ad.

WRITING YOUR ADWORDS ADVERTISEMENTS

Writing the actual ad for which you will be paying per click is not all that difficult if you follow a rather short set of requirements. These are:

Put your keyword in the headline (possibly copy the vendor's landing page headline if appropriate);

Put the biggest benefit in the ad;

End every ad in a "cliff-hanger", such as "and ....".

Have a strong call to action (cannot use the word "click");

Capitalize the first letter of each word in the ad;

Capitalize the first letter of each word in the URL;

If possible make the ad into a question;

If possible write the ad as a first-person testimonial.

Putting all of this together manually is good practice for you to learn the entire system. There are programs such as ppckeywordtoolz.com and speedppc.com that greatly speed up the process. Because time is money, they are well worth their cost.

LAUNCH YOUR CAMPAIGN

With AdWords you will know pretty quickly how well you are doing. Should you be getting strong traffic and sales, BINGO! At this point see which keywords are converting and deep six the rest. There is still some tweaking and optimization to perform, but you are well on your way!

If you find that your traffic is good but your sales are weak your landing page probably stinks. Change it. See what happens. You might be pleasantly surprised! This is especially true if you have established that others are succeeding in that niche.

If you find you have lots of traffic and zero sales check to see whether your links to your vendor are live (you or a third-party should be checking all of your links viability periodically anyway). If they are live, you probably have a dud project on your hands and you should drop it like a hot potato!

This could also hold true if you have lots of traffic and only one or two sales. You might be bidding too low, or on the wrong keywords, but if you followed everything above that should not be the issue. Not all campaigns work. Not all those that work to some extent can be made profitable with all the optimization in the world. Cut bait and move on.

MISCELLANEOUS SETTINGS IN YOUR ADWORDS CAMPAIGN

In the course of setting up your AdWords campaign don't make the mistake of selecting "All Countries". This may be tempting, but don't succomb. This is a common newbie error. "Wow, 7+ billion people can see my ad".
Not.

At the very most choose first-world English-speaking countries: USA; UK; Canada; Australia and New Zealand.

The number of wasted clicks from elsewhere in the world will cost you far more than any revenue a few foreign sales from ex-patriot English speakers might bring in.

If you happen to be totally fluent in another language, and can set up your ads and your website in perfect colloquial whatever tongue, you could focus a campaign on that country if it has a high literacy rate and many internet users. Germany, France and Italy come to mind.

Do not even think for one instant about using a computerized translation, regardless of the claims that might be made for the accuracy of same. You will look like an utter fool, and waste all of your ad dollars.

Above we instructed you to write two different ads for each ad group. For this to be of value, set your "Ad Serving" option to "Rotate". In this manner, after your campaign has run for a while, you can check which ad was better at attracting visitors.

CREATING PPC ADS

The "daily budget" you set is not carved in stone, unless you click on the "Recommended Budget" link and see the message: "Budget is OK". Google wants a budget that, according to their algorithm, will "max out" the times your ad appears when your keywords match the search keywords. It is a good idea to accept their suggestion. If you do not there is no guarantee that your budget will not be exceeded.

In theory you can use hundreds of keyword phrases within your AdGroup, but you will make a lot less work for yourself by finding and using ten or so phrases that narrowly target your niche. This makes it far easier for you to track which ads work best with which set of keywords.

I have found that my click-through rate increases if there is an EXACT match between a word in my title and the phrase the user typed in. Not only your ad title but your ad body MUST contain relevant keywords. Try to run five to ten sets of ads that match closely to the keywords in each group.

Note that Google prohibits what they call "double serving". If you happen to have multiple products that are all relevant to the same keywords you cannot have more than one of them showing up on the same page of search results. This prevents a creative advertiser from crowding out the competition by dominating all of the choice positions.

In writing your ads follow good "AIDA" principles pointed out above. Google is not exactly generous with the space you are allowed. You get 25 characters for your headline, and 35 characters for each of the two lines in the ad body. The "Display URL", your web address the user sees below your ad, is also limited to 35 characters, but that should be no problem.

The "Landing URL", which must send visitors directly to the information sought without a second click, can be 1,024 characters. This allows you to use whatever extensions and tracking codes you might wish to add to your display URL for tracking purposes.

Your ad may very well result in an "Editorial Disapproval" email. You have somehow violated one of Google's written, implied, or seemingly made –up-on- the-fly regulations. Violations of minor editorial rules are common. **Things such as unnecessary punctuation, misspelled words, all capitals, and capitalizing the first letter of each word in the ad are all no-nos.**

It isn't worth the time and effort to disagree with Google's finding and try to convincethem to allow your ad to show as written. Just clean it up and move on.

Ads can get immediate results, but there is a Google ad-review process which can delay the appearance of your ad. This delay could be a week or more if you are using very popular keywords, or your ad is placed at a time (such as Christmas) when lots of ads are under review. Always allow for a few weeks delay.

Although we have discussed aspects of Google elsewhere in this book, we need to revisit the important features of the AdWords platform. There are three major syntax forms available to you within your AdWords account:

EXACT MATCH: The user's entry must exactly match a word or phrase in your keyword list. You force exact matches by entering your keywords between brackets ([xxxxxxx]). (The [ ] are unnecessary with single keywords.) The more words in an exact match the better targeted the user will be, but the number of visitors are fewer in proportion to the number of words bracketed.

PHRASE MATCH: Putting quotation marks ("xxxx") around a phrase will trigger your ad when that exact phrase appears somewhere in a user's search. It does not matter what other words a user might enter in the search preceding or trailing the chosen phrase.

BROAD MATCH: Keywords entered without any punctuation will trigger your ad if they appear anywhere in the user's search.

Only your own experience with your ads over time will dictate how syntax focus relates to the success of a particular product campaign. There are no hard and fast rules because there are so many possible variables. Just test, record results, and optimize over time.

Google search any keyword term. Check out the first four websites that come up and then go to the AdWords Suggestion Tool , enter a keyword: adwords.google.com/select/keywordtoolexternal. The program will suggest related keywords. You can also click on "Site Related Keywords" where you can enter an actual website address, and Google will suggest keywords based on that address.

If you are representing a vendor as their affiliate, it is a good idea to register a URL with the exact vendor product name if it is available. This would be something like: "makebigbucksfromhome.com", where the title of the eBook is "Make Big Bucks From Home". If the .com version unavailable, you could try the .net or .org version. Alternately, you could make a minor change in the URL such as "makebigbuckfromhome.com" or "makebigbucksfromhome1.com".

If you want some FREE ideas for a domain name to register for a particular keyword or keyword phrase in connection with an affiliate campaign go to: 123finder.com. Enter your keywords, up comes a list of URL ideas.

Keyword research is critical to your success. Start by using Google's own "AdWords Keyword Tool". Click the " Tools" link on the "Campaign Management" toolbar to access the page containing links to the various AdWords tools. Click the "Keyword Tool" link to open the list. It helps if you have already put a keyword few phrases into your Ad Group. This tool does NOT give you the frequency of visitor searches for the suggestions given.

Once you have done this, and chosen a number of phrases you believe would be useful, it is time to go to "Plan B". This is the use of third-party tools. Probably the most used such tool is Word Tracker at wordtracker.com. It provides critical search data on millions of search terms. There is an inexpensive short trial available. Personally I have used

Brad Callen's "KeyWordElite" (keywordelite.com) product for years and find it serves my purposes quite well.

What you hope to find are relevant keywords that have significant search volume for which you are the only bidder and can buy for the minimum $0.05 per click. The more such phrases you can weave into your account the better your return on investment should be.

It pays to snatch the low-hanging keyword fruit first. Getting into a bidding war for a single common term makes no sense at all. You can readily bid small amounts for multiple obscure-long-tail-keywords that will in combination generate as much or more traffic for a lot less money!

The big mistake many newbies make is to list too many keywords in their AdWords campaign. They'll spend $50.00, see $30.00 income, and consider the item a loser, drop it, and go on to the next vendor. What they fail to do is to analyze which keywords produced the $30.00 profit. Very often it is one or two out of ten. No brainer.

The very best general strategy is to spread yourself very thin at the start.
Choose at least ten, better twenty, products to represent, but spend very little money in AdWords on each.

Drop non-performing keywords, focus a second sum on the winners, and the chance of achieving a fine rate of return is excellent.

There are certain useful nuances that can be applied to keywords. These include:

Plural vs singular form;

Verb forms and related nouns (e.g., repair, repairing, how to repair);

Common misspellings (e.g., weeding for wedding);

Hyphenated vs non-hyphenated words;

Abbreviations (e.g. wkly for weekly);

Acronyms (you are allowed to put these in all capitals);

Phrase questions preceded by who, what, where, when and why.

On one hand Google is very easy to use and to start PPC advertising. On the other hand there is a fairly steep learning curve if you hope to maximize your Google AdWords results and not throw away cash.
Google AdWords has a valuable tool called "Traffic Estimator" that shows how much you would have to pay to get the number one position for a given keyword or phrase. You can access this without actually running a PPC campaign.

Set up a dummy campaign with an obscure term. 1. log in and "create a new campaign". 2. Create ad group "TEST" Headline TEST, descriptions TEST. 3. Enter a single keyword. & save. Google will now tell you the $ it will take the top position when you click "Calculate Estimate". To be sure the dummy ad never runs put in very low bid (as a second preventative safety) and "Pause" the ad forever.

The above three sites, Google, Yahoo! and Microsoft, are the key places where you can <u>buy</u> search positioning. It may be a waste of time and effort to run PPC ad campaigns on any of the dozens of lesser-known search engines. In fact, concentrating on Google alone will expose your efforts to 80% of search traffic based on present-day reports of search engine traffic.

TRACKING YOUR KEYWORDS

Google makes it possible to track every keyword you employ. They provide a snippet of code that you place as directed. There are also many third-party conversion-tracking software programs available. You must track the conversion rate of every keyword you use. Google's own tracking is FREE, and seamlessly integrates with your entire AdWords effort.

The problem with keyword tracking is that the software snippet must be installed on the VENDOR'S thank you page. Few are set up to do this automatically, though you may find a few that are. You will need to contact the vendor, tell them how great their program is and how badly you want to send them business.

Explain that being able to optimize your keywords will mean more visitors will be sent to buy their wonderful product. Provide your conversion code, and tell them how much you are looking forward to working with them. Many, not all, will go along with your request.

Tracking is so critical to your success that not being able to track individual keyword conversions should disqualify a vendor from having you as an affiliate. In fact you should never go to the time to formulate a campaign until you can determine absolutely that you will be permitted to track.

It is absolutely impossible to intuitively guess which keywords will be best. Two keyword phrases with only a tiny difference between them can have dramatically different conversion rates.

Google Analytics (GA) lets you track an unlimited number of sites. You can track your sales conversions with their "Goal Tracking" feature. GA also lets you track your AdWords listings against your organic listings in the major search engines.

OPTIMIZE YOUR PPC ADS

You optimize your ad wording by "split testing". Using this technique you try variations of your headline and text such as: "Free Widgets Fast" (get your widget NOW); "Order Free Widgets" (order today for fast delivery); "Compare Widget Offers" (don't just buy but compare available offers); "Free Widget Offers Reviewed" (here's what I think of widget offer a, b or c). Get the idea?

Because you are paying per any click it doesn't matter on which of these split-test ads someone clicks. Over time, looking at your visitor statistics you will be able to tell which wording works best and focus your entire budget on paying for clicks for that particular ad.

Never pre-assume which ad and headline will work best. Personal intuition doesn't cut it. My gut feelings on a given ad is usually proven wrong by split-testing! You will very often be amazed to see one wording pulling five times the clicks of another for absolutely no obvious reason. **Just test, test, test. Then test again.**

If you see a competitor's ad at the top of the Google results day after day, (when you enter a particular keyword or phrase) week after week, and know they are paying a high PPC rate, you know they are easy crazy (and enjoy losing money every day) or they are making money at the PPC rate they are paying.

It is a bit of a chore to track one or more sites on a daily basis, but needless to say there is a company out there who will do it for you...for a price. This valuable resource to access is at: spyfu.com. They maintain a database so you can go back a month and see who has been bidding on what for how long. This is a great way to see whether your competition is making money with ppc.

One VERY important last thought in your PPC ad writing. It is a key tip that has been shown time and time again to increase clicks. It is called the "Cliffhanger". **EVERY ad copy, that which the web surfer sees, should close with "and ...."** *as if it were cut off by the character restrictions.* **It is human nature to want to learn "and WHAT???"** It has been shown by split testing to increase clicks. Easy and important to do.

Skill in advertising creation and placement is vital to your success in internet commerce. Of course you can have the perfect ad and generate oodles of clicks, but if visitors do not take the desired action on your landing page (whether it is email address in exchange for a freebie, or direct link to an affiliate offer) your click payment was wasted.

That is why your landing page is the single most important aspect of your overall internet marketing campaign.

There are a few useful rules to follow as you evaluate problems that might occur during your campaigns:

If certain keywords show very few clicks, drop them at once.

If you are getting insufficient clicks overall, it is possible that traffic does not actually exist. It is also possible that you have a bad ad, insufficient keywords, or too low a position in the search engine (<3) for anyone to see your ads.

If you get lots of clicks but low or no sales your landing page sucks. Perhaps your offer sucks too.

If your clicks are too costly lower your bid gradually to see how it affects your position. Perhaps Google doesn't like your site and hasn't told you yet (The "Google Slap"). If you see a sudden hike in your click costs delete the ad group and start from scratch.

AS mentioned earlier, if your ad is disapproved, delete it and try again. Don't argue. You cannot win.

If you get a "Final Warning" for something take it seriously, suspend the campaign, and make logical changes. It is always a good idea for your wife or partner to have a backup account!

If your excellent click-through rate suddenly plunges, search your keyword terms and see if someone decided to copy your ad.

If your impressions and clicks drop suddenly you may have been the victim of the dreaded "Google Slap", best avoided by following the rules outlined above.

Just follow basic good website practices and you will be rewarded by Google with lower click costs and higher search positioning.

POST LAUNCH CONSIDERATIONS

Once you are up and running and past break-even you now have to work on optimizing your program. Don't just sit back just yet, satisfied that you've won the war. The battle maybe, but total victory still lies ahead!

You have set up two ads in each ad group, and set the "Ad Serving" to "Rotate". This assures that each ad is viewed an equal number of times. You must wait until the analytical results have statistical significance. This would generally occur after the two ads combined have received 75 to 100 clicks.

Google will tell you the exact number of clicks on each, and the click through ratio (CTR) of each. If the ads have similar results, just leave them both. If one is clearly better, eliminate the weaker ad.

You can also split-test any element of your website. Your headline, your call to action, and even your color scheme can affect your conversion rate.

There is a software program at hypertracker.com that can accomplish this.

It costs around $15/month, but it can be more than worth it in improving your conversion rate.

What is hard to grasp intuitively is that a small change, such as going from singular to plural in a keyword, or from green to blue in an action button, can have a huge effect on conversion rates. There is no intuitive way to predict this. There is no clear pattern across campaigns. You simply must split-test if you hope to optimize your campaigns.

If you want to be lazy, "leave well enough alone", you may continue to profit but you could be leaving massive profits on the table. Your choice.

At no cost you can "play around" with your bidding. You can lower your bids for the top performing keywords by 15%, while raising the bids for the lesser converting keywords by 15%, and of course dropping the duds completely. This is all done in your AdWords Editor's "Advanced Bid" feature. (Be sure to check "do not set keyword maximum cpc bids to values lower than their minimum CPC bids" or your ads disappear!

Keep focus on you overall goal which is to earn one dollar for every dollar spent on advertising. (That is, every $1.00 worth of ads should produce $2.00 in revenue.) Some campaigns do far better than this, but it is an achievable goal. You want your average cost per conversion to be half or less than your vendor's commission.

Do not ever start messing with anything in your campaign until you have data that is statistically significant. **This is where many newbies fail.** Until a campaign has run for a month it is unlikely that any analytical data will have real value in directing adjustments anywhere. Once you can begin to make changes, make them based on cold hard statistics, never on emotion.

There are thousands of affiliate programs out their making many affiliate marketers very rich.   Start slowly, learn all you can, follow all of the above advice, optimize you programs, and you will be well on your way to earning more than you probably ever thought possible.

MORE GOOGLE WISDOM

Fairly recently Google came up with the idea of "First Page Bids". This is the minimum amount you must bid to appear on page one. There is no way you can get on page one at a cost below what Google decides. Bad change for advertisers.

In their never ending quest to enhance its bottom line, which they are very good at doing, Google has created "Pay Per Call". This allows companies with a call center to bid on phone calls generated by their Google search ads. Google patches the calls through to the advertiser's designated phone number. This is not exactly a program for newbies or even small companies. What effect if any this will have on page rankings has not yet been determined.

LOWER YOUR NET PPC AD COSTS

There is a very clever way to mitigate your PPC advertising costs. Once you have a successful website getting lots of PPC traffic that you can document you can sell advertising space on your website to offset your PPC bid costs.

You will need to show your average Cost Per Click (CPC) rate (under $0.05 is great), Alexa rank (under one million is great), Google page rank (4 or better is fine), and your average or previous day's page views.

And of course your ads need to show up at or near the top position for your chosen keywords.

Once you know your average cost for your PPC ads on a monthly basis, divide by the number of ads you choose to sell to get a good idea of your "break even" point in pricing your ads. Ads on a great site can easily be sold for $97 a month and possibly a lot more. It is a good idea to offer proportionally lower daily, weekly and two-week rates as well.

Even if you find you cannot cover 100% of your ad costs, you can certainly lower your costs dramatically and greatly increase your return on investment. Remember, simply cutting ad costs in half doubles your advertising ROI!

Selling five to ten ads should do the trick. Preferably these should be text ads, because banner ads are proving to have reached the point where people seldom click on them. You can try selling both, but you will have happier and longer-term advertisers if you steer them to text ads.

Use unsold space for your own ads. Don't overwhelm your own primary offer with other's paid ads. You can set your page up so that your offer or offers clearly dominate.

To get visitors to purchase your ad space, simply include something on your website that stands out and shouts: "HOT!! Your Banner Here For Just $3.13 A Day!!! Reach Google's 100-Plus Million Daily Buyers Here!"

You may be very pleasantly surprised to find that you not only cover your PPC costs but can actually turn a profit that could end up exceeding the profit from your primary offer! By purchasing a dropped website with favorable analytics you can save all of the time it takes to create an "advertising worthy" website. Definitely consider that route to riches.

Free traffic is wonderful, but the majority of successful infopreneurs have found that PPC advertising, cost-mitigated or not, over the long term is their best route to internet riches and a massive stream of alternate income sources.

GOOGLE ALTERNATIVES

Google is king. No one questions that. Most internet marketers focus entirely on Google. Many other search engines have PPC programs, and some are making good use of these, even though traffic is a small fraction of what Google generates.

There are many smaller search engine possibilities. They get far less traffic, but your cost-per-click can be dramatically lower, and it is much easier to achieve top position for long-tail keywords. Check out: adbrite.com; clicksor.com; searchfeed.com; 7search.com; looksmart.com; validclick.com; kanoodle.com; enhance.com; miva.com; abcsearch.com; search123.com and ezanga.com. For a full directory of PPC search engines go to: payperclicksearchengines.com/directory/.

Note that 7search.com can geo-target 240 countries. They offer FREE conversion tracking. There is NO minimum bid. They even give you up to a $25 match on your initial deposit as an incentive using code "WEBMAG" compliments of *Website Magazine.* You can go to *Website Magazine* at: websitemagazine.com/digital to see a PPC bid matrix showing average bid prices across many different various PPC search engines.

Pay per click marketing must be done deliberately and with caution. Use low bids and low daily maximums. It is a fact that there is no faster way to drive business to a website. You simply have to be certain that your revenue generated exceeds your ad costs. It just takes practice. Tread lightly at first, but **DO TRY PPC**. There is no way to achieve faster results.

Similar to paying per click is paying for "impressions". You pay purely for exposure, to have your ad seen regardless of whether it is clicked on. **Do not overlook CPM (cost per thousand impressions; M=1,000 in Latin). Tribalfusion.com and Albrite.com are affiliate networks specializing in CPM advertising.** Many very high traffic websites offer this alternative to PPC.

With CPM you are hoping that someone who had absolutely no idea they want what you are offering is sufficiently motivated to click on your ad. These people may not even be shopping at all. If you can find a relevant site where visitors might logically be interested in your offer CPM can work well. How do you find good relevant sites?

Take a long, hard look, at Quantcast. Quantcast.com is a site dedicated to internet demographics. Study this site in detail, because it can be of great value to you in all of you internet marketing. For example, do a search on a product niche to find related sites to what you are offering. Here you can check out the sites where your product niche gets great exposure. Taking the time to learn Quantcast will be time very well spent.

Well worth considering is a technique called Cost Per View (CPV). It is easy to implement, and you do not even need a website! What's better, your cost can be a penny per click, and you are advertising on other people's websites. How great is that? The two most popular programs are DirectCPV at directcpv.com and LeadImpact at leadimpact.com.

A direct quotation from the DirectCPV website says it all:

"Give your online marketing campaign the jolt it needs with DirectCPV's pay per view advertising solution. Starting at just $0.015 for URL, keyword and category campaigns and $0.004 for run of network advertising, DirectCPV offers the best value for your advertisement dollar. With a minimum deposit of only $100, DirectCPV is sure to fit any marketing budget. Discover the power of CPV advertising now with DirectCPV. Try something different with DirectCPV, the leading online CPV and PPV advertising network that delivers the highest converting results and increases ROI for all advertisers. Extend your reach by targeting relevant keywords, URLS, locations and channels to ignite your income and generate higher conversions. **We guarantee performance."**

Essentially, you simply write your ad and launch your campaign, sit back, and look for positive results. I know of a number of infopreneurs who use this platform successfully. The key to success is writing killer ads with killer headlines.

Paying to get your traffic, PPC or CPM, or CPV, done properly and carefully, can be extremely profitable. For an internet marketing newbie it is best to develop traffic in the cost-free ways until you are comfortable in knowing that you have a winning affiliate vendor product.

CHAPTER 25
EZINES AND ARTICLE-MARKETING SECRETS

An internet "ezine" is an "**e**lectronic maga**zine**". These are publications offered by internet infopreneurs for the purpose of keeping in touch with individuals who have shared their email addresses and requested such periodic information. Ezines are also often called "newsletters".

Aside from the "keep-in-contact with my buyers" aspect, ezines are your perfect advertising medium.

When you find an ezine that focuses on your niche topic approach the owner and ask to advertise. Many have three kinds of ads: the most expensive is where they will feature your ad at the top of their newsletter (or even send out a special issue with only your ad)., Less expensive are classified-type ads that appear at the bottom.

Between these extremes are ads where the ezine author favorably reviews your item and recommends it. With the right offer and a well written ad placed in the right publication you should be able to get many multiples of the cost of any of these three types of ads.

Ask the author how many names are on his mailing list, and whether new names are added by double opt-in (as they should be). And remember, a smaller list (say two to three thousand recipients) that is focused on the niche of your product is a far better vehicle for your ads than a huge list (thirty to a hundred thousand or more) that has poorly qualified subscribers relative to your niche.

A Google search for "ezine directories" gives you about three million choices! Personally I use Ezine-DIR.com which has over 1,400 ezines listed in 40+ categories. Something for everyone!

There are a number of things you must consider when choosing an ezine in which to place an ad. For starters subscribe to the ezine. Look for ezines with good solid content. Check out how many ads are shown. The more ads the lower your chance of having your ad seen (four or five ads in an issue is acceptable). Ask the author how many names are on his mailing list, and whether new names are added by double opt-in (as they should be).

And remember, a smaller list (say two to three thousand recipients) that is focused on the niche of your product is a far better vehicle for your ads than a huge list (thirty to a hundred thousand or more) that has poorly qualified subscribers.

A Google search for "ezine directories" gives you about three million choices! Personally I use Ezine-Dir.com which has over 1,400 ezines listed in 40+ niche categories.

Launching you **own** ezine can be a financially rewarding venture. Aside from being able to include text links within the ezine that point to your own product websites and those of your affiliates, you can sell advertising space to others.

Having your own ezine is a great enhancement to having your own eMail list. You can even swap ads with other ezine publishers. And having your own ezine creates the impression to visitors that you are an expert in your niche.

When you list your ezine in ezine directories, you will not only get subscribers, but you may get requests from authors to have their articles published in your ezine. To acquire ezine content, aside from writing it yourself, check out Ezine Articles at: ezinearticles.com.

It can also be very profitable to list your best quality articles at EzineArticles to enhance your exposure and build credibility. The key is that you can add a short but powerful blurb in a resource box at the end of your article. This can deliver pre-qualified visitors to your website squeeze page with potential click-throughs to your affiliate's websites.

Over time, as you write ezines, and answer visitors questions in eMails, you can create an archive of ezines and a FAQ ("Frequently Asked Questions") section of your website.

And if you want more information on ezines than you could possibly ever need check out The Ezine University at: ezineuniversity.com. Advertising is a two-way street. You can run ads to get more visitors, but you can also accept ads to get more money! Sweet.

If you are having trouble creating ezines you can always pay a third party to write them. Elance at: elance.com is very popular, but there are literally hundreds of similar sites and hundreds of thousands of willing ghost writers. As always, check out fiverr.com to see what is available for just five dollars. You will often be pleasantly surprised.

As an alternative to ghost writers check out the "Ezine Article Creator Pro" by Jimmy D. Brown. This is a template based "answer questions and fill in the blanks" system that is easy to use. A Google search will turn up many affiliates who offer this program, most for under twenty bucks.

ARTICLE MARKETING

Perhaps the single most powerful and FREE approach to making any internet product sales is called "Article Marketing". Each week you submit at least one short article (250 -350 words is a good range) on your niche topic. Do not write this as "sales copy". Make it informative in some valuable way. Although we have mentioned this earlier, it is so important that you must read it again and again.

Never try to pitch your company or product in the article itself. Article directories are looking for information, not promotion. You want interesting articles that people will read to the very bottom where they will find your profile and your link. Write articles that are "timeless". Avoid current events. You want your articles to be read for years to come.

Once written you must submit your articles to some "article directories". When website owners and ezine publishers want free useful information-rich material to reprint they turn to the article directories.

For getting this free content they agree not to alter your article in any way. Most important they must leave your resource box, which you placed at the end of your article (with the link to your website or your affiliate offer) as is.

A Google search for "Article Directories That Allow Links" turns up 242 million results! You do not need quite that many. The following two are the "must list on" list. Google seems to favor them.

Ezinearticles.com (By far the biggest, but you must link to a squeeze page or pre-sell content website page. Many smaller directories will spider-search this site and place your article on their site as well.)

USfreeads.com (Not exactly an article site, but you can link directly to your affiliate vendor, a **HUGE** plus.)

The following are excellent additional directory choices: affsphere.com; goarticles.com; articlecity.com; articlesbase.com; articledashboard.com; articlesfactory.com; newfreearticles.com; and sitepronews.com.

You should also try: articlecube.com; articlealley.com; articlesnatch.com; easyasrtcles.com; articlebiz.com; theleadingarticles.com; buzzle.com; and isnare.com.

Both FREE and paid placements are available at: ideamarketers.com; contentcrooner.com; and distributeyourarticles.com.

Keep in mind that some of these article directories get tens of thousands of visitors every day. When someone uses your article, others to whom they send it might also use it. This is known as "viral marketing", because your article with its links spreads like a virus across the internet!

The word "viral" carries the negative "virus" connotation. No one wants to be sick. No one wants their computer to be sick. For these reasons I prefer to use the term: **"Auto-Effective Marketing"** whenever referring to "viral" marketing techniques.

Other useful article directory choices are: articlecube.com; articlealley.com; articlesnatch.com; easyarticles.com; articlebiz.com; theleadingarticles.com; isnare.com; hubpages.com;technorati.com; buzzle.com; brighthub.com; thefreelibrary.com; suite101.com; ideamarketers.com; ezau.com; contentcrooner.com; distributeyourarticles.com; articleclone.com; articlegems.com; articlerich.com; associatedcontent.com; fastarticlefinder.com; findarticles.com.

Incidentally, throughout this book I offer a large number of website addresses in many different categories. These are all active as I write this, but websites come and go and some may no longer be active for one reason or other. I do suggest, however, that you take the time to visit ALL of the live sites. Yes, it is time consuming, but there is a great deal that can be learned by visiting the various vendors and studying their tutorials and reading the Question and

Answer (Q & A) sections. Overall you will acquire an understanding of the immensity of the entire internet marketing experience.

Many article site owners do not want you posting duplicate content that you posted to other similar sites. Always read the "Terms and Conditions" and/or "Article Guidelines", and follow them.

In general, once you submit an article it usually takes about a week to appear on the first page of search results. It will remain there a month or two. **I suggest you submit at least four new articles every day if you hope to make this business model your primary source of internet income.**

There are also over 150 specialized article directories that focus on a single topic or niche. Do you have a product related to dogs? Post an article in: bestdogarticles.com. How about hair care? See: haircarearticles.com. Product related to college? Check out: youronlinecollegeguide.com. Do a search on Google for "Specialist Article Directories" and you will find one on just about any imaginable topic.

<u>Your resource box, which is your earnings-key, placed at the end of your article, should look something like this:</u>

"To learn more about (your niche product) check out my website at (your domain name). Here you will find many more tips on (your niche product). Feel free to distribute this article in any form you choose as long as you <u>include</u> this resource box. "

There is the MAJOR ancillary benefit to using the Article Directories. Many of those listed above have high Google Page Ranks. (You can find the Google Page Rank [PR] of any website by installing the Google Toolbar at toolbar.google.com). Back-links to your website from a PR 5 or higher website will increase your search engine ranking considerably.

Instead of spending the time to post your articles to each directory yourself you can pay a nominal sum to have someone else do it for you. There are many directory submission vendors. One with which I am familiar is at: seoster.com. Check it out. They have many plans available. For example, for under $20 they will submit your article to 100+ high page rank directories.

If you do a Google search for "Directory Submission Tools" you will find that there are many software programs available that you can install yourself and do mass submissions of your articles to directories. You may find that some of these are cost effective.

IDEAS FOR YOUR ARTICLES

There are at least a dozen "article categories" you can exploit.   Within these categories you can create infinite variations:

Answer A Question: "What Does xxxxxxx Mean?". "xxxxxxx Answered at Last!". "What Does It Mean When Someone Says xxxxxx". "Why would someone xxxxxxxx".

How To: "How To Prevent xxxxxxx".   "How To Build A Better xxxxxxx".   "How To Get Rid Of xxxxxx In A Week!".

Hot Trends: "Top Five Trends In xxxxxxx."   "3 Super-Hot Trends In xxxxxxx." "Are You Missing These Three Trends In xxxxxxx".

Free: "5 Places To Get Free xxxxxxx." "Why Pay For xxxxxxx When You Can Get It For Free?" "3 Places To Get Free xxxxxx For Your xxxxxxx".

Cheap: "3 Ways To Get Cheap xxxxxx". "Five Of The Cheapest xxxxxxx". "Are You Missing The 7 Cheapest xxxxxx?".

Easy/Fast: "Seven Easy Ways To xxxxxx". "Don't Struggle. Use these three easy ways to xxxxxx". "Five Of The Fastest xxxxxx". "3 Ways To Get Faster xxxxxx".

Avoid Problems And Pain: "3 Ways To Avoid The xxxxxx Trap". "Never Do This If You Want xxxxxx". "7 Things Not To Do If You Want xxxxxx."

Reviews: Thinking Of Buying xxxxxx? Read This First". "xxxxxx And xxxxxx Compared Side By Side." "Should Beginners Buy xxxxxx". "Is xxxxxx Really User-**Friendly?".**
Rules, Laws, Principles: "The 7 Laws Of xxxxxx". "Three Success Rules Of xxxxxx". "Do You Know The 5 Basic Principles Of xxxxxx".

Top Tips: "7 Top Tips For Avoiding xxxxxx". "Five Top Tips For Better xxxxxx". "Do You Know The Top Three Tips For xxxxxx?".

Experts: "3 Ways The Experts xxxxxx". "What The Experts Recommend For xxxxxx". "5 Expert Tactics For xxxxxx".

X vs Y: "Should You Buy xxxxxx or xxxxxx?". "xxxxxx vs xxxxxx, Which Is Best?". "Why Is xxxxxx Better Than xxxxxx?

Still need an idea for an ezine or article? Google search the keyword "TIP". This will give you a wealth of ideas. Add these three words: "learn", "training" and "buy" to open up a Pandora's box of internet commerce possibilities.

To see articles that have actually been published in a particular niche go to ezinearticles.com. Plug in any term and see a list of articles related to that term. Click on an article and you will find the date that it was published and the number of times it was viewed. This can be a great eye-opener, and an indicator of the traffic you could expect for your articles.

The following is a list of ezines that accept advertising. You can get many ideas for your own ezine ad solicitation from studying these:

Ezinehits.com/ad-rates.htm;

Thegurumarketer.com/ad-rates.htm;

Goldbar.net/advert.html;

Gmhnewsletter.com;

Workathomenews.com/advertising.html</a>;

Bizweb2000.com/ads.htm</a>;

Inetexchange.com/inet-mailer.html;

Themoneymakingaffiliates.com/advertise;

Netincomesite.com/ezineadrates/ezineadrates.htm;

Superpromo.com/optadorder.html;

Rimdigest.com/ads.html</a>;

Topliving.com/marketing/fmailing.htm</a>.

You can go to ezinesearch.com for a comprehensive list of ezines that accept advertising.

CONCLUSIONS

Of all of the possible FREE ways to promote your products or your affiliate vendor's links, and obtaining quality backlinks, using popular Article Directories is one of the easiest and most profitable. Be certain to focus a significant amount of time on this one of many possible multiple streams of internet income. You won't be sorry that you did. JUST DO IT!

CHAPTER 26
MAKING EASY MONEY WITH ADSENSE

AdSense is basically Google's way of displaying their paid pay-per-click "AdWords Ads" on **your** website. These are the same sort of ads that you paid for in your PPC marketing. The ads Google chooses to put on your website are based upon the keywords in your domain name, keywords in your title, and keywords in articles on your site. When one of your visitors clicks on one of the AdSense ads you get paid a percentage of the cost that the advertiser is paying Google for each click.

Google AdSense is a very simple business model. You create a website and drive traffic to it. Google places advertisements on your website and pays you a commission every time one of your visitors clicks on one of the ads. Simplicity itself. It is the other face of the AdWords PPC model.

AdWords marketing is not always the best business model for a vendor buying clicks from Google. The reason for this is that many AdSense marketers drive visitors to their vendor's links but do not always provide the visitor with content that would result in a "better" quality click-through for the vendor. What PPC advertisers ultimately want are relevant visitors. By using Google AdWords, and by Google placing AdSense ads on your websites based on **relevancy**, advertisers can get a better quality visitor.

AdSense is the "lazy persons'" way to earn money from ads on a website. It relieves the time and aggravation of you selling ad space on your website, negotiating price and placement, and ultimately not being certain of getting paid.

If you choose to send visitors to your AdSense website by paying per click on Google AdWords you are now doing a Google "arbitrage". There is nothing wrong with trying this tactic. You need to spend less on your AdWords clicks than you earn on your visitors' AdSense clicks to show a profit. It can be done. With a properly designed website with keyword-rich articles it is reported that individuals using this arbitrage as a business model earn a return on investment (ROI) of 2X to 4X. It is well worth a try. I have found that it works quite well.

Of course, if you can drive traffic to your website by free means instead of PPC your AdSense revenue is pure profit! Many internet entrepreneurs make all of their considerable income entirely from the presence of AdSense ads placed by Google on their websites, and paying nothing to drive traffic to their sites with various kinds of free promotion.

You may not (Google's rule) set up a website **entirely** for the purpose of running AdSense ads. You need at least one other reason for your website to exist, such as offering a product of your own or presenting a vendor affiliate link.

There are, in fact, many internet mavens who use AdSense as their primary source of income. And it can be a very large income. But to do it right is not quite "simplicity itself". There is a modest learning curve, as evidenced by the fact that there are many hundreds of pages of "how to get it right" information on the Google AdSense website itself. It's not rocket science, but there is much to learn before you can sit back, relax, and collect an endless stream of checks.

Keep in mind that AdSense is a very important revenue source for Google. They keep a part of the revenue paid by the advertisers (reportedly between 32% and 60%). Because of that, they do backflips to see that you have every widget imaginable to make your AdSense experience successful. Your task is to learn how to take maximum advantage of what they have to offer.

Incidentally, the AdSense program is FREE as far as your relationship with Google goes. Any expenses you incur are those related to creating your websites and driving traffic to them.

To get started go to google.com/adsense, fill out the simple forms, and open an account. As with all things Google, if you have any other Google account you can sign in with that user name. Then go to "Newbie Central" and you will be guided through the entire process of setting up ads on your websites. (Of course you must actually HAVE a website before you do this.)

You may place three AdSense ads and three AdSense link boxes on each page of your website. There is also an "AdSense For Search" function (you get paid for clicks on that as well) that can be added in two positions on a page.

Learning where to physically position AdSense ads on your site's pages is more a matter of split-testing trial and error than it is science. Google offers a lot of guidance, but it is up to you to optimize the potential earnings from your website. It is worthy of note that the guidance they offer can be valuable knowledge that you can apply to your other website work outside of the AdSense platform.

The conventional wisdom for placing AdSense advertisements from the standpoint of the psychology of visitor attention is the following:

NO GOOD: Top right above navigation bar; lower right at bottom.

OK: Top left and center above nav bar; right along content, lower left at bottom.

BETTER: Upper right and center below nav bar. Bottom center.

KEY SPOT: Center above content, below first ad under navigation bar.

With Google constantly changing their ranking algorithms, and their likes and dislikes, the above conventional wisdom may well not be what Google prefers to see when you read this. Lately it seems that Google would prefer all ads of any kind be **below** at least the opening text on your landing page.

It is a good idea to change the overall width of your web site. Make the white-space reading area narrow (see "love-poems-love-poems.com for a good example of this structure). It focuses a user's attention. AdSense ads should be the first thing a visitor sees. You should put your navigation bar BELOW the AdSense ads. Because Google changes their ranking algorithm often, it might be a good idea to split-test with the navigation bar above the ads.

When you are setting up your AdSense ads you have total control over color schemes, size, shapes, and fonts. They also provide default settings for these parameters which they have found to be optimum. Personally I opt out of ego-satisfying creativity in favor of Google's experience! Go: "Default".

Google then decides which ads to place on your website based upon the relevant key words on your site pages. Ads can be beautiful image ads, or simple stand-alone text ads, or "contextual" ad links that become integrated within the text on your web page.

A certain familiarity with the placing of HTML (Hyper-Text Markup Language, a basic computer code used throughout the industry) coding on your web server can be achieved through the AdSense tutorials, or from your web host's help desk. You do not need to create any HTML code yourself. Be thankful!

Even before you submit your website to AdSense you can put it through a mock test at: tools.digitalpoint.com/adsense-sandbox.php. It will give you an idea of what ads you can expect to see, and also estimate your earnings from those ads. Google's own "AdSense Preview Tool" at: googleadspreview.blogspot.com/ allows you to see what ads Google is most likely to place on your website.

From the perspective of Google and their advertisers it is important that your website contains relevant content that adds value to a visitor's experience. They want you to focus on relevant and concise content. They do not want to see repetitive or irrelevant keywords.

Google has a tool in AdWords called the "Placement Tool". This allows advertisers to find websites where they want their ads to appear. You can use this in your research. It can show you how your competitors are presenting their websites.

Take note that the AdSense website is very useful in choosing the wording of your potential URL before you even register it. You want your URL to be keyword sensitive, but you need to know that it can be used profitably with AdSense. And you need to test whether your URL is search engine friendly.

When building an AdSense website consider making the "whitespace" reading area narrow (for an example see love-poems-love-poems.com). You also could try the innovative approach of having your navigation bar **below** your AdSense ads. Whether this technique is still viable, with Google presently wanting visitors see relevant content first, is anybody's guess. Google changes their various algorithms so frequently that it is virtually impossible to out-guess them!

To do this, go to resultsgenerator.com/adsense. Fill in your potential URL and click on "Show Me Samples". If no samples show up your potential URL is NOT search engine friendly. You want to see two or more ad samples shown. You can tweak the URL by hyphenating or re-arranging words. If that does not help, you need to try a URL with different keywords.

If Google is good at anything (and from their incredible success they are in fact good at almost anything they do) they are good at providing analytical data. The "Google Analytics" function in AdSense allows you to track all of the data you could ever need relating to a particular ad, group of ads, or web page. And it's FREE! Thanks Google.

There are also AdSense products designed for mobile applications, RSS feeds, and video. I have not yet used these, but I am told that they can be helpful in generating even more revenue. Of course the Google AdSense website has tutorials on the use of these additional products.

In order to attract advertisers Google has set very strict policies regarding what you can and cannot have on, and do with, your website. Google thoroughly electronically monitors every website very closely to insure compliance. Don't even think about violating any of their policies in any way. You cannot win against Google. They rule!

For starters, do not personally click on your website's ads to generate revenue. Do not encourage friends, family and neighbors to do so. Do not pay anyone or any service to do so. Do not enlist third-party "adbots", robots that create ad clicks. These are all great ways to be banned from Google **for life**. You definitely do not want that. They go out of their way to protect their advertisers from artificially inflated costs from "fake" clicks. Would you want to spend your ad PPC advertising and find that your "visitors" were fake?

You are not permitted to have any content on your site that violates Google's written policies. These policies enumerate the usual "no adult content", "no violence", "no racial intolerance" and similar repugnancies. Be sure to **read** their Terms and Conditions. Ignorance of Google's T&Cs is no excuse.

You must be certain not to have any copyrighted material on your site for which you do not have the legal right to display. There are landing page guidelines that must be followed. You may not alter their code in any way such that, for example, a new browser window is launched. AdSense ads cannot appear in pop-ups or pop-unders, or in emails. There should be no re-directs ever.

Although you are actually required to run ads (at least one) on your site other than those provided automatically by Google AdSense, such ads must not use the same layout and colors of the AdSense ads on that page.

In your "Privacy Policy" website page you must disclose that third parties may be placing and reading "tracking cookies" on your visitor's browser. I know people hate cookies. But I also know that very few actually read privacy policies and Terms and Conditions pages. So it is unlikely that a "cookiephobe" would avoid your website because you allow Google's cookies.

Google owns a blogging platform for building websites called "Blogger". They have set up AdSense in such a way that using Blogger to create your ad pages simplifies the entire procedure.

A very useful feature Google has provided for you is the tracking of your AdSense results. Once you have your free AdSense account, log in. Select the "AdSense for Content" tab. Click the "Manage Channels" link. Select a Channel (pages used for reports) from the dropdown menu. In the URL text field enter the URL you wish to track. Click "Create New Channel", which adds your URL to the

Channel. Check the small box to the left of your URL, then click "Activate". <u>Data tracking begins almost immediately.</u>

Again, even before you submit your website to AdSense you can put it through a mock test at: tools.digitalpoint.com/adsense-sandbox.php. It will give you an idea of what ads you can expect to see, and also estimate your earnings from these ads. Google's own "AdSense Preview Tool" at: googleleadspreview.blogspot.com/ allows you to see what ads Google is most likely to place on your website.

There are, however, some negatives to using AdSense ads. You have <u>zero control</u> over what ads Google might run on your site. You may not even be able to see the ads on your site because some ads are geo-targeted. A visitor in Oregon may well see different ads from one in California. If you live in New York you might not see either ad!

It is not beyond the realm of possibility that you might find some of the AdSense ads not to your liking for one reason of the other. And your visitor might find that the destination the ad sends them to is not at all what they expected, and this can reflect poorly on you as the owner of the website that carried the AdSense ad.

Regardless of whether you set up sites exclusively for AdSense or not, you should always consider supplementing your income with some ads from the Google AdSense platform. You just might find that they generate an unexpected amount of additional income. The most compelling reason to engage in Google AdSense is the creation of yet another of the possible "multiple streams of internet income". The more "streams" you have the less likely you are to be blind-sided by some event beyond your control that can have a massive effect on your income.

Case in point: For years many infopreneurs made a great living selling downloadable ebook products through eBay auctions. It was an extremely easy "no brainer" business model. That is until one day not so long ago, out of the blue, eBay said "no mas". Absolutely   prohibited. End of easy money. It happens.

When eBay made this decision, shock waves ran through the ebook publishing industry! Many were totally out of business, UNLESS they had other internet streams upon which to fall back.   Some did, some did not. Those who did shrugged it all off and simply changed focus. Those who did not either gave up entirely or were forced to play catch-up with unfamiliar marketing processes that they were too lazy to learn and apply earlier on.

The more ways you create to earn internet income the better. It offers both protection from the unexpected and the opportunity to evaluate which business model provides you with the best return on investment.

CHAPTER 27
PROFIT WITH YOUR OWN AD WEBSITES

Do you need to have a product of your own of any kind to make big money on the internet? <u>Absolutely not!</u> You do not have to rely on Google Adsense to run advertising on your website. You can "do it yourself". You will lose their instructional guidance, and their analytics, and the ease of setting up your ad pages. You will lose the fact that you can start with Adsense immediately on a new untested website. **What you gain is the opportunity to earn 100% of the ad revenue, half to one-third more than with Google Adsense, all else being equal. And YOU control which ads appear on your site.**

Many internet entrepreneurs have found this to be a very profitable business model. For it to work, however, you must develop (or buy) websites optimized to the point where advertisers will drool over the opportunity to be <u>permitted</u> to buy space! This takes time and effort, and is certainly not for someone totally new to the internet.

It's all about traffic. No one will pay you to run ads on a site that gets little or no traffic. Once you create your keyword-rich/information-rich website you must apply every technique possible to drive traffic and enhance your Alexa ranking and search engine positioning. This can literally take a year or more, but once you receive monthly ad revenue from a dozen or so advertisers on ten or more websites you will find that the work and time were well worth it.

The following is from earlier in this book, but needs repeating here: "Once you have a successful website getting lots of PPC traffic that you can <u>document</u> you can sell advertising space on your website to offset your PPC bid costs. You will need to show your average Cost Per Click (CPC) rate (under $0.05 is great), Alexa rank (under one million is great), Google page rank (4 or better is fine), and your average or previous day's page views."

You can also run a combination of paid ads and AdSense ads in an effort to capture both worlds. An old friend of mine from the very early days of internet commerce in the mid '90s, Charles Carboneau (a successful ex-accountant who found that the internet was his answer to lifetime financial security) has a website worth visiting as an optimized advertising model. Go to cashconnection.com to see the results of his many years of ad page optimization.

Once your website is "advertiser ready" you have to decide the various positions on your site on which ads will appear. The best (and therefore most expensive to an advertiser and the most profitable for you) positioning is "above the fold" as it is known in print media. In the internet world it is above the text-line where the visitor must begin to scroll down to see additional content. Your most valuable and profitable ad space to sell is above the fold.

But some people do scroll down web pages, so paid ads can be placed there as well. It is a good rule of thumb to have at least two ads visible no matter where on your page a visitor happens to be.

Once you have a fully developed website getting lots of traffic, you own a vehicle that can provide you with income for life! Besides SELLING ad space you can:

Rent or trade display advertising space;

Rent or trade classified ad space;

Sell, rent or trade links to other websites;

Run your own auctions;

Sell the entire website.

It is actually easy to get started on a small scale selling a single ad at very low startup cost. Get a domain name, set up a simple generic gateway website with a keyword rich article (from a ghostwriter, Fiverr.com, Private Label Rights or Public Domain). Add a couple of free relevant ClickBank affiliate ads. Then prominently post a simple text link that reads: "See Your Ad Here Now! This is a very limited spot – Get it NOW before it disappears! Click Here". Then drive some free or paid traffic to the site and prepare to be surprised! Try getting at least $197 or $247 for the ad spot. You can create an endless number of these sites over time.

It is important to note the positioning of ads on your website. In fact, you can charge more for the "prime real estate" positions. Many studies have been done to determine the ad positions that bring in the most revenue. The least desirable positions are the top right above navigation bar and the lower right at the bottom.

OK sites include the top left and center above the navigation bar; right alongside of your content, and the lower left at the bottom. Prime real estate? Upper right, and center, below the navigation bar, plus bottom center. Single Most Valuable Spot: **Center above your content, but below the first ad under the navigation bar.**

As you progress in your internet wealth building, always keep in mind that some day you will want to have a number of websites set up exclusively to sell advertising space. Magazines and newspapers have survived on advertising revenue for years. In the incredible world of cyberspace so can you!

MODULE SIX – PUBLISHING IN THE DIGITAL AGE

CHAPTER 28

THE FOUR BASIC PLATFORMS

No book on internet marketing would be complete without a discussion of the single greatest culture shift in modern times. Even before the Chinese invented the printing press hundreds of years ago people held hand-printed books in their hands. The electronic age and the internet has changed all of that within a single decade! It is now reported that more ebooks are sold for electronic download than hard-back and paper-back printed books combined!

And even the world of printed books itself has changed dramatically. It is only within the past few years that an author could write a book or report, upload it to an Amazon publishing platform (Chapter 33), and have books printed **one at a time** as they are ordered! It is beyond understanding to me how conventional publishing houses, who pay an author a paltry ten percent royalty or less, can survive in a world where authors now earn as much as 75% of retail!

There are four basic self-publishing platforms that I have used successfully. There may be others, and more will surely be created in the future. Self-publishing **is** the future. One can see evidence of this in the recent purchase by huge Penguin Books, a traditional publishing house, of a self-publishing company.

The four key publishing platforms are:

Amazon Kindle ebooks;

Smashwords ebooks;

Amazon CreateSpace paperback books-on-demand;

Downloadable .pdf files from your website.

There are three basic **formats** in which you will be selling your books : electronically downloaded on various devices; print-on-demand; and downloadable .pdf files. **You can cover the first two of these with accounts at Amazon Kindle Direct Publishing and Smashwords. Amazon Create Space is the print-on-demand platform. Your own website sells the .pdf downloadable copies.**

What complicates matters is that each of these four platforms requires you to create somewhat different text elements to upload.

There are seven elements to consider: **the cover (front for ebooks, front + spine+ back for printed books); the barcode; the ISBN number; the book text upload; the text description; about the author; and the locator tags.** Each platform requires a slight but very important variation of each.

In the Chapters that follow I will share with you all of the information **that will save you hundreds of hours of frustration and aggravation.** I will also share what I have learned in each step of your writing and publishing, most of which is anything but intuitive. Learn from my mistakes. Don't try to reinvent the wheel.

If you are a "teckie" and really know every nuance of your computer and word processor you will have a major leg up on non-teckies such as me. I'm a writer. I am not particularly computer literate. Yet I have become very proficient in getting my stuff published very quickly. You may very well develop your own shortcuts over time. Again, it isn't rocket science, just a bit confusing at first.

Each of the electronic publishers has **extensive tutorials** on their websites, extensive videos, answers to common questions, and user forums. They are very time consuming to watch, and some are difficult to digest. Follow my simple how-to instructions in this book and save yourself a lot of learning-time.

One very strong word of advice. Do NOT **ever** try to work on more than one book at a time. You will end up in a padded cell, on drugs, or in an AA class! It is extremely difficult to keep everything straight and organized working on just one single book at a time. There is a strong inverse economy of scale! Finish one book, every publisher platform, every step, all marketing, **then and only then** go on to the next book. This is one piece of advice for which you will thank me later!

May you have a fun, long, and profitable self-publishing career!

CHAPTER 29
THE PIECES OF THE PUZZLE

To sell your books you must pay attention to the classical old-time marketing truisms. People are motivated by a very small set of human needs (in no particular order):

The need to relieve pain, physical or psychological;
The desire for wealth;
The desire to have people like them, personal acceptance;
The desire for health and longevity;
The desire for happiness, with one's self and in relationships (The shrinks   call this "self-actualization");
The desire for knowledge.

Whatever ebook or report or article you create it must in some way <u>address one of these human needs</u>.

The basic steps that are common to each book or report project you begin are:

Decide on your business type, (sole proprietor, C-Corp, LLC, etc) and register locally if required by law;

Get multiple free email accounts (Yahoo! mail or Google gmail), ten recommended.

Get a logo for you or your business;

Create your manuscript, fiction or non-fiction;

Carefully proof-read and make all corrections;

Chose a title (VERY IMPORTANT);

Decide on who will be the author and publisher;

Buy four ISBN numbers from Bowker (our use free ones as discussed below);

Create a list of keywords;

Write a copyright and disclaimer page;

Write a dedication;

Create an Index, with pages un-numbered;

Study a general list of "power words" and insert them;

Write descriptions of the manuscript, long and short;

Write "About The Author" descriptions, long and short;

Create a two-dimensional front-side book cover;

Create a rear-side book cover and spine;
Get a FREE PayPal business account;

Join each of the book publishers platforms; it's FREE;

Get your manuscript converted into the accepted formats;

Upload your manuscripts to the publishers;

Upload your cover and other required details;

Choose your pricing;

Choose how you will be paid;

Obtain a relevant domain name;

Create a mini-website;

Market aggressively;

Sit back and collect royalties!

Next, there are many marketing steps you must follow to insure that your book sells well. The more of these you pursue the more you will earn. You can greatly multiply your revenue by focusing on all of the following marketing steps together. Details of marketing techniques are discussed in detail throughout this book. These include:

Outsourcing marketing steps as required;
Press releases, free and paid;
Articles sent to article directories, free & paid;
An eBay store;
A CraigsList account;
A blog;
Forum participation;
Social media participation;
Online classified ads, free and paid;
E-Newsletter (ezine) ads;
Conventional off-line advertising;
Organic website traffic (visitor types in your exact Domain name);
Google AdWords pay-per-click traffic.

You can do 100% of the above entirely on your own, **OR**, you can outsource almost all of it for far less cost than you might imagine.

In regard to outsourcing, the "classic" bid-for-work sites have for many years been elance.com and rentacoder.com. They have many thousands of freelancers ready to bid on any job you can imagine. Fairly recently I discovered Fiverr, at fiverr.com. You simply must visit the site, if for no other reason than the entertainment value of seeing thousands of individuals worldwide willing to do almost anything imaginable for five bucks! I use them often for a wide variety of tasks, and almost always I am 100% satisfied with the results.

CHAPTER 30

CREATING KILLER COVERS

When writing anything the idea is to **STAND OUT** from the competition. **Differentiate or die.** You do this with not only a killer title, but also with a **killer <u>COVER</u>**. This cover image is first seen as a tiny rectangle next to your description, then in a larger version once a potential reader clicks on it. **The cover is your "For Sale" sign.** It's the first thing that catches the visitor's eye. I suggest you visit kdp.amazon.com and click on some Kindle covers so you can see how a larger image of the cover appears. You must admit that some of the covers sparked your interest. You can also see how some are terrible.

<u>Your cover MUST tell the reader what your book is all about.</u>

You have a few choices here. The first is creating the cover yourself, using cover-creation software programs, and images from various sources.

I suggest that you create your covers yourself in "Microsoft Paint". This program is pre-installed in most computers, or it can be downloaded for free. It is a simple program, and all you need in order to do a great job. If you happen to know how to use Adobe PhotoShop, the most popular image-manipulation program, by all means use it. Personally, anything that comes with a one-inch thick instruction book never makes it onto my hard drive! I buy cover background images at Fotolia, upload them into Paint, and overwrite my wording from a very similar taskbar as found in Word. The cover of this book was created in that manner.

Even though I actually enjoy creating my own covers, there is another choice. For under ten bucks for each cover you can outsource the work to a professional graphic artist. Go to vworker.com (or any similar company) and ask for bids. Explain the intention of your cover, your title, your sub-title, your by-line, and your content description. Offer some general cover-design ideas if you have any.

Some other well-known outsourcing options mentioned above are: elance.com and rentacoder.com. You can also try: getafreelancer.com; onlinejobs.com; odesk.com; guru.com; and getacoder.com. You can get an excellent professional-looking cover this way. It's a good idea to mention in your bid solicitation that if you like the cover that the artist provides there will be a lot more cover business down the road.

But there is a quicker and easier way to acquire decent covers at **very** low cost. There is one site that I consider to be **the most valuable resource on the internet,** not just for covers but for websites, advertising, press releases, short articles, marketing, and many other time-consuming tasks. It is called **"Fiverr",** mentioned earlier. It is FREE to join! Go to fiverr.com, open an account and be prepared to spend a day on the site!   It is highly addictive. For just five bucks you can have absolutely anything you can possibly imagine related to graphics, video, writing, advertising, audio, or technology done for you! It is an amazing resource. Need a Kindle cover? No sweat. Need a video of someone dancing naked in the Fountain of Trevi? You can probably find it!

Fiverr has a provider-quality ranking system, expressed as a percentage of satisfied clients. It is seldom below 95%. More important, it has a "frequency of use" rating from "Unrated", through "Levels 1 – 3", and lastly "Top Level". Because of the greater number of clients involved at the higher production levels (they call assignments "gigs"), the percentage of satisfied clients usually is lower the higher the frequency of gigs. It is still seldom below 90%.

I will always select three Fiverr providers for a given cover. It's well worth the fifteen bucks. I supply each with a template of my cover with the title, subtitle and my by-line in appropriately sized fonts. In the middle of the page I write "IMAGE", and then I write a general description of what I want, color, ideas, etc. I may end up with three great covers, but almost always one of the three outshines the others. One is occasionally laughably horrible, but worth five bucks for the laugh!

I always ask for a 4-pixel black border around the entire outer edge. This more clearly defines your book on Kindle's white-background pages.

The only thing I do not understand about Fiverr is why anyone in their right mind would do what they do for a net four bucks a pop, especially Americans. Four dollars might be a princely sum to a teenager in Mumbai, but certainly not to the average American. Some of this stuff has to take many hours to create. In the same amount of time they could make vastly more money doing simple internet commerce. Perhaps they do Fiverr gigs for practice or fun! Their loss, your gain!

CHAPTER 31
AMAZING AMAZON KINDLE

During my lifetime there have been very few "culture shifts". Certainly the internet in general is the major culture-shift that comes to mind. Social site interaction on Facebook, MySpace, Twitter, Pinterest and YouTube is the major result of this culture shift. But there is another true culture shift happening today at an incredible pace. **This is the shift away from printed books to electronically downloaded eBooks.**

The reading "Tablet", led by Amazon's "Kindle" and its latest iteration "Kindle Fire" are found and used everywhere. It is reported that in excess of 20 tablet readers are sold every **minute**! You are on the cutting edge of something **HUGE**. In terms of dollars, and in terms of the number of Best Selling Titles, eBooks are **rapidly** pulling away from printed books.

Amazon sells one million Kindles a week, and loses money on every one of them! But as with Gillette giving away razors to sell blades years ago, all Amazon cares about is the money they can earn selling eBooks....**YOUR** ebooks! The eBook market is reported to be between $2 and $3 BILLION annually!

In Amazon you have a multi-billion-dollar world-renowned corporation promoting **your** virtual product for FREE and paying you handsomely for the privilege! Sounds too good to be true? Believe me, it's true!

Now let's look the Amazon "Kindle". It is that flat little piece of electronic gadgetry that Oprah Winfrey went bonkers over a few years ago. You buy it, and can read books that are pre-programmed on it. Then using it you can buy just about any book you could imagine, and download it to be read on the Kindle device whenever and wherever.

There is no limit to the number of books it will store because, unlike the iPad, it does not depend on internal storage. Everything is downloaded via cell phone towers, and stored permanently on Amazon's "cloud" servers. Pretty cool.

What I was very surprised to learn is that the Kindle-ready ebooks can also be purchased and downloaded on ANY digital device. On desktops and laptops. On cell phones and even on some gaming devices. They have applications (apps) for iPads and Blackberries. You don't have to buy the Kindle Tablet thingie at all. This means that your potential customer base is in the billions, a pure "numbers game". I don't need a small slice of the Kindle-universe pie. I just want to lick the knife. Even a small lick will suffice!

I was most surprised when I learned that Amazon is drooling over having anyone, you, me, anyone, write books and booklets and articles and reports for them to advertise and publish electronically. They call it "**Kindle Direct Publishing**" or KDP. Exciting? Hell yes!!!! And you are getting in on the ground floor.

Above I suggested you check out Kindle to look at ebook covers. This may seem like putting the cart before the horse, but I want you to **immediately** open up a totally free absolutely no obligation account with Kindle Direct Publishing (KDP) at this time. I have many reasons for asking you to do this.

First of all if you aren't sufficiently committed to take this small early step I think it unlikely you will ever actually work on **any** of the programs in this book. This one is an absolute no-brainer. It costs ZERO, and Amazon promotes everything for you. Can there be a better business model?

More important, going through the very simple account setup process, and reading the various notices, and drilling down into the content of the site will give you a very good feel for what the KDP experience entails. You will actually sense being a part of the program, and much of what follows below will make a lot more sense.

What I want you to do is click on many of the ebooks that are for sale. Look at the number of pages in the books and what price they are asking. Especially pay attention to the book "cover", the book title, and the book description. Make special note of the books you would buy on impulse because of the cover, title, and/or description. Again, the reason I am asking you to do this now is that what follows below will make much more sense. Please don't skip to what follows until you thoroughly acquaint yourself with the site and its offerings.

Some books allow you to read part of the content. Do so. Study the "Best Sellers" section. Look at both the "Top 100 Paid" and "Top 100 Free" titles. Study the Titles, the book covers, and the authors' descriptions. When you click on a book be certain to read the feedback section. Try to get a feel for what people think about different books, and why they rate them as they do in the one (worst) to five (best) "stars" rating.

Check out the various categories on the side, especially focusing on those in which you may have some interest or special knowledge. All you are doing at this point is looking for IDEAS, and (hopefully) getting excited. Be sure to visit the Forums.

So please go to kdp.amazon.com and follow the simple sign-up procedure. Aside from personal info, you will be asked for your social security number. Don't be hesitant to give it to them. Amazon has one of the world's most secure encryption of data, so personally I had absolutely no fear of giving them my SSN or company EIN (Employee Identification Number.)

KDP is one of the internet's best kept secrets. I only know of a few internet entrepreneurs who use this method of generating profits. I am one who does, and I found that it is extremely easy to generate significant income, which, incidentally, increases exponentially over time as you publish more and more books.

This is a "set it and forget it" business model. It is reliably reported that some individuals make in excess of $30,000 a month selling simple "how-to" reports on KDP. One lady who I believe writes gothic fiction has been written up in national magazines as having earned well over two million dollars, verified, from KDP!

THE KEY FUNDAMENTALS

The key to making this KDP program work is RESEARCH. You have to be ready and willing to spend a great deal of time at the outset before you can think about posting content to your KDP account. Personally I find this to be fun and interesting. If you look at it that way, and not as a "chore", you will greatly increase your chances for big-time success.

KEYWORD RESEARCH is the single most important aspect of marketing ebooks. You actually have two basic choices to consider. You can focus on a very broad-based market with a large number of searches. This may intuitively seem like the best way to go. Most internet infopreneurs, myself included, look for specialized "niche" markets, highly focused, but with far fewer searches.

Here is where internet marketing experience comes into play. I look for 15,000 to 40,000 "collective" monthly searches for a topic. Fewer is too limiting, more is too broad a market. This figure may not be optimum in other internet marketing efforts, but it seems to hold true for KDP. By "collective" search numbers I mean the total combined searches for any wording that you can imagine that is looking for the exact same highly-focused niche product.

For example, if you are writing on "hunting deer with a crossbow", searches for "deer hunting with a crossbow", "hunting deer with a crossbow", "crossbow deer hunting", deer crossbow hunting" would all be added together for the "collective" monthly search figure.

When your buyer is searching Kindle for an ebook to buy the following are the sorts of terms with which they will lead:

I need help with (training my emu); (fixing my garage door); (my pistol aim).

How do you (fix a leaky faucet?) (make a Doberman obey?) (find a hot date?).

How can I cure (my slice?) (a bad case of acne?) (my husband's snoring?).

What can I do to (lose weight?) (find cheap airline seats?); (find a wife?).

In addition to these four, eight other common "lead-ins" are: "How to stop....?"; "Help me to...."; Help with....": "Get help with...."; "Where can I ....?"; "How should I ....?"; "How can I ....?"; "How would I ....?".

Use these twelve lead-in phrases in your keyword search. Obviously there are infinite possibilities, but I find sticking to these twelve helps me stay sane! Let's take a look at what Google has to offer.

There are five basic ways to make money with KDP:

Sell original ebooks and reports.

Sell the entire business as you would sell a developed website. Build up your Kindle site with a number of different items on your Kindle "bookshelf". If you can document decent earnings, you can sell the entire site! Include the valuable 100% rights to all of the ebooks. I have heard of such sales in the $40,000 range.

You could offer your services to others helping them create covers, great titles, and great descriptions.

Use your ebooks to drive traffic to vendors as an affiliate marketer.
Use your ebooks to drive traffic to market your own products on your own website.

THE BASICS

You will be selling "INFORMATION" to individuals who are looking for "How To...." reports and books on almost anything you can imagine. They search for the information on Amazon by entering their needs in a search box. Your job is to learn what people are searching for, produce a product that fulfills their need at a price they will pay, and then seeing to it that your product shows up prominently as a search result.

Why do people buy information? Primarily because they are either too busy or too lazy to find it for themselves. They are willing to pay a nominal sum for the instant gratification of pressing a button and finding what they want effortlessly and without wading through pages of fluff. And many individuals like you and me can get rich guiding them as to which button to press!

Beyond information-oriented written reports, people also buy all sorts of fiction, (especially romance novelettes), children's books, poetry, science fiction, and just about anything else you can imagine. You will need to decide whether you prefer to offer non-fiction or fiction works. Personally, I provide a mix of both. And both can be wildly profitable.

DECIDING ON YOUR TITLE

It has been proven time and time again that people **buy the TITLE**. This is a critical piece of information to know. There are documented cases of books that hardly sold at all until the author changed just the title and it became a best seller! In fact, if I have an item listed in KDP that isn't selling well I simply change the title. It often changes my results to multiple sales.

You are allowed a Title at KDP but not a SubTitle. My preference is: "How To (keyword/keyword/keyword)". Followed by (as part of my title substituting for a sub-title): "x# Tips To (keyword/keyword/keyword)". The "x#" should always be an odd number such as 3, 5, 7, 9, 11 etc. Split testing has proven time and again that odd numbers increase sales for whatever deep psychological reason. Don't ask.

WRITING THE KINDLE DESCRIPTION

Equally important to the title and cover is your book description. This is what can close the sale after your title and cover art have attracted buyer interest. You are allowed 4,000 characters. <u>USE THEM ALL!</u> Look at your keyword research. It is central to your Description.

You must pick a "Category". I always try to select mine based on the best selling reports in my niche. This takes a bit of searching through the KDP site. You will end up clicking through something like: store>books>nonfiction>(your general niche)>(your sub-niche)>(your refined sub-sub-niche).

In writing the Description use keywords that are highly relevant to your report content, not necessarily those with high search volume. Just study your basic keyword research and write your description accordingly.

You might try asking a question to which you know the answer is "YES". "Do you want to get rid of acne? If you do, than this is the book for YOU. In (your title) you will not only learn (see the Yahoo questions) but you will also learn (see again the Yahoo questions) to help you." **YOU, YOU, YOU**, used as often as space allows, addressing everything you learned for which readers in your niche are searching.

At the end if I have space I'll often add: "You deserve the best and it gets no better than (my title). Buy it NOW."

Always try to work in some enhancements: I frequently use "Limited Edition"; "Collector's Edition"; "RED HOT"; "The NEW BEST SELLER"; "LIMITED DISCOUNT EDITION", whatever you can think of. Be certain to add a "call to action" such as: "BUY NOW".

You can add a link here that is not overt selling. You could try: "Visit my website at (yoursite.com) and get a free title of equal value." Or you could redirect to one of your affiliate vendor's free offer. This can be a huge money-maker even if someone doesn't buy your ebook!

CREATING THE ACTUAL KINDLE PRODUCT

Believe it or not, the very last thing you need to do to do is to create the actual book or report itself. From a time standpoint this is actually only about half of the entire process of posting content to KDP. The preliminaries above are FAR more important. A lot of weak copy is sold successfully because of a killer cover, killer title and exciting description.

There are four ways to create your ebook. Writing from scratch, using the Public Domain, buying Private Label Rights, and paying a ghostwriter. It is unlikely that you are a professional writer. You may not even be a good writer. But for some, the easiest, fastest and cheapest way is to simply write naturally from personal experience. Write about things you know well. Write about your personal passions. Remember, your material isn't being read by your High School English teacher. The chances are that anything you write is being read by an average individual with limited detailed knowledge of English.

The good news is that you do not have to actually write anything original yourself! (It would save you some time and money if you or a relative or friend could string together sentences that make sense, but even that isn't needed). With computer "spell check" you don't even need to be able to spell!

SETTING YOUR PRICE

Though this was covered in an earlier chapter, it is worth repeating here. If you are paying $100.00 for a report that you plan to sell for $0.97 you will need to sell over a hundred copies to break even. But selling at $9.97 you only need to sell eleven to be making a profit. Ah, decisions, decisions. You will only know after a great deal of experience how to price various offerings. Personally I sell almost everything at the $9.97 price point. I can always adjust downwards if I am unhappy with my results.

Some KDP authors take other pricing approaches. They will start at a low price, such as $3.97 for a few weeks, then raise the price by a dollar periodically, and keep doing this until sales decline over a given period. This is known in economics 101 as finding the "point of diminishing returns".

There are other authors who do "Kindle Shorts" which sell for $0.99 to $2.99, hoping for high volume to obtain maximum revenue. I believe that properly packaged any worthy item can be sold for at least $9.97. I've never experimented with Kindle Shorts, but you may wish to experiment. In general I believe most authors under-price their products.

Here is a helpful hint that has stood the test of marketing time since the days of mail order shopping: <u>ALWAYS END YOUR SELLING PRICE WITH A "7".</u> Your price is $3.97

not $3.99. It is $9.97 not $9.99. I have split-tested on a number of occasions and have proven to myself that this conventional wisdom is real. (Its origin is reportedly *Life Magazine's* original subscription price of $7.77).

Even though ending a price with a "7" has been shown to increase sales, you might also wish to try an "odd" price, such as $9.31 which might, for some obscure psychological reason, cause someone to buy your item out of either curiosity or pity!

<u>Be sure to have self-confidence in your products.</u> Have the guts to believe: "This Is <u>Worth</u> More". "It's a bargain at <u>twice</u> my price!". If you are providing something of value, don't be shy, up the price. You can always lower it if sales are poor.

Bear in mind, many KDP ebooks sell thousands of copies. Alas, many do not, in fact some do not sell at all. What separates the winners from the losers is the research you do on your niche, and the title, the cover and the description.

Compared to the royalties book authors are accustomed to getting from publishers (5%-10% is common) the commissions (i.e., royalties) authors get from Amazon KDP are outstanding! Anything you price below $2.99 pays 35% commission. (Personally I do not sell at this level.) Anything you price between $3.00 and $9.99 the commission jumps to <u>an amazing 70%!</u>

I price most items at $9.97, and receive about $6.67 net commission per sale. Sell a hundred, get a check for $667.00, a thousand (not at all impossible) a check for $6,670.00! That is for ONE single item. Some Kindle marketers have hundreds of titles for sale and make a great living.

The 35% royalty option is for any book you price between $0.99 and $2.98, and over $9.99. The 70% option is for books you price between $2.99 and $9.99. Testing by many KDP marketers have found the best price points to be $3.97, $4.97, $7.97, and $8.97. Personally I use $9.97 for almost anything.

If you sell at any price $10.00 and above, the commission drops back to a respectable 35%. If you do the math you will see that the first higher price at 35% that brings in more commission than $9.99 at 70% is $19.99.

I have seen individual ebooks commonly offered at $49.97 and $147.00 and $197.00. I have seen many ebook courses sell for $997 and higher. I buy lots of this stuff, and so do others. I have always believed that paying for valuable information is the best investment I can make. Kindle is NOT set up for sales at these levels.

It is a truism that almost anything will sell at $2.99, the figure at which almost any viewer will click to buy. People don't think twice buying at that level. This is what most Kindle buyers "expect" to pay.

Amazon does deduct a "delivery fee" per megabyte of upload to their users' devices. While it is relatively small amount per mb, if you are selling a very long item you should look at the possibility of a higher price at the 35% option.

I do not like the fact that Amazon can sell your material at any price they choose. Although commissions are paid based upon the price you set, you might find yourself competing with Amazon if you are selling your ebook elsewhere at full price.

THE RESULTS TO EXPECT

Keep in mind that you cannot expect a huge amount of royalties from any single book or report. Consider $20/month from Kindle to be excellent for one book. Once you begin to post items to KDP, DO NOT GET DISCOURAGED BY SLOW EARLY RESULTS. In fact, you can count on them. It could take a month before sales start to materialize. DO post at least five books or reports before you worry about getting results from the first offering. Or better yet twenty-five! It is not as hard as it sounds once you get the hang of it. Over time there are some KDP authors who have hundreds, even thousands, of titles in their accounts and earn a fortune!

The important thing to remember is that every title remains in KDP **forever**, so it just becomes a matter of compounding results. My personal goal is to try to double my KDP revenue every month. I base this on the old bet where the loser readily agrees to pay the winner a penny each day and then double it each day for a month. On the face of that it seems like you are risking very little. Not quite! **If you take $0.01 and double it each day for 31 days you end up with an astounding amount close to _twenty-five-million dollars!_** Check that out on a calculator and prepare to be amazed. This is why my goal is to double my revenue every month. If this means I have to produce a few ebooks a day and post them to my Kindle account then so be it. Never lose sight of the fact that a saleable ebook can be created in a couple of hours once you get into the habit of doing them. The time to start is **NOW.**

THE SUCCESS TEMPLATE

At first it will take much longer to post an item to your KDP account. You will find that each successive effort takes less time. This is because you will develop a "template" mentality. You have an eight-part template to repeat over and over and over:

Find a niche of "starving" buyers;

Do your keyword research; (You will be doing exactly the same sort of keyword search as for any well optimized AdWords campaign or website);

Create a killer title (Try to match your title to an EXACT search term for maximum sales.)
Create a killer cover;

Create a killer description;

Create your content;

Price the content;

Upload to your Kindle Direct Publishing account. NOTE: The upload process can take many minutes; do not get worried or impatient.

PROMOTION TRICKS OF THE TRADE

Posting favorable reviews of your work is important. You should be able to get favorable reviews from friends, family and associates. You can also go to go to fiverr.com and actually pay someone to write a favorable review for five bucks! Personally I consider this to be highly unethical, but your competition will probably be using it so you decide how you want to proceed.

Join some Kindle forums. Check out eReadForum.net and KindleBoards.com. You can even add a link to your book in your forum signature, or even an affiliate link to some free offer relevant to the content of your ebook.

Follow some of the other KDP authors' blogs and reply strings. You can learn a lot. Eventually start your own blog.

Unless your ego rules your pocketbook, it is a good idea to use a different pen name as the author of **each** ebook you create. Pen names and ghostwriters are used throughout the publishing industry (not to mention Hollywood) and are perfectly ethical and legal.

As mentioned above, always end your price with "7". Deviate from this at your peril!

Split-test everything. Try different prices. Try different Titles. Try different covers. Try different descriptions. Try substituting a male pen name for a female one (I always start out with a female pen name. For whatever reason it pulls more sales over the exact same item with a male pen name.) Most highly successful KPD marketers I know split test as often as possible.

Load up your Title and Description with keywords relevant to the information in your ebook.

Be certain to create an eye-catching cover. This is critical.

Create **QUALITY** ebooks. In the long run it trumps "easily created QUANTITY of crap" every time.

SET YOUR KINDLE TITLES APART WITH "BOOK EXTRAS"

This is a technique that is used by very few Kindle authors. Perhaps they are unaware of its existence, or perhaps they are just plain lazy. I am talking about adding "Shelfari Extras". These are "curated factoids" that provide potential buyers with helpful information that can influence their decision to buy your book. To Add Book Extras to your title, follow these steps:

Go to **www.shelfari.com** (It is an Amazon.com subsidiary.)

Log in using your Amazon.com username and password;

In the top search bar, enter your KDP title or author name;

Locate your title from the search results

Add, update or correct the community contributed set of Book Extras for your title.

This all takes very little time, and can definitely influence a prospective buyer to click that all important "Buy Now" button!

CHOICES WITHIN YOUR KINDLE ACCOUNT

There are a number of others choices you will be asked to make within your account. Here are the responses I use: Always check "Worldwide Rights". Use "general" if you have nothing specific for the separate chapter option. NEVER use a publication date unless you must. You want your material to be current forever.

TAGS=KEY WORDS. ISBN or other recognized ID numbers are not required for ebooks. Only list "Other Titles" if they are in your same niche and you used the same pen name; and don't check "Part of a Series" unless it actually is.

Kindle has devised another possible revenue stream. They call it "KDP Select". Amazon claims that: "KDP Select gives you a new way to earn royalties, reach a broader audience, and use a new set of promotional tools". The concept involves Amazon setting aside a fixed pool of money to be divided among authors based upon the number of times their "US Amazon Prime" members borrow a particular book in a calendar month. These special members can borrow books for free with no due date. The number of borrows of your ebook is some percentage of the overall total of all borrows in the KDP Select universe for that month. You receive a proportional percentage of the money pool. **DO NOT EVER JOIN KDP SELECT!**

Why do I say that? Because Amazon requires **100% exclusivity** if you join this new program. When you publish on KDP you have the right to publish anywhere else. But if you join Select and publish elsewhere you will get a letter from Amazon terminating your account! You don't want that. Until they drop that exclusivity requirement, avoid KDP Select.

UPLOADING YOUR MATERIAL TO YOUR KINDLE PLATFORM

Creating your product for Kindle, finding keywords, designing a great cover, and writing a killer title and description is no different for KDP than it is writing for any other marketing purpose. The exposure you get through Amazon is greater, however, than anything you could create for FREE by yourself.

But creating your book for Tablet readers requires that it be converted to a format that is compatible with streaming text on a small hand-held device. It is best if you write your material with an eye towards easy Kindle conversion. Purely text-based books, without fancy tables, charts, formatting or images are by far the easiest and least costly to convert.

The biggest concern is formatting your ebook in a special manner that allows a person reading your book on a hand-held reader to click on a chapter in your Table of Content (known as your "TOC") and be taken directly to the top of the desired chapter. The process of creating a "clickable TOC" is explained on the Kindle website. It requires downloading some software and learning how to use it. As a dedicated non-teckie I choose the chicken out of that process and let someone else do it for me! That someone else is located at fiverr.com. Just as with covers, there are many individuals at Fiverr who will, for five bucks, do the conversion for you and send you a perfect file with a clickable TOC. **Don't even think of trying to do it yourself.**

The key is to set up <u>as many different publishing income streams</u> as possible, and to eventually automate almost everything so that you have the free time to enjoy your internet wealth. This is why you want to publish your material in platforms other than KDP. We will discuss this in the Chapters that follow. This falls into the "Don't Put All Of Your Eggs In One Basket" category.

What if, for example, you did nothing but promote Amazon KDP and they stopped taking in new material, or decided to charge outrageous fees, or for whatever corporate reason decided to shut it down entirely? You are OUT OF BUSINESS. You must diversify. As Gordon Gecko said to his future son-in-law: "Money is a bitch that never sleeps. One day you wake up and she's gone"!

One last thought. Do not concern yourself with buyers requesting refunds. Yes, there are "Refund Bandits" out there. Fortunately there are far more honest buyers. You can expect around 1% to 2% refunds, irrespective of your material quality.

Remember, everything you publish on Kindle **is <u>eternal!</u>** It stays active forever! This means you have the potential for residual income for life, added to every time you add a new book or report to your catalog. The opportunity is literally limitless.

JUST DO IT!

CHAPTER 32

EVERY OTHER EBOOK DEVICE OUT THERE

Amazon is king. No single other publishing platform is even close. There are many additional non-Amazon outlets on which to sell your eBooks. <u>Collectively</u> they represent to many authors as much income as they earn from Kindle.

Barns and Noble Booksellers have come out with a product of their own to compete with the Kindle. They call the device a "Nook". Their formatting process is called "Publt". Customers can go to bn.com, enter search terms, and find ebooks, which can be bought on a Nook, or on any device or computer, same as with KDP. For all intents and purposes it is almost identical to KDP. Go to: pubit.barnesandnoble.com/pubit and print out "Questions About Pubit" and also the "eBook Publication and Distribution Agreement – Pubit". After reading these you will have a thorough understanding of the Publt to Nook process.

The Publt commission payout is a bit different from that of KDP. On the plus side, for those ">$9.99" items they pay out five percent more, 40% vs 35% for KDP. If you are selling many $197 items this could add significantly to your revenue over KDP all else being equal. For the less expensive items, which greatly dominate most publishers' marketing efforts, their payouts are equivalent.

Nook has a few ugly features that really turn me off. They call these programs: "Read In Store", "Lend Me", and "Samples". Worst of all is "Read In Store". Anyone visiting a B&N store can read your entire ebook for <u>FREE</u> for one hour! I have no idea what impact this might have on your revenue, but for now I personally choose not to find out. Virtually everything I publish can be read in an hour, notes extracted, and the reason to purchase obviated! Not happening. Their rationale is that it provides the publisher better exposure. Thanks, but no thanks.

As with KDP, you can set your selling price and get paid your commission based solely on that price. As with Amazon B&N can sell your ebook at any discounted price they choose. This in essence puts you in competition with selling through other channels such as KDP or your own website.

It has been reported in the media that B & N has considered shutting down the Nook program. The competition from Amazon KDP has just been too great.

There is a publishing platform besides KDP that you **must** consider using. It is called Smashwords, and many publishers have derived as much or more income from it than from Kindle. The reason for this is that Smashwords converts your book to a number of unique formats so that your books can be accessed at many places beyond those that Amazon reaches. I always publish at **BOTH** KDP and Smashwords, though I find the latter to be a bit of a pain to work with for a number of reasons.

Though Smashwords sells your ebooks directly from their own site, once you have properly formatted your manuscript for inclusion in their "Premium Catalog" (not exactly an easy task!) your ebook will be available for purchase in places worldwide you've probably never even heard of!

Owners of the popular Apple iPhones and iPods will be able to buy your books through Stanza. Android devices can be used to purchase through Aldiko and Word-Player. The Barnes& Noble Nook Reader is covered, as well as Sony and the Diesel ebook store. International coverage is through Kobo. And the important library distribution is covered through Baker and Taylor's Axis 360 service and the blio.com store. **That represents a lot of potential sales!** So do not overlook publishing at Smashwords.

Go to smashwords.com and follow the intuitive instructions to open a free account. That's the easy part. Before I proceed, let me tell you about a few (!) things I dislike about Smashwords as compared with Kindle.

First, there is no way you can contact them by phone if you have a question. You can send an email, but I challenge you to find the email address anywhere on the site in under a half-hour! (It is: mc@smashwords.com, deeply buried in obscure fine print). They do respond fairly quickly, but their responses often do not answer my question on the first try. Very frustrating to say the least.

Second, the required book upload format is, at least for me, virtually impossible to create by myself. They have a "Style Guide" which is literally almost an **inch thick** when printed out! I have spent dozens of hours on three occasions trying to follow it to no avail. Were it not for people at fiverr.com who have some magic way they do this quickly I would never attempt to publish at Smashwords!

Third, and perhaps the most annoying thing about the site, is the fact that it does not **retain** anything you input if you need to go back to fix something while you are inputting data. If everything does not go through first shot, and it frequently does not for me, or you make an error, you have to start from scratch and input everything all over again. Seriously annoying.

Next, though this may not seem important, I find it irritating that every time I add a new title (which I usually do under a variety of pen names) I need to create a "ghost author" on a separate part of their website every time I use a pen name or a nickname. Then later on in the submittal process I need to remember to match the pen name to the book title from a drop down list at the appropriate time. If I forget to do so, it defaults to the name used for the first book I published there. In the Amazon sites you just add the author of the book you are publishing right under the book title immediately after you enter it. Perhaps I'm too picky, but I find it irritating.

Fifth, but not least in the gripe category, often the site rejects my book manuscript upload and my cover upload as being "in an unacceptable format" when they are **positively 100% in conformity.** If you make enough attempts you can get it to work, but you can get an ulcer doing it. Sometimes just changing the **name** of the file you are uploading, making no other change, makes a difference. I have been unable to identify the problem. Nor have they.

I use three browsers: Microsoft Internet Explorer, Google Chrome, and Firefox. Each one shows a slightly different Smashwords website, and each interacts differently with it. But there are times when I cannot get an upload "lock" with any one of the three. They claim Chrome works best. I see no difference between the three....no single one works as well consistently as I would like!

Lastly, they pay you your royalties quarterly and if the timing of your orders hits the calendar off-cycle, you might not see your royalties for a lot longer than that.

With all that said, I still think **it is important to publish at Smashwords** if you can endure the frustrations. For starters, get all of the following together before you start:

A 400 character short book description, which has to be created from the description on your back cover, which probably exceeds that size.

A 4000 character book description. If I'm happy with my book rear cover description I use it as is. If you want to greatly expand upon that length you can.

As large a list of key words as you want to find. You cannot cut and paste these. They must be entered one at a time, so I usually stop at the twenty with the highest Google traffic volume. There appears to be no limit. **This to me is a very significant plus over the Amazon KDP site which accepts only a few keywords.**

The sample % you want to offer your potential buyer. You need to allow the potential buyer to get far enough into the book to want to buy it, but not so far that they don't **need** to buy it!

The book price you want to charge.

The text of your book as a .doc file specially prepared at Fiverr.

Your front cover .jpg file, adjusted to 1,400 pixels on the short side (easily done in Microsoft Paint).

Now once you have all of this together it **SHOULD** take you about ten minutes maximum to complete the upload. There are five steps, listed as Step 1 to Step 5.

Step 1 is your title, your short and long description, the language your text is in, and certification that your text has no sexual content.

Step 2 is your pricing and sampling. When you enter a price three pretty colorful pie charts appear showing how the retail prices is split up between you and Smashwords on different platforms. If the pie charts do not appear **instantly** STOP and re-login using a different browser. It is a certain sign that your later uploads will not work.

Step 3 consists of two drop-down category menus, which are quite complete. When you choose "non-fiction" or "fiction" a second drop-down menu should instantly appear. If it says "searching" don't bother to wait. You'll die of old age! It will never allow you to upload your text. This is the same situation as with the pie charts mentioned above. Re-login with another browser and start the whole darn process over from scratch.

Step 4 is your search tags. You must input these one at a time. It is tedious and the most time-consuming part of the whole process, because you can have so many of them. There's never a free lunch!

Step 5 is a list of formats into which Smashwords converts your book upload. Delete "Kindle". It is advantageous to do Kindle directly at Amazon KDP....if nothing else Kindle pays you more frequently.

Step 6 is the upload of your cover image. You must adjust the cover size to be 1,400 pixels on the short side and the keep the 6:9 ratio on the long side. This is very easily done in Microsoft Paint or any other image manipulation program.

Step 7 is the upload of your book text, in specially prepared format and as a .doc file.

Step 8 is your agreement with their Terms & Conditions.

Step 9 is where you connect a "ghost author", previously added elsewhere on the site, with the book title.

Now click **PUBLISH**. This is where I find it close to a miracle if everything is accepted. If the only problem is one of omission of some item, you can go back and add it without losing data. But if the problem is an "unacceptable format", you are screwed. You need to try again, uploading a differently-labeled but identical file. If this still does not produce an acceptance, you need to start from scratch in a different browser.

I have managed to publish many titles at Smashwords, but every one took far more time and aggravation than it should have. Compared to Amazon's KDP platform, it's a pain in the pooper to use. ALL I CAN SAY AT THIS POINT ABOUT SMASHWORDS IS STAY PATIENT, BE PERSISTANT, AND **GOOD LUCK!!!!** HOPEFULLY, your bank account will thank you!

Incidentally, because you do not see the buyer's identity or email address, KDP, Nook and Smashwords all have the unfortunate weakness of preventing you from directly creating a mailing list for your future marketing efforts. This speaks very highly for selling your books on your own website.

Once you have your ebook created in various formats there are also a host of other virtual bookstores from which you can sell: Booklocker.com; Ebooksonthe.net; Mypublish.com; Ebookmall.com; Ebooksnbytes.com; Ebooksubmit.com; Download.com; Ebookcrossroads.com/ebook-sellers.html; Ebooktags.com; Ecourseweb.com; Ideamarketers.com; Ebookpalace.com; Jogena.com; Published.com; Ebookjungle.com; Cyberreadcom; Blish.com; Ebookbroadcast.com; and Bowindex.com.

A Google search for "virtual book sellers" or "where to sell my ebook" will turn up more than you will ever need. As pointed out above, **PEOPLE BUY INFORMATION**. It is a fact proven over and over by successful infopreneurs. Millions of dollars have been earned by authors of virtual material. It isn't difficult.

JUST DO IT!

CHAPTER 33
AMAZON PRINT ON DEMAND

I have been writing and publishing since 1970. There is nothing quite as ego satisfying as holding a book in your hand that you spent many hours writing and proofing and re-writing and re-proofing. Just seeing it and feeling it and being able to give copies to family and friends trumps anything you can do with an ebook. It's the equivalent of holding a cute puppy!

Until Amazon created their print-on-demand, one book at a time publishing platform called CreateSpace, self-publishing required spending large sums of money to print "minimum" quantities of books (think "thousands") and then praying that somehow you could manage to sell them before you added them to the growing pile of "remainder" books cluttering up your attic or garage. And, being anal retentive, I have thousands of my "remainder" books cluttering up **both** my attic and garage! I find it impossible to part with remainder books. It's like tossing out that cute puppy!

Create Space enables you to publish hard or soft cover physical printed books on Amazon on a "print-as-you-sell" basis. There is no inventory required either by you or Amazon, which is a **huge** advantage. My garage and attic will surely outlive me!

It is important when publishing anything at CreateSpace to choose "Amazon Retail" as a sales channel. If you fail to do so your content will only be available through Create Space directly, which most shoppers do not recognize as an arm of the highly-trusted Amazon brand. You can also create your own eStore at Create Space, but you have to drive traffic to it as you would any website.

Let's start from scratch and publish a print-on-demand paperback book through CreateSpace, to be sold through Amazon.

For whatever reason, it is recommended that you use the Firefox web browser. Other browsers, particularly Google Chrome, are not as compatible with the CreateSpace platform uploads. If you do not have Firefox, just Google "Firefox download" and get a free copy. Then use it to access createspace.com, and open up a free account there. Then just follow the account-creation prompts, which are intuitive.

Once you have set up your account, log in. You will see "Start your New Project". Enter you book title, check "Paperback", and choose "Guided" for the uploads. Once the entire process becomes "second nature" the pro-quickie upload option might save you a minute or two. Hit "Get Started". You will then see a very intuitive four-part "dashboard":

"Set Up" includes your Title Information, ISBN, Interior, Cover and Complete Setup steps.

"Review" includes File Preview and Proof Your Book.

"Distribute" offers you six channels (you want them all), Pricing, Description, and Publish On Kindle.

"Sales & Marketing" allows you to Track Sales, use Marketing Services, and Get Ideas In "Resources".

For "Trim Size" I have found through experimentation (as well as the experience of other authors) that 6" X 9" is a perfect size for **all** of your print-on-demand books and reports. (Though you will not be asked for this information, I use 16 point type for shorter books, and 14 point for longer ones. Using 16 point makes any book a bit thicker and thus more pages. Bigger is better in the mind of the buyer, but it is also a bit more expensive to produce yielding a few cents less profit.)

The next step is the most critical. If you do everything correctly to this point it will go very smoothly. You have various options for the upload-file format. After much trial and error and agonizing over repeated rejections I have found the following process to work 100% of the time: Write your book in Microsoft Word. Then in Word go to "Page Layout" > "Size"> adjust to 6" X 9", with 3/4 inch margins all around, and a 0.2 inch gutter. Don't ask me why this works, it just does!

After you do this, proofread the resulting text to be certain all of the Chapters begin at the top of a page. This is the file you upload to CreateSpace by clicking "Browse", locating and opening the appropriate file, uploading the file, and waiting a few minutes while CreateSpace converts your 6"x9" .docx file into a their preferred .pdf. If I try to do the conversion to .pdf myself **before** I upload the file for some reason it greatly complicates the process. Do so at your own risk.

One item is very different from creating an ebook. Your cover, instead of just being the "front cover", now needs to wrap around a real physical book. Thus it requires a back cover and a spine. And the spine has to be the right width, which will vary depending upon the length of your book. To get the correct width, after you have converted your Word file to 6x9 format, hit File (upper left), and look under "Properties" where the number of pages magically appears! Microsoft Word is damn clever! You take this figure and multiply it by a formula given to you on the CreateSpace website. This multiplier varies with the type of paper you choose (I always choose white) and whether you book is to be printed in black and white (mine always are) or in color.

Your back cover and spine will contain certain elements. There is a certain recommended formula for the back cover. There are essentially seven elements: Upper left corner; upper right corner; about the author; about the book; testimonials; lower left corner; and lower right corner.

If you can access a copy of the entire cover of this book on Amazon.com do so and follow that format. (Of course if you bought a printed book-on-demand copy of this book the back cover is a bit easier to access…just flip it over!)

UPPER LEFT CORNER

In a small rectangle put two lines of text which tells the search route by which someone would find your book on Amazon. This could be: non-fiction/business>real estate, or whatever matches your book.

UPPER RIGHT CORNER

A short, two line "teaser" about the book, ten to a dozen words at most, as an uncompleted sentence followed by …….

ABOUT THE AUTHOR

Across the cover write a seven to eight line blurb, which can be the same as you created for uploading to your ebook platforms. Be certain that you include a few "power words" from Chapter 8. Put the underlined black-letters heading above it: "About The Author". Use 12 point Arial Black-Enhanced font.

ABOUT THE BOOK

Across the cover write a keyword-rich power-word-rich description of the book. Here again, you may wish to use the description you already created for the ebook platforms. This can be ten to a dozen lines. As a heading for this section use the title of your book. Use 12 point Arial Black-Enhanced font. On the line above the description I put the book title in white letters against a red background.

TESTIMONIALS

Below the book description, under the heading "Testimonials", place two very short one line testimonials. At this point in time it should be from the friends and family to whom you already sent preliminary text files for comment and can document their comments if challenged to do so.

LOWER LEFT CORNER

If you have one, (or if not just use your initials), this is where you put your logo. If you need a graphic artist to create a logo, I strongly suggest fiverr.com. There are many "Fiverrs" that do excellent logos for $5.00. This would be the same logo you would use on your book's website.

LOWER RIGHT CORNER

This is reserved for your bar code. You can create one yourself with barcode software you can buy over the internet. But why bother? Amazon CreateSpace designs one for you, and doesn't charge a dime! Let Amazon do it. Free is good. Just leave them a sufficient blank corner space.

Last but not least is the book's spine. If your book is not 1/3rd inch or wider leave the spine blank. Otherwise your logo and your book title go horizontally across the spine. You'll know the spine width after you convert to 6"x9" in Word, hit "File>Save" to learn the page quantity, and then plug the number of pages into a formula provided by CreateSpace.

THE ANXIOUS MOMENTS

Once you upload your 6x9 text file, here is where crossing one's fingers seems to help! What you are hoping to see is a message that says: "Our Automated Print Check Didn't Find Any Issues". There is a God! (If there **are** issues they will explain them to you for correction. You don't want issues.)

You are now ready to "Launch Interior Review". The first time I did this I was blown away! There, on the screen, is your finished book, open facing pages, with the ability for you to click-and- flip through the entire volume one page at a time! Do so in order to be certain that none of your text is cut off at the edges in the final version. If you proceeded as instructed above you should never have a problem.

If you see a message on the right side that refers to a possible problem with fonts just ignore it. As long as you wrote your book in a sans-serif font such as Ariel this message is irrelevant. I have never explored exactly what they are trying to say here, and ignoring it has never caused me any issue.

Now go back and on the left side choose "Cover". You want to choose "Upload A Print-Ready .pdf Cover", the one you had Fiverr construct as a single rear/spine/front combination as described above. You do not want "Professional Cover Design" unless you want to pay an arm and a leg for something over which you have no direct control. You also do not want "Build Your Cover Online". They do have a very fine free cover-design function, but you are VERY limited by the available templates and I found it not to be worth the bother.

Use Fotolia/Paint for the front cover, and someone at Fiverr for the rear and spine. Upload your cover. Amazon will provide you with a free bar code for the back cover, but you must have left them a space in which to print it. This is a great feature, because bar codes are rather expensive to create by yourself.

Now click on "Submit Your Files For Review". You will then be taken to the "Distribution" page. You are automatically and at no cost enrolled in three distribution channels: Amazon.com, Amazon Europe, and Create Space Store. You are then presented with a $25.00 add-on if you want to include "Bookstores & Online Retailers" plus "Create Space Direct" and "Libraries & Academic Institutions". **I am quite certain that over time the twenty-five bucks is a bargain, so I always go for it.**

Let me digress and talk a bit about "ISBN numbers" which is actually an incorrect manner of speech because the "N" stands for number! This is the International Standard Book Number system. Contrary to a popular misconception, an ISBN does **not** convey a copyright. It is simply an identifier of the publisher that facilitates listing of a book in various data bases. Why then would anyone want one, especially in light of the fact that they are rather expensive? That is a **very** good question.

How expensive? Anywhere from $1.00 each to $125.00 each, depending on how many you buy from Bowker, who has a monoply. Talk about a quantity discount! If you buy one ISBN number you will pay $125.00 for it. Buy ten for $250.00 and you're down to $25.00 each. Buy a hundred for $575.00 and it's now $5.75 each. Want a real bargain? Buy a thousand for a thousand bucks and it's $1/125^{th}$ the cost of buying one at a time. Costco beware!

Don't want to buy your own ISBN number at these exorbitant prices? Well, you don't have to! At Amazon Kindle they do not even require one, because in general an ISBN serves no purpose for a "not physically printed" ebook. Smashwords does require an ISBN for ebooks because certain of their distribution platforms want one for indexing purposes. (If you do not have your own, Smashwords supplies one for free, though you cannot use it anywhere else.)

For **FREE** Amazon will assign you an ISBN number. You can't beat the price! This number is unique to this one book edition and cannot be used anywhere else. You MUST allow Amazon to assign this ISBN to your book when you apply (as you should) for "Expanded Distribution – Libraries and Academic Institutions". You cannot ever use your own ISBN for this particular distribution channel. For all of the many other Amazon distribution channels, you can allow CreateSpace to assign the free ISBN number. When they do, the "Imprint of Record" that shows up as the "publisher" in all data bases will be "CreateSpace Independent

Publishing Platform".   Neither you, nor any publishing company you own or are working with, shows up as the publisher.

You can, however, for only $10.00, buy an ISBN number from CreateSpace (who buys them in bulk from Bowker) that will allow you to show whoever you want as "publisher".   You cannot use this ISBN number anywhere else, and you still must allow Amazon to assign their own ISBM for "Libraries and Academic Institutions", but you do get your name in lights!

Want an ISBN number of your very own that you can use anywhere in addition to Create Space but don't want to pay Bowker $125.00? You can save $26.00 at CreateSpace who will sell you a "Custom Universal ISBN" for $99.00! (But you still need the CreateSpace assigned ISBN for "Libraries and Academic Institutions".)

What if you want to have your very own ISBN number for all of CreateSpace's platforms, but still want library distribution? You will need to open up two separate CreateSpace accounts, one exclusively for the library option using their assigned ISBN, and one for all other distribution channels using your own ISBN. CreateSpace has no mechanism within a single account for accomplishing this ISBN split.

So this gets back to: "Why do I want an ISBN number at all?". The answer is, you don't, sort of! You do not unless you become a serious publisher of multiple titles and want all of your books to show up in data bases with you or some designated company as the publisher. Will this help you sell a lot more books? Probably not. Will it help you keep your various titles and various distribution channels separate and organized within your own accounting records? It does for me. But the point is, when you are just starting out and on a limited budget just "keep it simple" and accept the free ISBN.

Go through the intuitive secure payment process using your credit or debit card for the $25.00, and if you have used an Amazon-assigned ISBN you are now in **all** six distribution channels. If, however, you have used your **own** ISBN, as pointed out above you **cannot** be included in the Library+ channels. For that one distribution channel you **must** use an Amazon-assigned ISBN.

Because I use my own ISBNs, I open up a parallel CreateSpace account using a different email address exclusively for this special distribution channel. (I love to complicate things; it's my engineering background!) I must be very careful when I upload the text in that channel that I have **their** ISBN on the title page (they assign it before you upload your text and you must go back to your 6"x9" Word document, erase your own ISBN, and add theirs). Now hit "Save and Continue".

You will be taken to the pricing page, where you must decide what you are going to charge for your print-on-demand paperback. I generally charge $10.00 more than for my ebook versions. You can have fun playing with the calculator they provide, which automatically populates your net royalty for various ways a customer might make a purchase. It also populates the same information in both British and Euro currencies. Incidentally, you can change your pricing at any time in the future.

IMPORTANT NOTE: Once your book is available, and you are advertising it, be certain you promote only the link that gives you the greatest commission! This will be obvious from the populated royalty calculator. You can find that exact link once the book is available for public purchase.

Next you will have the option of uploading the "Author's Bio" information. Here I use the long text from inside my book, not the short version on the rear cover. They allow about five times as much text space as needed for your rear cover if you choose to use that text.

After this you will add "English" for the book language (or whatever language in which you are publishing) and your "Country of Publication", which for me is United States. You will next enter a publication date. I always use the date I am in the site, but if permitted you can leave this blank. Many feel that not stating a publication date makes your book "ageless".

Finally, you will be asked for keywords. Unfortunately you are only allowed a scant total of **five** keywords and keyword phrases. I use the top five most-searched relevant phrases according to Google. Because Amazon makes money when you make money it seems to me to be self-defeating for them to not allow you to enter far more keywords. I'm sure they have their reasons, whatever they may be.

After completing this section you will be presented with a tempting: "Publish On Kindle" option. I never use it, preferring to do all of my Kindle publishing on separate kdp.amazon.com accounts. I tried doing Kindle once through CreateSpace and it just made it more complicated as far as I was concerned, and much harder to keep things separated for my accounting purposes. Feel free to try it both ways. I just ignore it.

Now click on "My Account", choose "Member Dashboard" and you will see your Status: "In Progress". In about two days this will switch to "Available". **Hallelujah! Rejoice!** This is your signal to buy some ego-building copies for friends and relatives, and to begin your serious marketing efforts.

Incidentally, even though you have chosen "black and white" for your book interior, your covers will always be printed in full living color. If you want color pictures or illustrations within the pages of your book you have two choices. If you leave "black and white" alone the pictures will be reproduced quite well in gray scale. If you want interior pictures in color, you must choose "color" for the interior. Doing so puts you in a totally different pricing structure wherein making a profit is far more difficult. Once you play around with the numbers in the website this will become very clear.

What I especially like about CreateSSpace is the availability of a toll-free number and very courteous 24/7 service. (866-356-2154). You are connected very quickly to highly-literate English-speaking consultants who are very knowledgeable and helpful.

Once you have all of your ducks lined up in a row the actual submittal process should take well under a half-hour. And when you order a book on Monday, do not be surprised if by Wednesday shiny new very professional-looking paperbacks appear in your mailbox. How they manage to print these books on-demand and ship them out seemingly the same day is yet another Amazon miracle! The books are generally printed at a facility in South Carolina.

Selling ebooks on various platforms is overall more profitable, but there is something extremely ego-satisfying in seeing and feeling your masterpiece in the palm of your hand! A physical book with a great cover is certain to impress friends and family alike. **YOU ARE NOW A _PUBLISHED AUTHOR_! CONGRATULATIONS!!!**

This sets you far apart from most of the rest of the world's population! YOU ARE SPECIAL!

JUST DO IT!

CHAPTER 34
HOW MUCH MONEY CAN I MAKE?

Understand this up front: You cannot <u>expect</u> a huge amount of royalty income from any *single* book title. Of course there are exceptions to this. You might come up with a one-in-a-million super-best-seller, but the odds are strongly against that happening. <u>Your success will depend far more on your own **marketing skill** than on the quality of your books themselves.</u> Many very mediocre books sell very well because they are **marketed** very well. Never lose sight of the fact that the average intelligence of the average buyer is not quite in the genius category!

You should consider earning $20/month/title from Kindle to be good. Add in Smashwords and CreateSpace and combined $50/month/title is quite possible. Ten titles, $500/month is realistic. One-hundred titles? How about $5,000/month! **This is a pure numbers game.** How quickly you can publish material is entirely up to you. It is reported in major media that some self-publishers are getting quite rich, becoming millionaires, with 1,000+ titles!

As I said above, this is a "set it and forget it" business model. It is reliably reported that some individuals make in excess of $30,000 a month selling simple inexpensive how-to reports on Kindle. One lady who I believe writes gothic fiction has been written up in national magazines as having earned well over two million dollars from Kindle alone!

Remember, at zero out-of-pocket cost to you the biggest and most powerful book marketing company in the history of the world, Amazon, will bend over backwards to help you sell anything you can produce in writing! Then they pay you up to 70% of the retail price you set, <u>100% of which is profit for you!</u> And they keep marketing your item **forever!!!** This is an absolute <u>NO BRAINER.</u>

Amazon helps with exposure, does all of the customer billing, and provides marketing that would take the average internet marketer years to perfect. You simply provide them with the digital ebook or report content and they periodically send you royalty checks! Awesome!

Once you begin to publish books, **DO NOT GET DISCOURAGED BY SLOW EARLY RESULTS.** In fact, you can count on them. It could take a month before sales start to materialize. DO publish at least five books before you worry about getting results from the first book. Or better yet twenty-five! It is not as hard as it sounds once you get the hang of it. At some point in time you must begin your own marketing blitz.

As I said above, over time there are some self-published authors who have hundreds, even thousands, of titles in their publishing-platform accounts and earn a fortune! The important thing to remember is that every title remains in these programs **forever**, so it just becomes a matter of compounding results.

My personal goal is to try to double my self-publishing revenue every month. I base this on the simple math behind old bet where the loser readily agrees to pay the winner a penny each day and then double it each day for a month. On the face of that it seems like you are risking very little. Not quite!

Take that one penny and double it every day for a 31 day month. Can you guess how much money you will have? It is unlikely your guess will be close! After week one you'll be up to a staggering $1.28! By the end of week 2, almost half way home, you're up to $163.94, not exactly life-changing.

But by the end of week three, almost done (?) we have a nice tidy $24,192.32. Not a retirement fund, but not exactly chump change either. But guess what? At month's end, just 31 days after we started with a penny, we have just under <u>twenty-five-million dollars</u> ($24,774,039.84 to be exact)!!! I never cease to be amazed by this simple exercise in arithmetic.

This is why my goal is to double my revenue every month. If this means I have to produce a two ebooks a day and post them to my accounts then so be it. Never lose sight of the fact that a saleable short ebook or report can be created in a couple of hours once you get into the habit of doing them.

Incidentally, people who buy Kindle ebooks have seven days to return them. Do not concern yourself with buyers requesting refunds. Yes, there are "Refund Bandits" out there. Fortunately there are **far** more honest buyers. You can expect around 1% to 2% refunds, **irrespective** of your material quality. Of course, if your material is truly awful you can expect many more refunds and some pretty ugly comments.

<u>The main thing is to stick with the self-publishing program</u>. This is not a get-rich-quick system. But it is a way to create, over time, a residual income stream that can be counted upon indefinitely, and passed on to your loved ones after you get to that great library in the sky!!

MODULE SEVEN

SOCIAL SITE SUCCESS

CHAPTER 35
BIG PROFITS MARKETING ON FACEBOOK

I recently learned a startling statistic. Everyone knows that Google.com gets more visitors than any other website. But I had no idea that Facebook.com is number two with around two-hundred-million unique visitors every month, and four times that many registered members! That is over one person in seven on the entire planet! Facebook grows in popularity every month, and is expected to EXCEED Google in a few years.

Of course there are MANY other social sites, which we will discuss below. General marketing techniques shared in this report are applicable to any of the social media sites, but the overwhelming traffic at Facebook makes it a no brainer for marketing focus. Don't you want your shot at those 200,000,000 monthly unique visitors? As I've said before, I don't even want a tiny slice of that humongous pie. I just want to lick the pie- knife!

The good news is that it is possible to market virtually any products on Facebook. There is a lot of technique to learn, but the net profits can provide a huge income stream. I know a number of internet entrepreneurs that focus 100% of their efforts marketing on Facebook.

Because of the sheer volume of users of Facebook, it is also probably the best vehicle for adding names to your email list. One problem you will face is the natural impulse to get very involved in the social aspect of Facebook, which can be a massive time drain. <u>Never lose site of the fact that you are joining Facebook for the sole purpose of marketing your products, **not to socialize.**</u> Don't get caught in the "social media time trap" if you are serious about earning big bucks with internet marketing.

Also don't lose site of the fact that we are interrupting people using social media for socializing. They do not access their accounts with the intention of being sold something. For this reason your ads MUST be properly crafted. Do not overlook the word SOICIAL because social networking is all about connecting with people, not about connecting with the marketplace.

Facebook marketing can be FREE. You can also pay for advertising. You can do both, though just as with Google AdSense paid advertising gets much quicker results.

For starters, go to facebook.com and open a personal account. It is free and very easy. (Do <u>not</u> open a "business" account because it will limit what you can do.) If you already have a Facebook account for social purposes do not open a second account, because this violates Facebook's "Terms Of Service"…one account only. Of course your significant other can have their own account as well as you having yours.

With Facebook, as with any sites that I may suggest that you link to, there is a wealth of "how to use this site" information. You absolutely MUST read and understand all of this guidance.

For me to repeat this extensive material in this report simply adds pages of "fluff". This all might make this book have greater perceived value because of its increased length, but it adds nothing to your ability to learn Facebook marketing techniques. I am teaching you to fish. The rest is up to you.

I suggest you glance at some of Facebook's unique terminology which is shown below at the end of this Chapter.

You will want to create a user name that is the same for both Facebook and Twitter. The more name recognition you have the more people will want to work with you.

Your first job is to create a page in your Facebook account that promotes your website and your affiliate activities. Once you have an account look for the "more" button, and within the menu that drops down click on "Ads and Pages", and then click on "Create a Page".

You will then be faced with a number of choices. It is a good idea to explore all of them. You can surely eventually find a "type" and "category" that best fits your niche.

Once you select these two parameters, enter them and click "Get Started". Now just follow the instructions to build your page. You can upload messages, ad copy, photos, links, even a video clip! Your goal is to have visitors "Like" your page so that your page with its links shows up in their own profile for their "friends" to check out.

If you can create an interesting page with good changing content, photos, some video it can quickly "become viral" with fans scattered all over the Facebook landscape, and lots of "likes". This can take you some time compared to the instant focused advertising route described below, but definitely should be considered as a long-term traffic strategy.

As soon as possible you will want to shorten the Facebook Page URL that you are assigned, which is long, ugly, and impossible to remember. Before you are permitted to do this you need 25 "Likes". You can get these usually through friends and family. If you must, you can buy "Likes" through our old friend fivrr.com. Do not do serious Facebook marketing until you have your short, recognizable URL in place.

WATCH YOUR EDGE RANK

You must stay aware of Facebook's EdgeRank algorithm. The results of this mathematical formula determines how many people will see, in their NewsFeed, any link or content item you have shared on your Facebook Page. Of course you want to maximize the reach of your efforts. To do this you have to make nice-nice to EdgeRank.

When any of your posts is shared it is seen as an "object" by the algorithm. Each interaction with that shared post, such as a "like", "share", "comment",
"tag" or whatever for that particular object is called an "edge" (as in "it gives you an edge"). The more "edges" an object collects the more likely it will show up in a user's NewsFeed.

Weight is given to relevance, which is the number of friends clicking, liking and commenting on your material. Weight is given to the frequency of posts. It even considers the user's own history of clicking and messaging within Facebook, so your own participation is important.

Your job is to follow a number of best practices, and pray that Facebook's algorithm thinks as much of your marketing efforts as you do!

If you manage to do most or all of the following you figure to keep them happy:

Do not forget to put a "Like" button on your Page. Duh.

Users are expecting some sort of interaction by visiting your Page. Offer useful, engaging information.

Ask questions much as you would in Forum marketing participation.

Post interesting articles from third-parties.

Reward your visitors by introducing some new product or information before they see it elsewhere.

Create a "Welcome" application for new visitors to encourage them to click on your "Like" button.

If you have videos, embed them in your Page as opposed to sending them elsewhere (as in YouTube) to view them. You can add a YouTube channel and videos to your FaceBook fan page using an app found at: involver.com.

If you are using other social media in some way be sure to incorporate content from these.

Be certain to be social! "Like" the Pages of related businesses, important vendors and customers. Many will "Like" you back.

Use the Facebook Logo wherever possible throughout any other marketing to direct visitors to your Facebook Page. This includes any website or blog to which you might be linking.

Obviously all of the above takes a good bit of effort and time. The positive thing is it costs you zero dollars. Many find this to be a good tradeoff! You might consider one of the available programs to help you with your "FREE" efforts, which of course are then no longer entirely FREE.

But time is money, so you may well find it worthwhile to seek assistance. Investigate HubSpot social media app marketplace at hubspot.com. This is an extremely valuable resource. A Google search for "Social Site Marketing Software" should turn up many other helpful software programs.

NOW LET'S SPEND SOME MONEY TO MAKE SOME MONEY

For you to launch a successful Facebook marketing campaign you need to understand their four basic ad formats. These are: Web Ads; Social Ads; Post Ads; and Sponsored Stories.

WEB ADS encourage Facebook users to visit your website.

SOCIAL ADS encourage Facebook users to engage with your internal Facebook media, including your fan page or promoted events.

With both Web Ads and Social Ads, where you are sending someone directly to a specific place it is relatively easy to track your metrics and measure your return on investment.

POST ADS are more personal, including content generated from Facebook media. This you change creatively into your ad.

SPONSORED STORIES are ads you create with content generated through the interaction you have with your audience. This would include "likes", "shares", and "check-ins". There are over 800 million members! You pair stories with ads that encourage users to "like" your business, then showcase your fans reactions in Sponsored Stories. Note that Sponsored Stories can only be shown to friends of friends.

Your Facebook ads can be set to target audiences by choosing location, language, education, work, age, gender, relationship status, likes and interests. You can also choose specific friends and connections. You can set daily budgets and bid prices through "Ads Manager". You can easily follow your ads performance with their metrics feature.

Now let's look at actually running your own targeted ads on Facebook. Direct linking of affiliates' links in social media is important because it bypasses the need for creating a website or a really killer home page. The downside is that direct linking precludes the use of a "squeeze" page to build up an email list for future sales.

You should go to clickbank.com and find yourself some suitable products to represent, get your affiliate links, and write some short compelling ad copy. You will also need a PayPal account so you can get paid by your affiliates.

You do not have to do any of the "FREE" stuff described above for marketing without advertising. You don't need a domain name. You don't need a website. Just go to the bottom of Facebook's home page, click on "Advertising" at the bottom, and set up an account.

Facebook is VERY particular about the ads they accept. They apparently do not see the advertising model as a pure money maker. If your ad isn't "cool" they don't want it. I'm told that far more are rejected than accepted. They have zero tolerance for bad grammar or spelling! After their catastrophic initial public stock offering they just might be rethinking this policy!

Nothing remotely sexually-suggestive is allowed. No pictures showing cleavage. No "Find hotties". No "Find well-hung guys"…get the picture? Many rejections seem to happen for no reason at all. They will NOT tell you why a given ad is rejected. Just don't ask and try again.

Believe it or not there is a "sneaky" way to greatly increase your chance to have an ad approved. After 8PM PST Facebook's USA ad-approval desk shuts down and all ad approvals are done in INDIA! Apparently they are much less sensitive to the nuances and certain colloquialisms in English that would kill an ad in the USA but gets a free pass in India!

YOU SHOULD ADD PICTURES

You should include photos in your ads. You can use "GoogleImages", which are free, but they do not tell you if a photo is copyrighted. I prefer not to run the small risk of copyright infringement.

I buy "small" photos from "istockphotos.com". Do not buy "extra small" or anything larger than "small". They cost around $1.70/picture depending upon how many you commit to buying. You purchase "credits" in advance and pay with the credits. A bit more expensive is fotolia.com, where I buy my front-cover background images. They have a mind-boggling number of excellent images at reasonable prices, though they have a minimum dollar commitment of around thirty dollars. There is another good source of photos called archive.org, but I find it too hard to navigate to bother with. Try it. You might like it.

If you know how to use "Paint " or "Adobe Photo Shop" software it is advisable to put a frame around your pictures. They catch the eye better. You could also try putting a gold star in the upper right corner of the picture, which it is reported to increases click-throughs, especially among women. Why that is true I cannot imagine.

LET'S DISCUSS HOW MUCH TO BID

For your bidding parameters, start with $5.00 a day. Facebook newbies are assigned a spending limit, usually $25.00. They want you to start slow and do it right. As you gain experience they automatically raise your limit to $2,000.00 a day.

Beyond that limit they will provide you with a form that you complete along with a copy of your driver's license to get increase up to $20,000 per day. You are a long way from that figure, but there are many Facebook marketers who hit this level. If I break even at their initial level I know this ad will make money as they lower my cost. As long as your ad gets clickthroughs Facebook is happy and rewards you with ever lowered costs.

Click on "Set A Different Bid". You will be doing PPC (pay per click) only, not CPM (cost per thousand looks at your ad). As a general rule knock off 25% from the minimum of the range they offer. For example, @$0.95 - $1.60, bid $0.81. ALWAYS bid in one-cent increments, not five-cent or ten-cent like most bidders.

If you bid $0.81 you will get preference over the regular bidders who use "even-number" $0.80! (I have heard that $0.71 is a very good amount to bid as a starting point regardless.).

Make sure you always show "External URL", which is your unique affiliate link.

YOU MUST SPLIT-TEST

Split testing is the key to Facebook riches. You can split test every variable, demographics, the ads themselves, and especially pictures. I know of one insanely-successful Facebook marketer who will split-test FIFTY or more different pictures until he hits on one that gives clearly better click-through rates (CTRs).

Many marketers get 100% - 200% return on investment (ROI) with well-designed affiliate ads. If you find an ad that gets this ROI at $5.00, $10.00, $20.00, $100.00, etc., why wouldn't you just keep increasing the daily limit? In general, if an ad is pulling under 20% ROI most Facebook marketers will pull it and work on more profitable programs. But ANY positive ROI is good!

Keep your niche focus tight. With ages, do not use "40 – 70"; use "40 – 42". Then split-test, "30 – 31", "32-33", etc. You will be amazed to find that one particular tightly focused parameter can have a massive effect on results. I've seen "38 – 39" outsell "40 – 41" by a factor of three! DON'T ASK! There is no way to intuitively predict this. You MUST split-test the age parameter.

As ridiculous as it may seem, if you focus a given ad towards "brunettes", "blonds" and "redheads" in three splits you may very well find vastly different CTRs! There is no way to intuitively predict this in advance. Don't even try.

Incidentally, some very successful internet marketers focus entirely on marketing to women. They are convinced that the CTRs are always higher than with marketing to men.

As important as split-testing is, you can end up spending too much valuable time if you overdo it. The various permutations of variables for any ad are almost infinite, so you must set some sort of limits on the time you spend split-testing any given campaign. Decisions, decisions.

Facebook does have excellent analytics built in to their program. With it you can easily track the number of visitors and your click-through rate. You can actually run multiple ad variations simultaneously to see which ones are making the most money.

SMART MARKETING

There is one awesome feature in Facebook called "Advanced Demographics". It allows pin-point marketing focus. You can even focus on individuals on their birthday!

Does that seriously limit your market? Not when you consider that on any given day there are a million individuals or so in Facebook celebrating their birthday!

Never lose sight of the fact that all internet marketing is a "numbers game".
To obtain the number of members in a focused niche put "#" sign before an interest to get a group figure. My bullseye group size is between 250,000 and 500,000.

Also you will find that the ability to target specific religions can be very valuable. There are many affiliate offers available that are specific to one religion, such as "Christian Dating".

Facebook makes keeping track of metrics easy. You will want to know your exposure rate (the percentage of your target audience being reached ---75% is very good), your frequency (the number of times the user sees a specific ad (optimum is reported to be six times), and your click-through rate (0.04 is good). Note that Broad Category Targeting (BCT) increases exposure rate, though many Facebook marketers prefer Precise Targeting (PT). The latter is not necessarily better to use.

A couple of important tips. If you are attracting visitors to "freebie" ads (which are zip code or email-requested programs) be certain to add: "Participation Required" or "See If You Qualify". This is to avoid implying that everyone gets the freebie, which would be a lie. Always use these qualifiers where the freebie is not guaranteed.

Also, in any dating ad be certain you check "single"! There is no Facebook category for "married but playing around"!

Facebook has created a new class of advertising: "Targeted Opt-in Customer Ads" (TOCAS). Ads are displayed only to customers who have decided to have a relationship with you by declaring that they "Like" your page. The key is that only you, the creator of the page, can specifically target everyone who has "liked" your page.

Facebook has rolled out "Facebook Exchange" that allows you to advertise your book by offering real-time bids for targeted ads. These can be targeted at users who have shown interest in a particular niche. This is based on cookies Facebook has imbedded TO TRACK WHAT THEY DO WHEN THEY LEAVE Facebook.

It is possible to "hire" third-party help with your Facebook advertising. The best known platform for this is at kenshoo.com/social. It is a site worth visiting if only for some ideas you might uncover.

You may wish to consider setting up a "Facebook Store". There is considerable disagreement over how useful this is because Facebook users do not like leaving fan pages and buying something in a "store". You can study this at shoptab.net/ and decide whether it is worth the bother.

For companies to be better able to interact with their customers in April 2012 Facebook committed to the Timeline platform. This opened Facebook up to all users and made this feature available to **brand pages**. Within two weeks over eight million company brands switched to the new format! The Timeline platform puts a premium on overall page design. Images can now predominate. Virtually any brand you can imagine, from Macy's to Coke jpounced on Timeline. A company can highlight and pin key content and add apps to the top of pages. They can interact with "fans" through private messages.

This represented a change in the Profile Page design. You are now able to feature (or hide) "Stories". These are the life events you feel create the best representation of your life. Where your personal history used to begin on your first day of joining Facebook, it now goes back to the womb! Be particularly careful what you divulge. Identity thieves are salivating over this new "feature". Always be vigilant about what you post. As Facebook evolves they are developing various means to allow optimum protection of personal information.

One of the most significant changes this brought about is that users can no longer use landing pages. You can no longer use a "like-gate" to get people to like a page before they actually view it. There are ways you can create **tabs** for your facebook pages using programs from: Pagemodo at pagemodo.com, or Wildfire Interactive (which was purchased by Google in August 2012.) In fact, at Pagemodo you can speed up just about anything you want to do with Facebook. Tabs are now much more prominent than they were previously, which is a big plus. This compensates to some extent for the loss of the Landing page.

Another big plus with the new Timeline is the ability to add a large "Cover Photo" across the entire top of your Facebook page. Be creative with this photo, because it is the very first thing visitors see. You cannot, however, use this photo along with "like" or "share" or any other calls to action.

Remember, as mentioned above, do not overlook the word SOCIAL in social site marketing. Social networking is not about connecting with the marketplace, it is about connecting with individuals. Participants are looking for a personal exchange. Just be certain that your socializing is product oriented.

GLOSSARY OF FACEBOOK TERMS

There is a lot of terminology that you will encounter in your Facebook marketing that might be unfamiliar when used in this social media context. You will encounter:

Applications: These are programs within Facebook that let users share content with other users.

Content: Items posted on a Wall, such as status updates and recent actions. Becoming a Fan would be an action.

EdgeRank: Facebook's algorithm that determines what content gets shown in users' News Feeds.

Fan: Users who choose to "Like" your business page.

Friend: As a noun, a personal connection. As a verb, to add a Facebook member as a friend.

Friend List: An organized group of friends.

Group: This is an aggregation of users having a common interest. You can create and/or join a Group.

Like and Likes: AS a verb, to "like" your business page means someone became a fan of that page. As a verb, to like others' comments on their Wall or News Feed. As a noun, "Likes" are the number of users who have liked your business page.

Network: An associated group of users based at a school or workplace.

News Feed: A collection of your friends' Wall posts published on your homepage.

Page: The official Facebook presence from which your business shares information and interact s with Fans.

Profile: Your personally stated information about yourself or your business.

Wall: This is the core of a Facebook Page or Profile that collects new content.

Facebook marketing can be FREE, or paid, or both. Properly used, Facebook can represent one of the largest streams of internet income, and one of the easiest for any newbie to conquer.

JUST START SOCIALIZING YOUR WAY TO INTERNET CASH!

CHAPTER 36
RICHES ARE A TWEET AWAY

BECOME A TWITTER TWEETER

Twitter is, behind Facebook, the second most used social media platform. They get about a quarter of the unique visitors that Facebook gets, which is still a very substantial number of people. And they have a pay-per-click advertising platform that can be tightly niche-focused.

"Twitter is a real-time information network that connects you to the latest information about what you find interesting. Simply find the public streams you find most compelling and follow the conversations". So begins the opening web page of twitter.com. Check it out.

There are basically four types of Twitter users. There are the **SHARERS** who seek out useful information and share hyperlinks to these articles with their legion of followers. These can also be "retweets" of tweets they find interesting. There are the **FOLLOWERS** who mainly follow sharers to get real-time news in their areas of interest. Probably the most frequent tweeter are the **CONVERSATIONALISTS** who spend endless hours blabbing with their followers and friends. Lastly are the **MARKETERS** who are either promoting themselves or some product.

Twitter can be a marketing challenge because of the sheer volume of people "following" Tweets (what the individual messages are called). With information streams coming in so fast it is impossible for anyone to read or even notice most of the messages received. But some internet marketers have found a way to make Twitter pay. It's a numbers game, as with all of your internet marketing.

Twitter's "Promoted Accounts and Tweets" selects users with similar interests to an advertiser's current followers and places the businesses' Twitter handle (identifying name) in the users "Who To Follow" section. You pay when someone follows your account or interacts with your Tweet. You can geo-target, and state your maximum dollars per day, dollars per new follower, and dollars per engagement action. If you want to create contextual ads for your Twitter marketing check out adix.com.

Within the Twitter website is a useful search function, search.twitter.com. Enter your niche keywords in the box and hit "search". Your job is to place tweets that direct people to your squeeze page where you can offer a free report or review article relating to the search topic. As always, the idea here is to gather email list names in exchange for the report, and then get click-thus to your affiliates.

Twitter is huge! A recent article in Science magazine reported that one-hundred- million Tweeters send two-hundred-thirty million Tweets a day. Numbers such as these definitely get the attention of the marketing community. It should get your attention too!

Twitter is actually a better vehicle for reaching the masses than email. Those nasty spam filters that can get in the way of email marketing don't exist on Twitter.

For starters, go to Twitter.com and set up a free account if you have not done so already. It is a very simple, almost instant process. Enter your email address, make up a password, click and done. Create a user name that is gender neutral, but a real name, not some idiotic pseudonym like "dietslogger" or "mucusdude". Don't laugh, an awful lot of Tweeters use absolutely nutty names. It has been shown conclusively that people prefer to buy from a real person. You will want to create a user name that is the same for both your Facebook and Twitter accounts. The more name recognition you have the more people will want to work with you and buy from you. And if you are a female with a pretty face they will want to work with you even more. Live with it.

Be certain that the requested little blurb about yourself would not turn off either a male or female visitor. A bit about your passion for your niche would be appropriate.

And now for the picture upload. It has been proven time and time again that whether you are a dorky looking guy or a gorgeous 280# bodybuilder, or an average looking man or woman, a picture of a really attractive woman pulls more clicks every time! Chauvinism aside, this is all about making money. If you happen to be a really attractive woman than by all means use your own picture . Most of us do not quite fit that profile. Remember, in ALL of your internet marketing, social site or otherwise, perception that the seller is a **woman** makes web marketing more profitable.

You will be setting up a Twitter account for every niche to which you care to market. You could end up with a hundred or more accounts eventually. Build up slowly, but once you get the hang of it you will find it quite easy to promote profitable marketing links to any number of Twitter accounts.

Marketing on Twitter requires a thorough understanding of how the Twitter universe works. Twitter is all about person to person communication. It was initially conceived as a way for individuals to let each other, friends and families, know what they were doing at a particular moment in time.

Each message is limited to 140 characters, and over time a "shorthand" vocabulary, to say more in fewer characters, evolved. Tweeting "4u" saves two-thirds of "for you". "LOL" for "lots of laughs" saves lots more. Get the idea? You will find you can get a lot of marketing communication into 140 characters!

Recently Twitter is beginning to go beyond this sacrosanct 140 figures in a roundabout way. Twitter is allowing some select groups (New York Times, BuzzFeed and the WWE among others) to add characters that are relevant to their content. The headlines in these super-sized tweets can be 70 characters long, and the added Tweets themselves 200 more, for an overall total of 410 characters. Time will tell whether the 140 character limit will be expanded for all Twitter users.

There is some Twitter terminology with which you need to be familiar. A "Follower" is someone who enjoys your Tweets or finds your account interesting and elects to follow you and get your Tweets automatically.

You can search for Tweets that relate to your niche. Twitter has a search function. If you enter "[your niche key words] :)" you'll find positive Tweets relating to your niche that you can use as testimonials. You do this with a Retweet.

A "Retweet" is used if you see a Tweet that is saying something nice about some product but they themselves are not selling it. If it is something you market you can send this Tweet to all of your followers, a Retweet.

Any time one puts a "d" in front of your user name a follower can send you a Tweet without anyone else seeing it.

If one of your followers has seen something you offer, or used the product you offer, and liked it, they can use "@". Putting @[your user name] you get a reply, all of your followers get the reply, and all of their followers get the reply.

Your job is to get as many Followers as possible. Remember, every Tweet you post goes directly to your

Followers' account, but also to their Followers' accounts as well.

It didn't take long for marketers to realize that they could post information about their products or special sales or giveaways or whatever to a massive audience.

The way we are going to make money on Twitter is to build a "following". If you keep putting out useful information, expertise, opinions and the like on a niche topic people with an interest in that niche will begin to "follow" you. Their followers will also see your Tweets and some will follow you as well.

The universe of followers grows like a virus, and it is not uncommon to end up with many thousands of followers, all interested in your particular niche! This can easily occur within a month or two, as long as you keep posting relevant tweets. And there is the rub. How can you possibly find the time to send out frequent Tweets, especially if you have lots and lots of Twitter accounts. I'm glad you asked!

Google to the rescue! If you do not already have a Google account for gMail or AdSense or a Google calendar, open up an account automatically at Google.com. It's free. (Or register from scratch if you have no other Google account.) Once you have any Google account (such as gMail) "user name and password" you use the same log-in for any other Google product forever.

Once you have your Google account go to: Google.com/Alerts. This is your niche-relevant auto-content system. Here's how it works with Twitter:

Not only does Google index billions of pages of web content, but it also indexes blogs! This is important for our Twitter marketing efforts because blogs are updated much more frequently than static websites. You need to enter, in a box requesting your "search term", your niche keyword search phrase.

Leave or set the "type" at "comprehensive" because we want content from everywhere. Then set the "how often" choice to "as-it-happens".

Lastly choose "feed" as the delivery method. Right-click the word "feed" and copy the special URL link shown. Now go to TwitterFeed.com. Give your feed a title, then enter the special URL you got from Google. Then go to the "advanced settings" and set "time" to whatever minimum they allow, for example, thirty minutes.

This is the frequency between posting cycles. Then set the maximum number of entries per cycle to the maximum allowed. Then hit "create feed". Presto! You have just become a super-efficient publisher!

Now it's time to make some money with our constant information feed. And we have TWO great choices. We can place links to our affiliate programs or to our website squeeze page, AND we can place special pay-per-click links from special Twitter advertising companies.

Check out the following three sites, and open up free accounts: revtwt.com; be-a-magpie.com; twittad.com.

These networks typically pay $.03 to $.05 per click, but remember, it's a numbers game.

Twitter accounts allow four ads per day, which is why it is important to have as many Twitter accounts as possible, and as to gather as many followers as possible. The power of big numbers is on your side, because the actual percentage of followers who actually go through with the process that earns you cash is historically less than one-half of one percent.

But if you had ten Twitter accounts each with a hundred thousand followers (not difficult to achieve) that is a few thousand individuals a day responding positively.

But it gets even better! Go to Revtwt.com and sign up for an account. This company pays you a 20% income for money paid to those you send to their network, and it is paid as a residual on an on-going basis. There is yet another step to finalize this process.

First sign up for a free account at: TweetLater.com. Follow the easy instructions to connect it to your Twitter account, and an automatic announcement will go out to all of your new followers. You place your RevTwt referral link into a message such as: "You Can Turn Your Twitter Account Into Free Cash". There is a referral link to RevTwt attached automatically which can get a high "out of curiosity" click rate. Again, a numbers game, but over time this can result in continual daily income.

Let us not forget our affiliate accounts, which pay much higher amounts per click than the examples above. Choose your niche offer, and post it to your Twitter account. Disguise it as a "non-ad" testimonial by saying something like: "I just tried xxxxx and thought it was great". The "xxxxx" product name is your affiliate link.

The easiest way to automate this process is to use your TweetLater account which can send pre-scheduled affiliate-linked Tweets to your entire follower universe. You can do this with multiple affiliates, and multiple Twitter niche-related accounts. The numbers can get mind-boggling: Have twenty Twitter accounts, dozens of affiliate links, and thousands of followers and your automated income stream can be quite impressive.

Check out: HootSuite.com. Study the site in detail This is a wonderfully useful and basic "Social Media Dashboard" which costs zero dollars to use forever and greatly simplifies you Twitter marketing effort. As you gain experience you can use their "all-the-bells-and-whistles" version of HootSuite for under six bucks a month.

All you do is enter your original post or article or Google feed on your HootSuite site and it is fed to Both Facebook and Twitter automatically, saving a lot of time.

Twitter itself provides literally hundreds of special applications (known colloquially as "apps"). These are intended to enhance the Twitter experience in one way or another. Feel free to check them all out. Frankly I have only found one that I thought would add a dime to my earnings.

Just stick to the basics I share with you and you will make more and easier money than you ever thought possible. The exception is the "Auto-Follow" app. This sets up your account to automatically follow any Follower you get. It pays to use it.

Recently Twitter cracked down on the creation of new apps much to the chagrin of the industry that creates them.

There is a tool that can help your Twitter marketing along, though it is not free. It is located at twollow.com. Understand that independent research has shown that almost half of the individuals you follow will follow you back, often without even looking at your account page!

What Twollow allows is for you to enter keywords and phrases to automatically follow any Twitter account that sends a post using these key words or phrases. This is extremely powerful.

Depending on how broad your key word terms are you might find thousands of posts every day with those key words in them. Any time the phrase appears on a site you are not already following you automatically become a Follower. And of course their Followers are added as well.

Bearing in mind that around half of these new people you are following will blindly follow you back, you can see that in a very short time period you can build a huge number of Followers.

Twollow.com has three levels of service: $15/month for 5 keywords; $20/month for 10 keywords; and $35/month for 20 keywords. Once you begin to earn money using Twitter you will be able to easily afford this program, which is well worth the price.

A new feature of Twitter is "TWITTER CARDS" that one can attach to their tweets. Twitter cards can give you control of how your content is displayed and can be used to drive traffic to your site. There are three types: summary cards (default) which includes a title, description, thumbnail image, and Twitter account attribution; photo cards; and player cards (which include audio and video). Card properties are defined by simple HTML code strings. You specify the type of card for your content by adding: <meta name="twitter:card" value="summary">.

Recently Twitter made their most significant design and functionality changes in their six years of existence. They focused on creating simpler navigation. They also launched commercial "Brand Pages" to allow more in-depth company profiles and are giving marketers control over the tweets a visitor sees when arriving at this business page.

Twitter recently announced to its mobile device users that they would begin to see sponsored advertising messages in their timelines. These are the "Promoted Tweets". I'm sure they were thrilled! Twitter also announced the acquisition of blogging platform Posterous. What the implications of this might be are not yet known.

Twitter isn't for everyone. But if you enjoy keeping in frequent touch with a universe of potential buyers you might well find that you can have fun and make a lot of money at the same time. That's not a bad business model to pursue.

CHAPTER 37
PIN YOUR WAY TO SUCCESS

THE PINTEREST PHENOMONON

As if Facebook and Twitter don't give us enough social marketing interaction, enter "Pinterest". Quite frankly, until you feel you have mastered Facebook marketing, moving on to any of the other social sites is probably counter-productive. Compared ebook publishing and Domaining (Chapter 44) the amount of time one can spend on social sites in general is just too much to justify economically, at least when you are first starting out trying to make money on the internet.

With that said, there are some marketers who are so grounded in social media outside of marketing efforts that profiting from their existing social presence is a natural transition. **If you are one of these folk then by all means go for it.** For the newbie just starting out to earn an internet living I strongly suggest putting social sites in general on the back burner until you are generating significant income elsewhere. They simply take too much time away from the more direct revenue streams.

When originally conceived Pinterest was "by invitation only". The marketing idea behind this was to build pent-up demand from the everyday user who wanted to give it a try. "Create Scarcity" is a fundamental marketing tactic, even if it is just an illusion of scarcity. With that said, Pinterest dropped the "invitation-only" model in mid-2012.

Pinterest is growing at an amazing pace. Within two years they have at least 40 million unique visitors monthly! Some marketers I know claim that it is providing more traffic to their marketing sites than other social media. In any event, it can't be ignored. It only started in late 2010, and began to explode exponentially at the end of the year when it began to rise above ten million unique visitors a month! That's serious traffic. The traffic to Pinterest equals the traffic to Google+, YouTube and LinkedIn combined! Pinterest is continuously evolving, and may be quite different by the time you are reading this Chapter.

The site itself can be addictive......and time-wasting. When I first visited it I spent an hour or so fascinated by the variety of images on the home pages. Then I realized that these social sites in general can be an horrendous waste of valuable marketing time unless you can focus 100% on marketing. Not easily done. They are as addictive as potato chips! On the other hand, I certainly suggest that you go to pinterest.com and spend many hours studying how marketing is being accomplished there.

Incidentally, you can visit compete.com and at no cost you can view the number of unique visitors received by any website. It's fun to watch the dual between Google and Facebook and other social sites every month for the most unique visitors. The numbers of unique visitors for all of these sites is truly staggering!

The Pinterest concept is to allow users to visually share their interests by posting, known as "pinning", images or videos on to "pinboards". Think of these as "virtual corkboards". Each pinboard holds to a single theme.

An image is called a pin. Adding something makes you a pinner. Adding that pin to a pinboard is called pinning. Reposting someone else's pin is called a repin (duh).

You can browse through pins that others have pinned. Then you can repin or "like" or leave a comment. You can share others' pins on Facebook or Twitter or even stick them on your website or include them on your blog.

Pinterest's website points out that they were conceived to: "connect everyone in the world through the "things" they find interesting." This is accomplished by means of the magic "Pin It" button.

When you have a "Pin It" button on your pages all of your pins will have a link back to the source. These links have no SEO linking value (they are "no follow" links) but the key is that they do have marketing value. Pinners find your content and visit your web pages in one quick click.

Pinterest is integrated with Facebook and Twitter for easy content sharing, though you cannot connect directly to your Facebook Business Page at this time. This may well change in the future.

The Pinterest Business Model (how they make their money) is a bit obscure. It is reported that they are relying on affiliate marketers to use Pinterest to drive traffic to their affiliates. When your link is found to drive that traffic they secretly add a code that enables them to get a piece of your action. How much do you lose? As yet no one knows for sure. It's enough for me to never use Pinterest until I can convince myself the additional traffic will offset my possible loss in commissions.

You should have both Facebook and Twitter accounts before joining Pinterest. Until recently, to open your Pinterest account you visited pinterest.com and clicked "Request an Invite". For whatever reason the site was set up to be "invitation only". At present, you can simply join the fun without being "invited" to do so. What **were** they thinking?

Provide your email address and wait for your link. Sign up through your Twitter account option to tie in with your Twitter business account. As I said above, at this writing you cannot connect to your Facebook business page, though I'm sure that will change in the future.

Once inside Pinterest, hit "Settings" and complete the all-important Pinterest Profile. Put in your company name, logo, brief description of your company, and whatever links you want seen. Because you want search engines to index you, turn off "Hide....from search engines".

Ah, Pintequette. <u>Pinterest frowns upon self-promotion, which complicates your promotion efforts a bit!</u> The idea of the site is to have entities share the lifestyles that their brand promotes. Selling hats? Show pictures of places to where people wearing different hats can travel. Showcase the lifestyle your brand promotes. You should not be spamming the site, overtly selling. There is a certain subtlety that must be mastered.

Initially, set up three or four cork boards, er….pinthingies, before you start your marketing efforts. There are two ways a follower can follow. When following a specific board you will be notified when any user pins something new to that board. When following a particular user you will be notified every time that user pins anything to one of his or her pinboards. Your task as a Pinter-marketer is to find a way to increase traffic at the levels of your pinboard and your account.

Set up a pinboard with items related to your primary keywords. Increase the content on your board with other user's pins. Then start following those users you think might want to follow you in return. When a user sees you "liking" or "commenting" on their content it is probable they will check out your pinboard. They hopefully will choose to follow you, and tell others about you.

I mentioned above having other social sites before joining Pinterest. To begin to get followers be certain to add the Pinterest Follow Button to your website. Promote your presence on all of your social sites, and your blog. The hardest part is creating exciting visual pins, because many products simply may not lend themselves at all to a visual format. A nice collection of your colorful killer book covers might work well.

Be creative. Use charts and graphs if appropriate. Create visuals that relate to your **written** content, which you cannot use. Every time you write an article or blog think of some image you could create that would relate to its "culture". You could pin the covers of your relevant books, which speaks highly for having covers that leave no doubt as to the content of the book itself.

As idiotic as it may sound, when you ask for testimonials for any product try to get a photo of your customer smiling broadly after using your product. That makes a great pin! You can also post videos on your pinboard.

The ultimate situation is to become the one **"go-to"** Pinterester, the ultimate Pinterest-star, about a certain topic related to your industry or special niche. **Whenever you can, be certain to imbed links in your pins that take the viewer to your commercial website or a "buy now" button somewhere.** When they arrive at your website they should see whatever they saw on your pinboard, and then you can expand from there to get some desired action that earns you a commission.

Keep in mind the primary Pinterest demographic: **YOUNG WOMEN.** **The most** popular pinboards display recipes and fashion. Of course in addition to promoting your own products, you can certainly use Pinterest for Affiliate Marketing of other merchants' products. Try to find appropriate products of merchants who are not yet represented on Pinterest pinboards.

One problem Pinterest encountered was people pinning copyrighted material from websites without the site owner's permission. They have tried to resolve this issue by providing website owners with a line of HTMNL code that lets them opt-out of being featured on Pinterest. If a Pinterest user tries to use an image or other site material from a "no pin" coded site, they receive a message to the effect that: "This site does not allow pinning to Pinterest. Please contact the owner with any questions. Thanks for visiting". Of course, those determined to do whatever they choose will simply ignore the message. I prefer: "Steal anything from my website and you will be tracked down for life and when located, immediately beheaded!". Whatever.

Of course an entire new industry has sprung up, inevitably, around Pinterest. This is the "we can make it easier for you" software solutions folk. Simply Google "Pinterest Software" and you will find many different software solutions available. At this writing I have not tried these, but some look interesting, such as pinterestsoftware.net. Thus far I feel I have more control if I do it all myself.

Whether you can effectively monetize Pinterest, finding creative ways of showing how your products integrate into your visitor's lifestyles, remains to be seen. Remember, this is 100% visual.....for example you can't use written testimonials. As mentioned earlier, the closest you could come to a testimonial would be a picture of a smiling customer actually using your product!

Your true cash investment in Pinterest is whatever part of your profits they are skimming. As with all other social site marketing, a thorough understanding of the monetizing process, and a continuous involvement in your presence are the keys to success. There isn't much to lose except time. Pinterest has yet to completely define its commercial marketing model.

If you are someone who is deeply engaged in socializing through any of the many social site choices, Pinterest might be right up your alley. If you have never engaged in Tweeting, and Liking, (or whatever) you are surely better off beginning your internet marketing adventures elsewhere.

There are some newer alternatives to Piterest that you might wish to visit. Check out: sparkrebel.com; stylpin.com; imagespark.com; designrelated.com; manteresting.com; gentlemint.com; and juxtapost.com. Each of these specializes in a different theme.

The entire concept of using electronic bulletin boards has taken off exponentially. If you want to get involved in social marketing it is not the worst place to start.

CHAPTER 38
CASHING IN BIG WITH OTHER SOCIAL SITES

Although Facebook seems to be the social medium of choice for many internet marketing pros, let us not overlook the many others. I do suggest, however, that all newbies start with Facebook marketing and establish success there before moving to other social sites.

Social site marketing is not for everyone. Because so many of you may already be involved in Facebook and Twitter it is a very easy transition to changing your focus from "social" to "business". There are unlimited ways to use social sites in your internet marketing. Today, virtually anything that is really funny, intelligent or intriguing has the potential to go viral and result in massive traffic.

Here are some of your alternatives:

MYSPACE MARKETING

Take MySpace for example. They only get around 0.02% of Facebook's traffic. MySpace attracts a generally younger crowd, the 13 – 16 age group being huge. The Facebook membership is a much older demographic, with a large percentage being the college student population.

One difference between MySpace and Facebook that I like is that while Facebook makes you create a personal profile to qualify to run ads, MySpace does not. Just sign up at MyAds.com and follow the easy instructions.

You must, however, carefully mask your marketing efforts because blatant advertising is not permitted on MySpace. I look at MySpace as sort of a blog whose layout you can customize.

Go to myspace.com, and follow the instructions to create a FREE account. You will need a separate email account for each MySpace page if you want to create more than one. You can use a pen name and profile if you want to protect your identity and try to be "simpatico" with your target audience.

On MySpace visitors want to know about YOU, not be sold a product. You will need a photo of "you", which can actually BE you, or can be someone you pick as your "avatar" out of istock.com or some similar photo site. Once you get to your Control Panel you will want to create a really professional profile customization. A few sites where you can download excellent FREE templates are: pimpmaspace.com; facepaintapp.com; and groovymachine.com.

You want to create a keyword-rich title, but it must sound personal. You can start to blog about your niche topic by clicking on "Manage Blog". Never blog about your product itself. If you are promoting a gardening product, you might say: "Last weekend I started to winterize my plants. If only I had followed the advice in (your product with contextual link) last year I wouldn't have lost so many plants to frost."

Make your page friendly and personal. Seek out MySpace users who have tags in their profiles that relate to your niche. Click on the "search" link and enter appropriate keywords. Visit the profiles that come up and send a friends-request to see if they will, add you to their list.

Once you begin to establish a list of friends send out personalized bulletins where you make announcements and drive traffic back to your site. You are also able to post Classified Ads and join specific groups to get added coverage.

You can buy traffic on MySpace, but you are charged differently than on Facebook. Facebook sets their charges based on the demographics you choose. Change a parameter, and you will see the cost change accordingly.

The tighter your focus, the smaller the niche you are trying to reach, the lower the cost.

MySpace on the other hand shows you the exact number of people in your chosen focus group and they charge you based on the size of that number. Fortunately there is a relatively easy "work-around" to save money.

For example, if you were to choose the 14-30 age group they would set a specific cost. But if you split this into three groups, 14-17, 18-24, and 25-30 the combined total cost will be MUCH lower! By running very focused ad campaigns it is possible to get your cost down to a penny or two.

Although its traffic is relatively small, there will be far less competition than on Facebook, so MySpace is certainly worth a try, especially if you have a college-student-oriented niche product.

ONE, TWO......SQUIDOO!

Facebook, MySpace, Pinterest and Twitter are household names. Literally billions of social interactions take place daily. Ask the average web surfer about Squidoo and you are likely to get a blank stare. Ask a select few rich internet gurus and you'll get a knowing smile. Simply, **Squidoo equals easy cash.**

Squidoo is a unique social environment where anyone can claim a FREE page (called a lens) and become an expert on that page. I guess it's got "squid" in its name because it puts out many tentacles for you to locate the right people that will buy your affiliate offerings.

You can blatantly market **anything** on your lens. Most have found that the best approach is to become a "teacher" on your topic-of-expertise, and work your links into your lessons text.

You can create as many different "Squidoo lenses" as you wish, which is a big plus over some other social sites. Sign up at: squidoo.com/member/registration. Enter the minimal requested information, log in, and choose "Create A Lens". You will be asked what your lens is about. This is your "Lens Title".

Be certain to include some keywords in your title, targeted for the product you plan to promote. Promote one product per lens. Shoot for a catchy title because you want to attract as many people as possible to click on your lens title. You can make the title as long as you wish.

Next you will be asked whether you want Squidoo to populate your lens with ads (called modules) of their choice. I prefer to add my own ads. Then you will be assigned a Squidoo URL, squidoo.com/(whatever you want). What you want are your best keywords, with a hyphen between them.

You next choose a category, and let the system know if your lens is safe for all viewers. Adult lenses are fine, but have their own category that restricts viewers. Then you will be asked for your "best keyword" and three additional ones. Enter the security code they show you and you are done!

Now comes the important part, editing your lens. The "Write Module" is the text section where you can write a brief introduction to your topic with a hyperlink to your website squeeze page. You should include keywords with around a 4% - 5% total keyword density (Google's general favorite for indexing).

Now click "Add a Module" and you will be presented with ten or so choices of ways to make money with your lens. Each has an explanation when you hover your mouse over it. They are self-explanatory. If you want you can have nothing but "Write" modules.

Sign up at squidu.com for great tips on using the site. Visit other lenses and sign their guestbooks. Ask people to add your lens to their favorites, and to please rate your lens "five-stars". The tiny little stars are located at the very top of the page, in case you can't find them!

You can drive traffic to your lens from anywhere you wish, your blogs, your articles, your MySpace pages, anywhere you would normally use for your marketing. Your Squidoo account has all of the statistics you will need, including your traffic, your ranking compared to other lenses, and how much money you have earned.

Be certain to download the FREE .pdf file written by Squidoo's creator Seth Godin, titled "Everyone's An Expert". Reading this, visiting other lenses, and participating in SquidU, will make you a Squidoo LensMaster in no time!

GOOGLE ENTERS THE PICTURE

Because of Facebook's phenomenal success, Google decided to get into the social site scene with its "Google Buzz" platform, but it was a flop and shut down. Smart companies cut bait fast and learn from failure. Google ain't stupid. This is a prime example of how internet marketing evolves over time.

Enter the "Google+" platform. Go to: plus.google.com and take a look at the site. Though it only began in June 2011 it received at least 10% of Facebook's traffic volume after only a few months and figures to grow rapidly as it continues to evolve.

Google is so popular because of its #1 search engine that their company executives have expressed the expectation (hope?) that companies will build entire marketing plans around the new Google+ platform.

Google+ is evolving rapidly, though not as rapidly as Google had hoped. Their "+1" button was created to compete with Twitter's "Follow" and Facebook's "Like". Internet marketers are working feverishly to learn to optimize their marketing on this newest Facebook/Twitter/Pinterest competitor.

To set up your personal business on Google+, first be certain to get a free Google "g-mail" email account. (They frown upon Yahoo mail!) Then go to plus.google.com/pages/create and follow the instructions offered by their page creation wizard.

You will need to decide on a category to classify your business. Some choices are Product/Brand, Company, Local Business, Arts/Entertainment/Sports, and Other. I suspect "other" will be further refined as the site develops.

You will need a website URL to be allowed to sign up, so be sure you have registered one. I suspect they would be pleased if you set up a very simple website and it contained a few Google AdSense ads. These cost you nothing and can generate revenue for both you and Google, aside from your marketing efforts on Google+. A Google Blogger site would be a great choice.

You will be asked to create a "Tagline" which should be a keyword-rich "Headline". Next you will be asked to upload an image. This could be your company logo if you have one, or something relevant to your niche.

Now comes the fun part! You need to optimize your page with valuable information and LINKS to valuable content. The more the better. As with your website, frequently-updated blogs is the best approach. Google takes care of "launching" your page. The entire idea is to get visitors to enter and stay with your "Circle", and only relevant fresh content can achieve this.

They have something called a "+1 button" which you should add to your site. It facilitates a visitor in sharing your information. Google claims having this button on your page increases visits four-fold.

A visitor to your page can see in advance how many others have found your site useful and might be inclined to check it out for no other reason.

One word of advice. Google+ apparently puts a lot of emphasis on visual images for sharing, such as charts, slides, PowerPoint type presentations and the like. This will become apparent as you search their site's participants.

An interesting aspect of Google+ is its emphasis on the use of online video communication between vendors and customers, sort of a Google "YouTube" (the video sharing social site).

The feature called "Hangouts" promotes group video chats among Google+ users. In theory this creates stronger inter-personal connections than does simply sharing links and images in continuous update streams.

Google has thought of another innovation to Google +called "Direct Connect". To take advantage of this feature you must add a special unique computer code to your page. Once you do, anyone can bypass the Google search engine results by simply adding a "+" before your company name in the search bar. Google uses a "secret" algorithm to determine whether your page will actually "qualify" for this gimmick, so it isn't automatic even when you imbed the code.

To what extent bypassing search engine results will impact others who use PPC or optimization by reducing their exposure to new visitors (those who "connect directly") is anyone's guess. It could be problematic. Time will tell.

Google + is focused on "Circles" of like-minded individuals, and on having members encourage sharing of your postings with their Circle members. This is much like encouraging "retweeting" on the Twitter platform.

A word of advice: include a "+1" button on your website. This button allows users to easily share links and promote results in Google search activity. Google claims that this button's presence will greatly increase your Google+ traffic. And if I had to take a guess it probably helps your website ranking position.

They have also created "Sparks", a feature which aggregates content in a specific broad topic. The information is presented in a magazine format. Also differentiating itself from Facebook and others Google+ incorporates a "chat" feature.

There are a few basic things that appear to be important considerations in marketing with Google+:

Set up a Business Profile. Here you can only add people into one of your "circles" once they have added you. Some people from your Personal Profile page will add your business Profile into their circles. Only then can you add them into your circles on your business page and market to them.

Set up a Personal Profile to interact with people and advertise your Business Profile. Here you can add anyone you wish to add into one of your circles. The person does not have to follow you for you to add them. You will then see all of their public posts and you can click the +1 button and interact with that person.

You can create as many circles as you wish and name them whatever you choose. Your circles are private. No one can see what you named your circles (e.g., "Prospects", "Clients", "Morons!", etc. though they can see how many members are in each circle.

For those of you also using Google's pay-per-click AdWords program you will see a +1 button next to the ads. When someone clicks on the +1 button their recommendation appears next to the ad, which hopefully encourages others to click on the ad.

Enable "Social Extensions". When you do so Google+ combines the +1s from your Google+ page with the +1s from your ad. The total shows up on both your Google+ page and on your ad. Lots of +1s make your ad and page look more attractive. You want lots of +1s!

Google really pitched our industry a curve-ball when they decided to integrate Google+ results into their search engine positioning. The long range effect of this major change has yet to be reconciled by search engine optimizers.

Google is in a never-ending quest to outdo other social sites. Enter "Search+ Your World". This newer feature automatically pushes results from Google+ up the search engines. Because of contractual matters, which may be resolved eventually if not already as you read this, Google does not show or rank Facebook and Twitter searches.

I don't believe anyone has quite yet mastered marketing with Google+. There are some creative ways you could apply it. These include:

Use the "Google Hangouts" feature to schedule up to ten people in a group teaching/learning environment. Clever entrepreneurs will surely find a way to monetize this feature.

Post a video to showcase your products benefits.

Be certain to choose the "Public" option when you post to Google+. You will be indexed by Google in their regular search results. No one knows what algorithm they use to rank these posts.

Search out people who need whatever it is you offer. If you respond to a question give away simple answers for free, but set yourself up as the "go to" expert in whatever it is you are selling. Soft-sell your paid services.

A key to Google+ is your ability to add key links to your "About" page (edit profile>about). You can tell your visitor exactly where the link will take them, e.g., your website, Facebook, etc. The five photos you are allowed at the top are the only site design elements over which you have any control.

Another key to Google+ success is to optimize the management of your circle. You can segment by geo-location, interests, whatever relevancy exists within your group.

Overall I see Google + as muddying the internet commerce waters to some extent because its use will have an impact on search results and to some as yet unknown extent on your search rankings for your regular websites.

It may make conventional Search Engine Optimization more complex by adding another layer of involvement to the equation. And it may force you to become involved in this new social site platform whether or not you care to do so!

At this writing Google has not created the paid advertising aspect that is so very successful with Facebook, MySpace and Twitter. It seems to me that if they hope to some day pass Facebook in marketing value to businesses they must employ that commercial model as well.

Although Facebook and Twitter have a huge head start, by its very size Google+ should be able to play catch-up a lot faster than any other company entering the social site field possibly could. Ignore Google+ at your marketing peril.

LET'S LOOK AT LINKING WITH LINKEDIN

Most internet marketers who do social site marketing focus their attention almost exclusively on Facebook. Google+, because of Google's immense size, has begun to attract a lot of attention as well. LinkedIn is often overlooked because at first glance it seems to be a difficult path to sales. Used properly, however, a few savvy marketers are realizing its potential for profits.

If you think of Facebook as the local beer pub, LinkedIn is a professional trade show. One way LinkedIn is used by its one-hundred-thirty-million-plus users is as a virtual employment agency where people post and find jobs. It is, however, also a business information site.

Before joining LinkedIn you should have a Twitter account and a personal website and a business website. Registering your "name.com" and setting up a simple "about me" website is useful for many reasons. If your exact name .com isn't available, try either a different top-level domain (TLD such as .net, .org, .info or .biz), a nickname, or your name followed by "internet guru" or whatever. You should also have a blog.

First off look at LinkedIn as an individual user. Browse to linkedin.com. Your first step is to create a "Profile". This is more like a job resume than a social page. Be certain to include: your full name and address; a good professional looking picture; a "Professional Headline" (such as "Internet Guru"); and your recent work history. Be creative.

Next you want to create a personalized LinkedIn URL. Click "Public Profile" >"Edit". Your domain name (URL) will be: linkedin.com/(whatever you want). Your name works just fine. The "Additional Information" section is self-explanatory. Just follow the prompts. You are asking people who know you and your work to recommend you to LinkedIn.

Last, connect your Twitter account, specifying in the check box that only Tweets that contain the LinkedIn tags (#in and #li) get through. That's it for your personal page.

Next you need to create a great Company Page. This is accessed through your Personal Page. You want to include a lot of good information about specific products you want to promote through discussions. The instructions provided by LinkedIn are quite easy to follow. Just make everything sound professional, and not sales oriented. Consider the following nine steps:
Make certain that your Company Page overview is filly synchronized with your company website. Be certain to include your product benefits.

Under "Specialties" you have 256 characters to use for your marketing. Be certain your primary keywords appear here.

You are allowed 25 characters for your headline, 75 text characters, and a 50x50 pixel image. Bids are $2.00 minimum. You can target a certain job title or function, a specific industry, geo-target, company size or name, seniority. Age, gender or Groups. You can do CPC or CPM.

Carefully pick your "Industry", which visitors will use to find you.

Also list up to five locations if this applys to your particular product
If you have one, and you should, enter your blog's RSS feed so that you can share your latest blogs.

Work on making your page dynamic. You do this by posting all manner of updates with links back to your product website.

Create a LinkedIn "Group", where people with similar interests to yours will meet to discuss news on topics of mutual interest.

Use the "Announcement" feature judiciously, ands infrequently. Used improperly and too often it is analogous to email SPAM.

Participate in "LinkedIn Answers" as the resident expert.

Under "Admintools" you can set up an ad campaign. The "Common Questions" box fully explains this feature. You will next turn on "Status Updates". This is where you will add news and content about new products and projects. You create leads on LinkedIn by engaging visitors as you would at a Chamber of Commerce mixer or a cocktail party. Communicate with your visitor about their interests and needs. Offer helpful advice and information. Eventually send them to a landing page where they can get a free report or sign up for your newsletter.

IMPORTANT: Be certain to include a LinkedIn logo button on your website so the visitor can virally spread your information.

There are specific functions within Linkedin that help you generate leads. Check out all of the following and use them all: "LinkedIn Direct Ads (not unlike Google pay-per-click); "Linked In Answers" (the most useful for initiating dialog); "LinkedIn Applications" (there's an app in there to add your blog posts to your Business Page); and "Linked In Groups" (join many, in and outside of your area of expertise). There are many others with more being added often.

The above discussion of marketing on LinkedIn leaves out a great deal of fine detail. If you go to: learn.linkedin.com and read everything there the entire Linkedin experience will become crystal clear. As with other social site marketing, this is a project that takes time and attention. For those who enjoy social interaction it can be a fun way to earn internet income.

YOU TUBE VIDEO MARKETING

YouTube.com just happens to be the second most visited website on the planet! Part of the Google family (what a surprise) it enjoys 160 million visitors a month viewing some **20 billion** video clips. These are astounding numbers, surpassed by only Google.com itself. It gets 50% more traffic than either Yahoo! or Twitter.

With this sort of traffic it seems as if YouTube would be a natural for marketing manner of products. The fact is, while some companies are learning how to capitalize on this massive traffic, very few have learned how to generate significant income.

There are ten general types of video clips that appear on YouTube. If you can find a way to tie your product in with one of these, and produce a 30 second to one-minute video clip that attracts a huge audience, you could have a real winner. The general categories of videos are:

An **instructional** video about a product and its application. Try to be interesting and informative, and to gain the visitors' trust.

A **demonstration** video of a unique and interesting product could go viral and attract many viewers. This would require a product that lends itself to an interesting demonstration. Try watching some late-night TV ads for ideas.

A video that creates **interest** and inspires a viewer to take some action such as typing in your domain name to satisfy their curiosity.

Hilarious videos rule YouTube. Babies and pets doing really funny stuff become classics with millions of views. Tying this in with a product offer is a challenge.

Spiritual and inspiring videos can be a hit, though here again tying in with a product could be tough.

Weird works. UFOs, conspiracy theories, whatever, if it's weird, people will watch.

Videos that have **shock** value often attract huge audiences. The key is showing that something improbable actually is real.

Sex sells. It always has and always will. Of course, laws and propriety dictate just what you can show without getting in trouble. Can you somehow portray your product as sexy? As making someone sexy?

Truly **gross** videos. Think "Fear Factor" TV. There is a very fine line between "gross" and "truly repulsive and disgusting" that you don't not want to cross. Tying this in with a product could be a bit dicey to say the least!

There are also many **personal** "This Is My Life" videos that have gone viral and attracted millions of viewers. From "look how boring my day is" to "look how exciting my day is" done well can be a winner. Showing you or a shill repeatedly using your product might be doable.

Google is constantly evolving YouTube. They are endeavoring to make the site more business friendly with better social media interaction, especially in conjunction with their Google+ platform. They have created another Google-mysterious algorithm, this time for a "Recommendation Bar" to better personalize viewer experience. What will they think of next?!

You can also add a YouTube channel and videos to your Facebook fan page. A good app for doing this is found at: involver.com.

If you happen to be one of the many who frequent YouTube and enjoy the concept, then using it to promote some product might be a natural for your marketing plans.

OTHER SOCIAL MEDIA

There are a large number of lesser-visited social sites that may still be worth your look. These include:

Yelp.com is a review site. Members write reviews about local businesses. If you are promoting a local business take a look at Yelp.

Delicious.com is a bookmarking site where members can save the links to favorite articles or websites. This is analogous to your browser's bookmarking capacity. The links can be shared and commented upon.   The more comments you make, the more people are likely to visit your profile page. This in turn can direct traffic anywhere you choose.

Digg.com is for sharing news. Links are posted to favorite news articles.
Members comment and vote on the articles they like the best. A good rating for an article that links to your website could be expected to increase your traffic.

Stumbleupon.com is another "recommendation site" where members rate websites, blogs, photos and videos. When they click on the "Stumble!" button they see a ranking of your material. The higher the ranking the more often your material will show in their results. Of course your material will contain links that send them wherever you wish them to go.

Other large general-interest social sites are: . Tumblr at **tumblr.com** (20M); and Flikr at **flikr.com** (20M);

Some of the smaller social sites are: Friendster at **friendster.com** (150K); Xanga at **xanga.com** (800K); Instagram at **instagram.com** (100K); Bebo at **bebo.com** (0.5M); FourSquare at **foursquare.com** (2M) and LiveJournal at **livejournal.com** (4M).

Beyond all of the above popular social sites there exists is a large universe of very specialized social sites directed at specific niches. These can be marketed to by accessing the forums that accompany each of these platforms.

The following are some of those specialized social media sites, with the value in parenthesis their approximate traffic in monthly unique visitors as of this writing (M=millions; K=thousands).

Athlinks at **athlinks.com** (130K) brings together joggers/ runner types.

Cramster at **cramster.com** (0.5M) is frequented by high school and college students seeking help with their schoolwork.

Two social sites that cater to music lovers are Last at **last.fm** (not .com) (5M) and ILike at **ilike.com** (300K).

Four social sites that are frequented by those interested in stocks and bonds and the like are: Tip'd at **tipd.com** (20K); Wesabe at **wesabe.com** (25K); SeekingAlpha at **seekingalpha.com** (2M); and Jigsaw at **jigsaw.com** (0.8M).

Dog and cat lovers share their love on Dogster at **dogster.com** (0.7M) and (you guessed it) Catster at **catster.com** (0.6M)!

With the great popularity of online gaming it was inevitable for specialized social sites would eventually be created. The two best known are Raptr at **rapter.com** (100K) and GamerDNA at **gamerdna.com** (50K).

People interested in sharing their opinions about films join Flixter at **flixter.com** (1M).

Book lovers can be found socializing on GoodReads at **goodreads.com** (5M) and Shelfari at **shelfari.com** (100K).

Want to find a social sites that share recipes and cooking advice? Check out BigOven at **bigoven.com** (200K), BakeSpace at **bakespace.com** (40K), or FoodPals at **foodpals.com** (2K).

A rather large social site that finds artists socializing and sharing their work can be found at DeviantArt at **deviantart.com** (5M).

Social sites that facilitate the exchange of travel experiences can be found at TripAdvisor at **tripadvisor.com** (a large site with 13M unique monthly visitors), TripIt at **tripit.com** (200K), and Doppir at **doppir.com** (5K).

Nitch.biz is a business to business social networking site that allows businesses to join with kindred spirits.

If you have a product that is focused on any of the above social sites interest areas it would be foolish not to join in and find subtle ways to gain maximum exposure.

A Google search for "social sites" will turn up more than you could ever hope to access. Just beware of becoming too involved in any social medium to the exclusion of you primary focus which must be getting people to buy your products.

A very important FREE resource is available to you at quantcast.com. Type in any social site domain name and you can determine not only its monthly traffic, but more importantly the demographics! What I find interesting is that the huge percentage of users who are under 34years of age. You won't be selling a lot of seniors'-oriented products here!

What I find even more astounding is the relatively low percentage of social network users who are reported to be Caucasian, especially when you consider that the population of this country is primarily Caucasian. African Americans, Hispanics and Asians predominate as users of social media across the board. I have no idea why this is true, but there have been many studies confirming this demographic.

A very long list of social media sites can be found at: wsm.co/rJK5F2. (Note that this is a special type of web address where the end part is case sensitive.)

Social site marketing is often overlooked as a potential source of massive internet revenue. The key here is the sheer massive numbers of individuals actively using these programs day in and day out. If I had just two marketing platforms that I would recommend to a beginning internet entrepreneur Facebook and Twitter fit the bill.

Happy and profitable socializing!

CHAPTER 39
BIGGER CASH MARKETING ON FORUMS

One of the best routes to gaining customers and backlinks to your website is through participation in the forums in your niche. In my experience participating in forums takes a great deal of time that might be better spent in marketing elsewhere. But there are many internet marketers who make a great living participating in forums, so don't let me stop you from trying. The best news is it is FREE!

If you happen to be someone who enjoys social sites such as Facebook and MySpace and love to Tweet on Twitter, and pin on Pinterest, and are on a zero or limited budget, you might just find it to be an enjoyable way to build a valuable focused email list, make sales, and improve your Google PageRank.

Your first step is to locate forums and discussion groups in your niche. Google search is my choice for locating forums. Just Google "(your keywords) forums" and you will find more than you might expect. The more specialized your niche the fewer forums you will find, but you will almost always find many more than you could possibly join.

Check out the number of active members, the more the better. Look for forums with lots of active members that have lots of discussions. As you look at various forums the differences will become obvious.
Also a search at: big-boards.com will show you a useful database from which you can derive market intelligence such as the number of members and the member activity in various forums.

Many forums, known as the "DoFollow" ones, will allow you to put your website link in your signature at the end of your post. This can be very helpful in your marketing because the whole idea is for forum members to click on your link just to see what you are all about. Don't disappoint them! Be sure they see a great freebie in exchange for their email address.

So you only want to post with forums that are in the "DoFollow" category. This allows for the prospect of getting those valuable backlinks. A good long rated-list of these can be found at: vtechtip.com/2009/10/list-of-dofollow-forums-with-high-pagerank-update-regularly.html.
Some general forums to which I would strongly suggest that you post to are: forums.mysql.com; bungie.net/forums/default.asp; forum.joomla.org/; bbpress.org/forums/; flickr.com/help/forum/en-vs/; forums.cnet.com;
forums.feedburner.com; affiliate seeking.com/forums; dnforum.com; htmlforums.com; webmasterforums.net; sitepoint.com/forums; webhostingtalk.com.

There are a number of other very popular forums that focus on a particular area of interest:

AssociatePrograms.com for affiliate marketing.

eWealth.com also for affiliate marketing.

WorkAtHome.com for home based businesses.

MoneyMakerGroup.com about making money.

InternetBased Moms.com for work-at-home moms.

DNSscoop.com is domainer focused.

The best affiliate marketing forum is at: abestweb.com. The best place to put anchor text backlinks by offering comments and advice can be found at: warriorforum.com. Their focus is on internet marketing. Enter subtly: "Did you see that great new 400 page ebook,,,,,,,,". Get the idea?

It needs to be noted that forum PageRanks do fluctuate rather widely over time. What may be a great active forum today could become almost obsolete in the future for a variety of reasons.

Forums can be used for research, subtle advertising, or even some paid advertising banners. Your job is to actively participate in discussions and over time build a presence that will ultimately result in visitors to your websites.

Be certain to read each forum's posting rules, and be sure to follow them. Many forums are not friendly to individuals who are openly trying to market products. You need to invest the time to wander through the various forum topics and determine what participants are asking about the most that may relate to your niche.

Your general approach needs to be subtle. You cannot appear to be "selling". People want to be helped, not sold. If you see a question your product addresses you could respond to the questioner with something along the lines of: "I saw this answer to your question and I think they can help you with your problem." The underlined portion is your "text link" which takes them to your website squeeze page or affiliate link.

You can put a text link anywhere is a short paragraph discussing a relevant topic by adding: "......and I found a report that explains it in detail here." This text link could take them to your squeeze page where they get a free report so you can get their email address for later use marketing related information.

If you find that you enjoy the forum universe there is an all-in-one platform that you can utilize. Go to ning.com. At this writing they have a free 30-day trial. Beyond that, you are looking at a substantial cost of between $300/year and $720/year depending upon which of their two programs you choose.

Ning includes the whole ball of wax: a hosted website, blogs for you and for your members, email list building and management, marketing to site visitors and members, and discussion forums for infinite discussions. In addition there is every bell and whistle you might ever need to have your own successful forum site.

Although a Ning site could be created within hours, consider this a very long term project before serious income might be generated. Properly executed it could be an absolute gold mine. It's at least worth a look.

There are five basic approaches to marketing through forums:

ANSWER QUESTIONS: This can work especially well for you if you have a great deal of knowledge on the subject in question.

ASK QUESTIONS: This is a fast way to initiate a stream of forum posts where you can eventually subtly market your product.

ASK FOR AN OPINION: Make a long list of affiliate programs from ClickBank and other networks. Then ask: "Has anyone had any experience with xxxxx". Not only can this start a stream of forum posts, but you will learn about the products you might wish to market.

ASK FOR A CRITIQUE: Write an article, post it in your blog, and ask peoples' opinion of the article. Not only will you learn about your article's popularity, you will be getting involved in that forum. AN ADDED BENEFIT ARE THE BACK-LINKS YOU GET FROM VISITORS TO YOUR BLOG WEBSITE.

OFFER THE ARTICLE AS YOU WOULD TO AN ARTICLE DIRECTORY: See Chapter 37) Go back to the forum and offer the article (assuming people liked it) for publication, with the proviso that they leave your resource box (at end of the article with your URL or affiliate link) exactly as is.

Regarding 1. above, Answering Questions. A rather sneaky trick that many internet marketers employ to promote their product or an affiliate product link is asking a question from one computer and answering the question **themselves** from a different computer.

Some Q & A sites frequently used in this fashion are:
answers.yahoo.com;
groups.google.com;   wiki.answers.com;   allexperts.com;
yeda.com; help.com;   askhelpdesk.com;
theanswerbank.com.

Two different computers must be employed because this sort of tomfoolery is immediately caught and deleted because each computer has a unique identification number. I guess the technique can work, but don't get caught doing it. Remember, your internet reputation is VERY important. Tricks aside, your participation as an "expert" on Q & A sites can help you build a reputation in your niche and ultimately lead to increased sales.

Click on all of the above, and sign up for a free account. Then study what others are posting and the replies they get. Do not advertise your products in your posts. You will eventually create a "signature" containing your affiliate or website link at each forum. That is what does your marketing for you.

One of the hottest niches historically, and one that will continue to be hot, is making money at home with a computer. (I didn't write this ebook just for the hell of it!) If you have an applicable product, look especially hard for posts that appear to come from a newbie seeking help on making money on line.

If you can buy a PLR article on-topic, or have a relevant affiliate vendor from ClickBank, do a post that says: "Check out this site (your link), it sure helped me make a lot of extra cash". And add a believable explanation of exactly **how** the site helped you.

In summary, your job is to appear in the forums as a "helpful" person. If it fits, you could even eventually establish yourself as the "resident expert". You must appear to be providing useful advice with the links to back it up. But don't just put links in everything you post until you perceive that people have trust in your prior no-link input.

You certainly do not have to have an all-inclusive solution such as Ning to start a forum, though you might find that approach to be time and cost effective. A WordPress website creation program has a plugin that allows you to create your own forums on the WordPress site itself.

Either through Ning or WordPress you can build your own multiple forums on sub-niches which over time can add more and more members to you email list. Never forget: "The Riches Are In The List".

You can also create and start your own forums using programs found at: vbulletin.com; vbadvanced.com; whoson.com (Live Chat program).

Forum participation, as with blogging, takes time and patience. You might find that this time could be better spent elsewhere. Just remember that forums are yet another rivulet into your giant stream of multiple internet income methods.

Good luck, and Happy Posting!

CHAPTER 40
FISHING FOR RICHES – NET'S BIG SECRET

This is another of the best kept secrets on the internet. Although there are costs involved, the potential for profit is extraordinary. It is a relatively new way for internet marketers to increase their profits, and I perceive that there is far less competition than there is on Facebook.

Plenty Of Fish (POF) is a very popular <u>dating site</u>. They have literally hundreds of thousands of members seeking romance. There are two critical keys to the site's importance to you:

<u>They accept advertising;</u>

<u>They make it extremely easy for you to target ONLY those individuals who are likely to be interested in whatever you have to offer.</u>

This is possible because of the extremely detailed 30+ question profile they have on every user of their site. This extreme targeting to the dead center of your potential customer bulls-eye is POF's big advantage in your marketing strategy.

Want to present your freebie offer to college freshman women who are interested in their skin's appearance? Bingo! No problem. How about men between 40 and 42 who play golf and also enjoy heavy-metal bands? Bingo! No problem. How about ….well, you get the idea.

All you do is post product links on the Plenty Of Fish site, tell them who you want to have view the links, and pay them a rather nominal amount to present your offer to the universe of potential buyers you have carefully selected as being interested in exactly what you are selling!

They make the entire process very easy. Remember, you are not asking someone to actually buy anything (although you could) but simply to click on a product link that takes them to some website to take some action to get something for FREE (or even buy something!).

Of course it doesn't take a lot of imagination to realize that you could send your targeted visitor to your website, gather their eMail address on a squeeze page for later marketing efforts.

You do NOT need to sign up for a Plenty Of Fish "lonely-hearts" account, unless you are looking for the love of your life (which in my experience is counter-productive if you are trying to increasing your wealth!) This Chapter is about the making the big bucks, not finding a creative way to spend them!

Once you have chosen to promote a particular product offer, and organized your title, description, and picture, you are ready to hit the POF marketing bulls-eye. At the bottom of the opening home page click on "Advertise Here". Fill out the information page, and choose for "Business Class" the "affiliate/network" choice. Now comes the fun part!

Your next page is the key to the entire process. There are no right or wrong answers. I'm going to tell you the responses to use when you are starting out.

Name your campaign;

Set start date, leave end date blank;

Minimum Bid $0.10 (ignore their recommendations); max. $0.25;

Maximum daily spend: $5.00.

"Distribute Evenly" (throughout the day) NOTE: 6PM to 2AM works best for dating programs.

Frequency Cap: The number of times a given ad is shown to a given person over 24 hours. 3X is minimum to use; If you find your CTR at this level is too low, scale up to "4X" or a maximum of "5X" and see if your CTR improves.

Ignore "Value of Conversion".

Some useful suggestions on targeting: <u>This is the heart of your ad campaign.</u> It takes a lot of thought, and a lot of split testing to optimize results. "Income": Ignore this because most lie about it!   (FYI, you will see as a choice "BBW". It means **B**ig **B**eautiful **W**omen.)

"Log In Count" start at "50", increase to "100" maximum. "Session Depth" use "3". Ignore "Employment" category. The "Creative" is whatever blurb your affiliate gives you, edited by you to fit the AIDA advertising formula discussed in Module Five.

<u>Now for the center of the bulls-eye.</u> There are almost thirty choices in the drop-down targeting menu. When you click on one, you have a further refinement choice, such as "greater", "smaller" etc. Once you begin to play with this Target List you will be amazed at how tightly you can focus who will actually see your ads.

For each choice, click "Add Target". This records your choice in a large box next to the choices. Then repeat until you have everything you want in that target box.

Next you set up your ad, using keywords and an action close. Always choose "small ad" 110x80, which have been shown to get a better CTR. Once you are done click "Create Campaign".

Follow the instructions, add your payment information, and you are ready to go live!   As you will see they have excellent tracking for you to follow your results. <u>And positive results can happen quickly!</u>

Typical of the product ads that have proven profitable are FTD Florists and 1800Flowers. Remember, this is a romance site. Consider special occasions such as Valentine Day, Mother's Day, Father's Day, Christmas,

Thanksgiving, whatever, ALL are ideal times to promote appropriate seasonal gifts. One author has made a fortune marketing a children's Christmas book "Noel's Miracle" for at least fifteen Christmases!

Overall, what works best for me 24/7/365 are "Free Trials". Create a free trial and present it to a tightly targeted group of potential buyers you believe would be interested and you will be amazed at the number of click-throughs you will get.

It is reported that "ZIP Code submit" offers get better CTRs than "eMail submit" offers by almost two to one. Keep this in mind when developing a website squeeze page designed to collect email addresses.

It is also significant that most internet marketers I know focus more on marketing to men than to women. This doesn't make a lot of sense because it has often been proven that the CTR with women, all else being equal, is higher. Perhaps this is because most of the original '90s internet gurus were male, and apparently were chauvinists!

Don't overlook selling you own ebooks on your own websites. If you create something like "Reasons Why A Guy Hesitates To Date A Woman Taller Than Himself And What To Do About IT" you can focus that in such a way that only tall college age women will see the ad!

In fact, you can "reverse engineer" your ebook by creating a very narrow profile from the POF list and then writing (or having someone else write) an ebook that only this tightly focused group will be interested in owning. Your possibilities boggle the mind.

Especially for a beginner, Plenty Of Fish is an ideal early choice as one of of the multiple streams of internet income on which to focus. **Cast you line and reel in a fortune!**

CHAPTER 41
YOUR EMAIL LIST – KEYS TO THE KINGDOM

There is a common truism amongst internet entrepreneurs: **"YOUR MONEY IS IN YOUR LIST".** There is absolutely no question that a list of your visitors email addresses, legally acquired by you over time and properly nurtured, is **your most valuable asset.**

There is one best way to acquire an email list. When you attract a visitor to your website find some clever and creative and legitimate way to obtain his or her email address.

The classic way to do this is by means of a "squeeze page". When someone visits your site before they view the site itself present them with an "offer they can't refuse"! This can be a lifetime free subscription to your newsletter or ezine, a special free report on a relevant topic, a free ten part course on a relevant topic, access to your weekly special "whatever"…….. something that has genuine **perceived value** and is **FREE.**

Let's talk about the creation of your "squeeze page". It is the foundation of the website-based portion of your internet income streams. Nothing is more important.

The **sole** purpose of this specialized website landing page is to **OBTAIN VISITORS' EMAIL ADDRESSES.** It is an e-commerce absolute, stated above, that your money is in your list. Show me an internet marketer with a ten-thousand name list of loyal customers and I will show you an individual who can become even more wealthy at will. Even a highly-focused list of 2,000 names can be a goldmine.

It is important to understand that the more "request-for-information" fields you present to a visitor on your squeeze page the fewer people will choose to give you <u>any</u> information at all. The only two fields you want or **need** to show are "name and email address". And don't even split the name field into first and second name. Having more than one name is irrelevant.

Within the request box is a short headline of some sort about your niche topic, and a statement in smaller font above the two information request boxes and below the headline that says: "send me xxxxxxxxxxx". Do not use a simple "submit" button. Better is a "send me the report now" button.

One last item of text at the very bottom helps get better resilts: "Your Privacy Is 100% Secure!" and/or "We Never Share, Rent or Sell Your Email Address!"

And a simple "no thank you" option button removes the "squeeze" entirely and takes them directly to your website offer. No email address secured but a shot at the purchase of your own information product or a link to some other desired location.

To actually physically create the landing page you will be using the program inside the web-building tool you are using at wherever you are having your domain hosted (such GoDaddy). You can also use a free tool you will find at: tucows.com/preview/.

Once your visitor sends you the email request, you respond instantly by (Aweber or equal) autoresponder) by asking them to confirm, by clicking on a link you give them in the autoresponder email, that they have actually requested the item you offered.

This is known as a "double opt in" which tries to insure that you will not be accused of spamming anyone. Once they hit that link you then automatically send them whatever it is you have offered, which is pre-programmed into your autoresponder.

Your autoresponder is a very important tool in your internet success model. It is not inexpensive, but it will pay for itself endlessly. We will discuss this valuable tool in Chapter 42 to follow directly below.

Obtaining email addresses through your squeeze page is free, but relatively slow. It is possible to have an" instant" list, by renting or purchasing one. This is a decision that requires some thought and analysis.

Benjamin Franklin is credited with creating a simple system of making decisions where two ideas each of which has its good and bad points. He would take a piece of paper, draw a line down the middle, and write "pro" on one side and "con" on the other. He would then list everything he could imagine for either opposing pole on each side. He would repeat it on other pieces of paper for competing ideas. Then he'd study them side by side. Going through this simple process often makes your correct choice a no-brainer.

There are pros and cons to renting lists of email addresses. Renting is very fast, and very simple. The addresses are of people who have responded to something before. You can choose how many names to buy. That's the "pro" side.

But on the con side: It is expensive to buy a good list. You are permitted a one-time use (they put a few of their own private addresses in there to keep you honest!). You have limited control. You are competing with others buying the same list. The list may not be a perfect fit for your offer; and, perhaps most important, the people on the list have no idea who you are.

Now let us look at building your own list as opposed to renting one. On the "con" side: It is a much slower process, building a list one name at a time. It is more complicated, and you cannot know in advance how many addresses you can collect.

Now let's see if the "pros" prevail. You have unlimited lifetime use of your list. You can fit your list perfectly to your offer. You have an established relationship with the listees...**they know you**. You have no competitors using your list; and your list has becomes a valuable commodity which you can rent to others (as long as you have not promised not to do so).

Notice that throughout this report I always use the word "marketing", not "selling". Marketing is generally defined as the science of encouraging interested people to buy. If you can properly present a powerful offer to an interested audience they should be sufficiently motivated to buy. <u>Just find the right audience (niche), find out what they want, then provide it.</u>   Ultimately you want to set up automatic, repeatable systems that create an environment wherein people actually want to buy from you as opposed to you having to "sell" them.

Just as with all of your internet marketing it is important that you keep track of your analytics. In analyzing your email results, the "recentness" of purchase, the frequency of purchase, and the average dollar per purchase are three key items of information that can guide your future efforts.

THE PRE-SELL

Whenever you create email messages it is a very good idea NOT to compose it in MS Word. Unfortunately the formatting codes used in Word do not show up consistently as you expect in various customer email programs. To insure that what you see is what they get use a plain text editor such as NotePad or Wordpad to create your cut-and-paste messages.

For starters, every email should be individually personalized. This is readily accomplished with the functions in your autoresponder that collect this information from your squeeze page and present it properly at the beginning of your message.

Once you have your established email list, tell all of the members that you uncovered something very exciting and will be sharing this with them in two days! Mention some benefit. The next day remind them that your big announcement is only 24 hours away. Mention a couple of other benefits. On the third day reveal your discovery, and offer irresistible bonuses to the first "x number" who order whatever from your link.

I have seen this technique carried out to extreme over a period of two weeks. You know what? I could not wait to buy the damn product! I didn't care what it was, I had to have it! After hearing all of the benefits I had decided in my head that the price had to be $297 at least and I would probably buy it.

If it just happened to be only $197 I was certainly buy it. When I received that final email and I found out it was just $97 and included "$697 worth of "valuable bonuses" I couldn't get my credit card out of my wallet fast enough! I had been pre-sold to the max. Believe me, this technique works, every time.

Aside from the pre-sell approach, you get attention to your emails with an enticing subject line, analogous to the critical headline in an advertisement. The idea is to actually get people to **open** up your email. Sounds basic, but it is critical.

Wacky headlines actually work. Consider: "Forget Making Money"; "This Is Not An Email"; "Don't Dare Lose Weight"; "You're A Bigger Idiot Than You Think". Wouldn't you open these just to see what the idiot who sent it had in mind? Emotion-oriented subject lines work well: "The Dangers Of......"; "Don't Risk......."; "Be Certain You Don't......". In fact, simply looking at your email inbox (and especially your SPAM box) will give you endless subject line ideas. Which ones would **you** open up?

Of course your email message **content is key**. Try hard not to be boring. Show excitement, which is infectious! Short emails can get a point across quickly. Long emails give you the chance to provide information, include links within the text, and have an action post-script at the end. It's a good idea to provide a balance between short and long emails.

Why is email marketing so important? It is reported that up to three out of four persons on line are not surfing the net and buying stuff. **They do so specifically to access their email.** This is why building your list, before being concerned about sophisticated search engine optimization of your website, must be your primary objective.

Aside from the classic "squeeze page" method of growing your precious email lists many internet marketers resort to "pop-ups", "pop-unders", and "alert boxes". These are great ways to annoy visitors! Many visitors have "blockers" installed on their computers so they do not have to even see these. In spite of this it is still common knowledge that these "annoyances" can actually help you build your email list over time.

Doing a Google search for any of these terms will turn up dozens of sites where the codes to create these "poppers" can be downloaded, often at no cost. In my experience "alert boxes" are the least intrusive and most effective. These appear after a visitor departs from your website.

You offer some enticing incentive for them to click the "OK" button, which sits alongside a "Cancel" button.

For incentives you can offer special reports, a short e-course, a trial membership, a subscription, a "$197 value" free bonus, or anything you can imagine. When they click "OK" it takes them to your double-opt-in form where you capture their email address into your autoresponder. The most common bonuses consist of collections of outdated PLR material (I've seen as many as 500+ reports!) which are available to you all over the internet for FREE!

There are other ways to build your email list. One of these is through the use of FREE "List Builders". Check out the following:

List Fire at: listfire.com. Their website claims: "With **ListFire.com**, you can have thousands of people building you a **targeted, double-opt-in list** (that means 100% SPAM Free) around the clock." It is a sort of multi-level marketing system where you post a website they give you and drive traffic to it.

Opt In Boom at: optinboom.com. Their system is based on giving you a bit of code to add to your website which creates an exit popover that is designed to get a high click-through rate. You earn credits based on the traffic you create for the popover, and it ultimately becomes a viral multi-level stream of visitors to your site.

You can also build your list with "pay-per-subscribe" services. They are not as tightly focused as the tiny-niche-focused lists you will create yourself, but they are worth a look. Check out:
List Builder Pro at: listbuilderpro.com. Most impressive is the long list of the top internet gurus who apparently use their services. I'm sold. They offer double-opt-in names for around four cents each. Worth a try.

Opt In Marketing Lists at: optinmarketinglists.com. They have millions of addresses available in many general-niche categories. You can get 4,000,000 of them for under $200.00! Check out your autoresponder costs before trying this sort of mass marketing. But even if you can find 0.05% (one-twentieth of one percent) positive response to add to your hot prospect email list that's a sizeable 2,000 names!

In the long run, a big part of your marketing will of necessity be email based. Done correctly email is perhaps your best marketing tool. Done incorrectly it can land you in jail! The legal implications of email marketing were discussed in detail in Chapter 3. It is so very important that I am going to repeat much of it here.

The "Can-SPAM Act" was passed by both houses of Congress in 2003 and became law in January 2004. It is an acronym for: "**C**ontrolling the **A**ssault of **N**on-**S**olicited **P**ornography **A**nd **M**arketing Act". From that date on all unsolicited email has been referred to as "SPAM".

Back in the '70s there was a famous Monty Python TV skit about SPAM, the Hormel canned meat product. The final punch-line was: "I HATE SPAM". I suspect some government genius reverse-engineered the acronym to create the name of the act the fit the universal hatred of unsolicited email.

For the ten or so years prior to enactment of the act, sending out unsolicited marketing emails was the **primary** source of income for most internet entrepreneurs. In fact, there were " How To SPAM " seminars galore, with names such as "Creative eMail Marketing", and "Email Your Way To Wealth". There were many serious written courses available for hundreds of dollars. I still have many that I purchased in the '90s gathering dust in my library. Back then you could even legally send pornography to a minor! There were simply no rules governing commercial emails.

And as I recall no one called it SPAM. It was called "internet marketing"!

It is your responsibility to study and abide by the "Can-SPAM Act". Check out: ftc.gov/bcp/conline/pubs/buspubs/canspam.shtm, the government's site with all relevant updates. Be **certain** to check this out. It is your sole responsibility to learn the letter of this law.

The following list is far from complete, but it represents areas that are most easily and often inadvertently violated in your email marketing:

For starters, NEVER use a false or misleading header. "From", "To" and routing information must be accurate to allow the recipient to contact you.

Do not use deceptive subject lines. Make the subject relevant to the content.

You should clearly identify your email as an advertising message.

You must include your current physical address.

Primary to the law is the requirement that if a recipient of one of your emails asks to be removed from your list you MUST do so. Neither you nor anyone affiliated with you may ever send another email to that recipient. To facilitate this you MUST have an opt-out link in your email (tied to your autoresponder), and you have ten days to comply. You are required to keep a list of everyone who has unsubscribed. This is known as your "Suppression List". And you may not sell, rent or give out this list to anyone.

Penalties for violation of the act are rather strict. EACH violation can cost you $11,000.00. The Federal Trade Commission (FTC) can actually seize your property! And should you involve minors, or do something particularly egregious, or are a repeat offender, you can do hard time in a Federal prison. You don't want to SPAM.

To check your email content to insure that it is free of spam triggers go to: ezinecheck.com/howitworks.html. This can help you stay out of the sort of trouble you really don't need.

Check out mxtoolbox.com to be certain you are not blacklisted for some reason, a certain way to not get your messages to the desired destinations.

Your email very often does not get delivered as hoped. It is reported that twenty percent, one in five, emails you send are blocked by various filters, even if you have permission to send them. You will also experience "hard bounces" where the recipient address no longer exists. You will receive "soft bounces" due to recipient's email boxes being full, or the delivering server being out of commission for some reason or other.

You should always ask your list members to "white list" your emails. The process for doing this is relatively easy, but it is different for each browser. A Google search for "How To Whitelist An Email Address" will turn up directions to offer your list members.

To learn about the deliverability of your emails go to senderscore.org. Their website states: "Like a credit score, a Sender Score is an indication of the trustworthiness of an email source. Return Path's Sender Score reputation rank, compiled through our cooperative reputation network, provides access to data that ISPs and other email receivers can use to determine whether to accept or reject email. The score will provide you with information about where that source stands in comparison to other email senders, and how it is likely to be evaluated by email receivers. If you are responsible for that email, a

Sender Score will tell you the most important factors you need to change about your program in order to improve your delivery rates." This is really important information for any serious email marketer to know.

Done correctly, email marketing has historically been the single key to internet riches by virtually all of the multi-millionaire gurus. There is no reason why you cannot become one of them.

JUST DO IT!

CHAPTER 42
THE AUTORESPONDER MONEY TOOL

Having a fully developed email list is a critical piece of your long-term internet strategy. Every wealthy internet guru makes full use of their personally-developed email lists. I know. I am on at least fifty of their lists, and, incidentally, very happy to be on them. I periodically get valuable free information, and occasionally get offers to purchase some ebook or other. And frequently I buy one, because I believe that knowledge is power and that one can never have enough of either!

The great Benjamin Disraeli is credited with saying: **"As a general rule, the most successful people in life are those who have the best information".** I have found this to be true. And the more I learn, the more I realize I don't know.

I know that certain of these internet gurus have as many as 50,000 double opt-in customers on their email lists; a few perhaps have even more. Top internet marketers on whose lists I happily repose, from memory, and in no particular order, include Anthony Morrison, John Reese, Marlon Sanders, Jim Edwards, Avril Harper, Alex Mandossian, Robert Allen, Donald Trump, Rachael Long, Socrates Socratos, Alok Jain, Brad Callen, Andrew Fox, Ewen Chia, Cody Moya, Gabor Olah, Jason Potash, and Jay Abraham.

Add to these Dr. Jeffrey Lant, Justin Blake, Ty Hall, Liz Tomay, Mike Glaspie, Matt Garrett, Sam Baker, Edmund Loh, Yanik Silver, Mike Filsame, Ty Cohen, Mike Mazzella, Marc Joyner, Paul Birdsall, Marc Ransom, Anik Singal, Sean Mize, Shawn Casey, and a very strange dude who goes under the moniker of "The Rich Jerk"! There are many others as well.

Over the years I have met many of these individuals in person at various seminars. Many of them are true marketing geniuses. Almost all are very nice people. I mentioned Anthony Morrison first above because a few years ago I had the privilege of participating in a thirty-minute TV infomercial with him at his request at CBS Studios in Orlando. Nothing quite like seeing yourself on late-night TV to boost the old ego!

There are also a great number of equally wealthy and equally knowledgeable internet marketing individuals who operate entirely "under the radar", use a variety of pen names, and choose for whatever reason to remain anonymous and unknown to most. I consider myself to be one of them.

What all of these very successful infopreneurs have in common is that they all use autoresponders to manage their email lists. I do, and you must eventually also. You simply cannot do successful long-term email marketing without one.
You know that you want to periodically contact each customer with some sort of message. You can do this manually for a while. But in a very short time as you begin to accumulate email addresses you will end up with too many addresses to handle manually. Enter the "Autoresponder".

A Google search for "autoresponders" will turn up a long list of available products. Some are free, some are expensive. Many have FREE trials. What you want is the least expensive autoresponder that will collect addresses automatically and send out sequential messages to each recipient in the correct order at the correct times that you choose.

Most internet entrepreneurs I know use an autoresponder program called: "Aweber" at aweber.com. They have a vast number of desirable features in their software. They offer a $1.00 one-month trial, then it's a reasonable $19.00/month to manage your first 500 customers. The next level, $29/month for up to 2,500 subscribers should be sufficient for many months of email list gathering when you first begin your quest for internet riches.

Here is the simple procedure for setting up an Aweber account:

Set up an account at aweber.com.

First, view their five-minute video "Getting Started", at aweber.com/videos/getstarted/.

Next, you will need to start with the "List Settings" information.

Hover your mouse over the "My Lists" tab and choose "List Settings"
from the drop down menu. Under the "Basic Settings" section, choose a
list name and description, and enter the "From" name and email address
that you would like subscribers to see when they receive emails from
you. Save "Settings" at the bottom.

Move to the "Personalize Your List" section of the "List Settings" by
clicking in the gray bar at the top of the page. Here, you will fill
out all "Company Branding" information and connect to any social
media accounts you might want to integrate with at a later point. Save
settings again.

Finally, move to the "Confirmed Opt In" section of the "List Settings"

(also by clicking in the gray bar at the top of the page). You will
need to edit the "Subject" line, the "Intro" section, as well as the
"Signature" part of this message. Save settings. For additional information go to: aweber.com/faq/questions/68.

Hover your mouse over the Messages tab and choose Follow Up from the drop down options. On this page, you will click the green "Create a new follow up message" button to create your Welcome Email. This is the email that subscribers receive after confirming. It should welcome them to your and explain what they can expect from you in the future. For more info go to the above URL with /questions/102.

Be sure to test your message(s) to make sure they appear fine
when you receive them. See /questions/310.

Create your web form. Click on the Web Forms tab in your account.
On this page, click the green "Create a new web form" button.

Now this is where you're going to ignore the editing options and simply
click save. Once you save your form the coding will be generated that you
need to hook your custom form from Aweber to your AWeber account. The guide below should be helpful to you and your developer when it comes time to set up the custom form integration. See questions/396.

If you need additional help: aweber.com/blog/live-webinars/, or go to their FAQ knowledge base: aweber.com/faq/. To view all of their tutorials go to: aweber.com/video-tutorials.htm. They have a toll free number for seven-day live support, as well as help via email.

At first you might do well to use a free or inexpensive autoresponder from a different vendor. As your list grows and you learn about and begin to appreciate Aweber's true value you will be happy to spend whatever is necessary for a totally automated solution with lots of bells and whistles.

There are other popular programs, which I have not personally tried. One is "I Contact" at: icontact.com. Their prices are quite similar to Aweber's. A second, which focuses on "newsletters" is Get Response at: getresponse.com.

Note that neither Aweber nor GetResponse will accept confirmed opt-in subscribers from any co-registration or lead generation service. As an alternative, Aweber and GetResponse users who want to use co-registration should consider searching for an alternative autoresponder service that will accept these email addresses if you do plan to go that route.

Many autoresponders will not permit their use in conjunction with affiliate marketing. Read all "Terms of Use" carefully. AWeber and iContact are OK with affiliate marketing. I am told that iContact offers better customer service by providing you with a personal account manager. Remember, a web page is nothing. Traffic is everything. Email is king. And keep in mind the main purpose of your website is to entice your visitors to sign your guest book and give you permission to contact them again via email.

Once you send them the first email and they have gone through the "double opt-in" you have your autoresponder pre-programmed congratulating them on their wise decision and giving them some special FREE goodie. Try to make the value of this item equal to or greater in value than other items you are selling.

Before you can create your autoresponder details you need to have it installed on your domain server program (or subscribe on the vendor's server). Make certain that the autoresponder that you choose has the double opt-in feature, and also provides an "unsubscribe" link in every email. Further, it must be able to accept each subscriber on their own unique "Day 1" and produce sequential messages accordingly so no one misses an installment.

Your autoresponder will present you with a dizzying array of options, header and footer files, personalization tags, message areas, and time sequencers. It will take you a good bit of study to learn how to properly use your autoresponder, but everything you need to know is found on the provider's website tutorials. It's not rocket science, but it is necessary to climb the learning curve.

There are two types of emails you will be sending. The ones that make you fast cash are the **Promotional Emails** where you feature a niche product and induce the recipient to click on a link to your affiliate so that you can earn a commission.

The other is an **Informational Email** that is educational or instructional in nature. At the end of this type you may or may not offer an affiliate link as a "P.S." afterthought.

Incidentally, your customers love to watch short videos, so do not overlook the opportunity to include one in an email.

How often to contact individuals is the subject of endless debate. Some marketers email every single day. Some every three days. Others once a week. A few once a month. You must keep track of your results, and especially the number and identity of opt-outs.

If lots of visitors are fleeing your list it is just possible you are annoying them to the point of distraction! Also, if your click-throughs and sales are very low, obviously you need to focus on better ad copy in your emails. Then there is the decision as to **when** to actually send the emails.

According to Aweber the most popular days for eMail marketing are Monday and Tuesday, with Wednesday, Thursday and Friday not all that far behind statistically. Most internet marketers have found that weekends and Holidays are the least productive times to send out messages, and few bother to do so. My in-box is almost empty on weekends.

As far as time of day, 8AM EST is considered to be best. Their statistics show a very sharp drop-off in results at 9AM EST, just one hour later! Go figure. The worst hours apparently are late afternoon, say 4-5PM EST. Many stick with Monday 8AM EST for every message.

You would do well to experiment for yourself. Buyers in your niche might for some unfathomable reason respond best to emails sent at 4:30PM EST on a Saturday! But don't count on it.

It is common knowledge in the industry that having an autoresponder send out a series of messages to visitors who sign up for your newsletter or study course will **increase your overall results about tenfold!**

While you will normally get 1% to 2% who actually buy your product on the first visit to your website, up to half will usually sign up for a periodic free newsletter or multi-part free course. Once they are on your list you should be able to induce at least one in four to eventually buy your product.

Personally, I prefer Aweber. Remember when choosing your Aweber autoresponder-list name to choose it carefully. Your list will receive email from "(the name you choose)@aweber.com".

Be sure you choose "Open Rate" in your account so you will know how many people have actually opened your emails. (You must be using the special HTML code that Aweber gives you for this purpose.) You will be shocked to find how many people use spam filters that will prevent your message from ever being read.

It is a good idea to periodically remind members on your list to "white-list" your eMail incoming address. The procedure for doing this is different for each of the many different eMail services out there. This will insure that your message gets through to their in-box. If you do a Google search for "How To White List eMail" you will be able to copy the result and send the white-listing instructions to your list.

In time you will find that your autoresponder is your best friend. Once you set it up properly you just sit back and let it do its thing, week after week, month after month, for as long as you are in this wonderful business.

CHAPTER 43

PROFITABLY RENT AND SELL YOUR LISTS

Your our own double-opt-in email lists are beyond a doubt your most precious internet asset. Most internet entrepreneurs would never part with their lists for any amount of money. Most have sworn to their visitors to never sell or share their email address.

Yet there are thousands of email address lists available for sale and rent, some very tightly focused. And every day you get tons of SPAM in your email box that had to come from some list somewhere. That "somewhere" is in the fine print of many, if not most, vendor's websites "Terms and Conditions" pages. That's the stuff that almost no one actually reads, a fact on which vendors count.

Most buyers simply check on "I Agree" and move on, knowing that to not agree will prevent them for buying whatever it is they are intent on buying. Nowhere on these sites does it promise not to sell or share your email address with third parties. And sell and share they do! In fact, it is a very significant source of revenue for many companies.

Because there is a very ready market for the sale of focused email lists, many enterprising internet entrepreneurs set up squeeze pages with the sole intention of creating email address lists to sell. It's just another business model, and there is surely nothing illegal about pursuing this income stream.
Beyond a doubt there are some, perhaps many, who swear on their squeezes pages that they will not sell or share your email address ever, "Scout's Honor". Apparently most were never Scouts! Then they sell your email address a short time thereafter, and again and again and again. I know this for a fact because I will occasionally use a free email address such as I can get at Google Gmail, or Yahoo!, or HotMail as an experiment. I will use this

address just one single time with a purposely misspelled name.

Sure enough, within a few days I'll be getting SPAM emails to my misspelled name at my never-used email box for everything from low cost loans to ocean cruises to sex toys! Don't get caught doing this sort of crap. If you are caught and someone cares enough to smear your name all over the social network as an internet fraud it will not be of any great help in your future internet endeavors.

Do a Google search for email list brokers. Check out a few and you will find that there is a very wide range of costs for email addresses. There is an almost endless range of niche-focused buyers email addresses available. These can range from a penny a name to $20.00 per name or more depending upon how current a list is and how tightly focused it claims to be, as well as how exclusive the list is for your personal use alone.

When you are working in sales in industries such as securities, mortgages, real property and any other "big ticket" item the email address of a hot ready-to-buy potential client can be worth a lot of money. The high price-per-lead can be easily justified.

Say you have a great eBook focused on people who need to locate a source of hard-to-find parts for their Ferrari (don't laugh....I have a friend who has made a great deal of money with a similar site). Would not a list of Ferrari owners email addresses be of real value to you? Would you pay a dollar or more for a name? Most likely you would.

When you access some of the list brokers as suggested above, you will see that they generally offer "one time use". They police this by adding a few of their own personal addresses to insure you only use the list for the contracted number of times. They do not want you loading it into your autoresponder.

They sell the use of the same list over and over and over. Some will offer a "fresh list" that has never been offered before at a considerably higher price. Next it is sold as a "used" list, then sold later as "used twice", etc., at progressively lower prices per name.

If you amass your own unique list of 5,000 names in a focused niche, you could probably sell these for one-time-use at $1.00/name if unused, $0.50/name used once, and say $0.10/name just once a month for a year. In this realistic scenario you just made $13,500 in a year from one list! Of course you can still sell your own products to the list as you would have anyway had you not shared it with others. If you can figure out some creative way to obtain email addresses in a tightly focused niche in a high-ticket industry you could have yourself a cash cow beyond almost anything else you could do on the internet.

The downside is that you may have created some competition for yourself. There is also the cost to acquire the list in the first place and the cost to advertise its availability for rent.   The net profit, which can continue for years with a single list, should far outweigh the acquisition costs by a large margin.

Another rather borderline-ethical approach is to swear not to SELL your email address. Then they either RENT it, or even SHARE it, and can say with a straight face that they didn't SELL it. Email list sharing (swapping) is quite common between companies in the same niche but with non-competing products.

Just be certain that you never promise not to sell, rent or share your list and then do so anyway. Disclosing your intentions to do so, buried in fine print somewhere, is sort of gray-area ethical, but it is done every day by major world-famous companies as well as smaller businesses everywhere. Just keep those T & Cs very long, very boring, and very hard to read! The "I AGREE" button is your best list-promotion-business-model friend!

Selling, renting or swapping your email lists for profit should be thought of as just another one of the many possible multiple streams of internet income. You could focus on it as an entirely separate business, or simply keep in the back of your mind that you are holding within your autoresponder an often-overlooked goldmine!

INTERNET DOMAIN PROFITS

CHAPTER 44
DOMAINING

WHAT EXACTLY *IS* A "DOMAIN NAME"?

Many of you reading this book already know that a "domain name" is an internet web address, an "http://" or a "www" followed by "dot [.] something" and a "dot [.] something else". These domain names are also known as "Unique Resource Locators", or "URLs".

These web addresses are the means by which any website is found on a computer. One types the domain name in the appropriate search box, hits "Enter", and as if by magic up pops a website! Damn clever I might add.

A domain name can be a single word such as "financial" followed by .com or .whatever, or multiple words such as "financial planning" or "best financial planning" or "the best financial planning"....you get the idea. They can be over fifty characters long!

The evolution of web addresses traces back to various government programs many decades ago (no, Al Gore did not invent the internet). There is actually some disagreement over the exact succession of events and to whom credit should be given. The fact is, it was a tortuous process over many decades involving many individuals in both the government and private sectors before internet web addresses were standardized.

Today, The Internet Corporation For Assigned Names And Numbers (ICANN) has been assigned the responsibility to control most but not all domain name "dot something" extensions. (.ws and a few others are exceptions, and these too may be valuable domain names).

Initially the extensions ".com" for commercial sites, ".gov" for government sites, and .org for academia, came into wide use in the early '90s, followed by ".net" and a few others. Today there are over a hundred "dot-somethings", such as ".info", ".us", ".biz", ".ws", ".tv", ".mobi", ".ca", ".cn", even ".xxx", and myriad others in additional to the original ones, with new ones added quite often.

As I am writing this ICANN is reviewing the applications for new gTLDs (generic top level domains) such as .Microsoft, .tiffany, and .amazon with major company extensions. Also .app, .blog, .baby, .deal, .pizza and about 2,000 others! At $185,000/submission it is hard to believe that Google applied for over a hundred, and Amazon 76! Obviously they believe this will change how consumers market. Is this the end of ".com" as the beloved commercial generic TLD? They are certainly betting on it.

At present there are literally millions of domain names already registered worldwide. But that is only a drop in the bucket compared to the many possible domain names that could be conceived and might actually have real value

The reported statistics from Verisign, which they update quarterly, serve to illustrate the immensity of the domain name industry. As of 2Q 2012, there were 225 million total TLD registrations, with over half of these being .com/.net combined. Over 8 million .com/.net domain names were registered in those three months!

It is reported that 88% of all .com/.net domain names lead to a website. Only 17% of these websites were single-page mini-sites.

The most startling statistic: There were **64 billion** domain name queries in 4Q 2011. That's about 710,000,000/day! To say the internet has totally remade our lives would be an understatement!

There are about 500,000 English language words, and hundreds of millions of possible two, three, four and five or more word combinations. Multiply that by hundreds of "dot somethings", and then consider the dozens of other common languages......Spanish, French, Italian, German, etc., and one can see that there are almost limitless possible domain names that could be registered and might have value.

This is why the business of flipping domain names is still in its infancy. Every day those in the know are buying domain names and flipping them for multiples of what they cost. **But the surface has just been scratched!**

Do not make the mistake in believing that you have missed the boat. The boat is still in the dock! In a few years people will be looking back at today and wishing they had gotten started back in "the good old days", i.e., **<u>TODAY</u>!** These ARE the good old days. The time for you to get started in this lucrative business is NOW.

The most coveted names are the .coms, followed closely by .nets and .orgs. Recently, .us, .mobi, .info, .biz, and .tv extensions have become saleable commodities. But potentially any extension with the proper wording or phrasing could be a winner.

Remember, each web address is totally unique, one of a kind. Let's say, for example, financial.com is in great demand (in fact it reportedly sold for $100,000). If someone else wants "financial dot something" they will have to settle for one of the extensions other than .com. The more people that want "financial dot something", the deeper into the realm of possible extensions they would need to buy, .net, .org, .info, .biz, etc.

Eventually all the financial dot-somethings are taken and the next person will have to pay more to induce one of the owners to sell. Simple supply and demand. Until someone wants your domain name for some reason, it cannot be "flipped.

SO WHAT IS THIS DOMAIN NAME FLIPPING BUSINESS ANYWAY?

If you are a complete newbie to making money on the internet, the concept of making easy money flipping domain names is as foreign to you as would be an advanced course in website search engine optimization or viral internet marketing.

But if you have had some exposure to internet commerce, perhaps even having purchased an expensive course or two, the concept of making easy money flipping domain names is probably still as foreign to you as to an internet newbie!

You see, few of the well-known internet guru's courses, even the all-time best-selling book on the subject of making money on line, even *mention* the domain flipping concept. The simple fact is that while thousands have pursued conventional internet commerce riches, and many have succeeded, relatively few have focused on domain name flipping.

Just what do we mean by domain name "flipping"? It is a very simple concept. Smaller "domainers" (what the folk who buy and sell domain names and websites are called) like you and me sell to bigger domainers. The beauty of the business is that anyone can participate and make money. It is estimated that there are around 100,000 active domainers.

It is worthy of note that the big players going after very valuable domains are relatively few, perhaps a hundred or so. This is because very few individuals have the knowledge and experience to evaluate a domain name properly. This fact works to your advantage because you can often sell a domain name or website to the emotionally-driven less-experienced buyers for far more than it may actually be worth.

In conventional real estate, speculators (known as "spec buyers") buy houses that need some sort of enhancement. This might mean mechanical repairs or simple cosmetic painting. Buying spec-houses for below market price for some reason or other, and then selling quickly for profit at a higher price, often *much* higher, is known in the trade as "flipping" of real estate.

But the flipping of houses most often requires a significant amount of money and risk (with due notice of the "no down payment" gurus), or stellar financial credit, or both. And then there is the expense of the actual rehabilitation, real estate taxes, and insurance. The fact is, it takes a great deal of knowledge and expertise, money and *risk*, to be successful flipping houses.

Domain names on the other hand are *"VIRTUAL Real Estate"*. They are under law real property in much the same sense that a house is real property. They are not "intellectual property" as is this book.

The big difference between flipping houses and flipping domain names is in the tiny amount of money it takes to get started in the domain flipping business, and the relatively shallow learning curve involved. The money involved, the work involved, and the risk involved, is minimal.

So why doesn't everyone do it? A simple absence of wide exposure to the concept explains why. It seems to me that once the secret is out a lot more work-at-home entrepreneurs such as you will get involved, and make their fortunes focusing on domain names.

HOW DO I GET DOMAIN NAME IDEAS?

There are two basic possibilities: original names that you think up off the top of your head, and "secondary market" names that someone in the past thought of that you can purchase from many different sources.

THROUGH ORIGINAL THINKING

It's really very simple. Just pick any word, add words such as "info" and "site" and "best" to make some logical word combination (e.g. "mortgage", "mortgage site", "mortgage info site", "best mortgage info site", etc. Presto, you have a possible domain name!

But before doing any serious buying, go to one of the many websites that list the results of recent on-line auctions and live auctions. From this you can get a really good feel for what dollar amounts domain names can be sold. And you'll get lots of good ideas for domain names as well. You can find results of recent sales from BigSpend at: bigspend.com

Remember, you are only paying only around $10.00 per name for a year of ownership. If you can sit there and think of just five names (which might take an hour if you're really slow) that you can list and eventually sell for perhaps fifty bucks each on eBay, and do this every week, you have just made $10,000 a year for an hour a week of fun! Dedicate more time, buy more domains, and potentially make much more money

SO WHERE DO I BUY THESE DOMAIN NAMES?

When it comes to buying domain names you have thought of, you have a lot of choices. All of the registrars shown below sell original domain names. In fact, there are literally hundreds of registrars approved by ICANN. All of the registrars shown, however, are not created equal. As with most things in life you get what you pay for. There are seldom, if ever, free lunches.

My favorites are godaddy.com and bulkregister.com. Both charge under $15.00/year of ownership for a domain name. All have lots of features that and in general offer very hassle-free service. You need to check them all out, but it is very important in my opinion to settle on a single registrar that you like, and eventually have all of your domains with that one registrar.

Do *not* be influenced by price, at the high or low end. One of the highest priced I know of, at $35.00 per year for .coms, has given me fits over the years and I have finally transferred all of the domains I manage out of there to a more user-friendly registrar.

Conversely, there are some "$5.00 and less specials" registrars that will drive you crazy with unwanted offers before you can even get to the registration process! Some make it very difficult or nearly impossible to transfer domains to another registrar, as you may have to when you sell a domain.

It took my wife and me almost *two years* of frustration to transfer JesusSonOfGod.com to a friend of mine! It took us five minutes when we sold BuffaloMilk.com at a massive profit. Obviously different registrars!

Some registrars are highly anal retentive.....yearly renewals are how they make their money in addition to the initial registration fee (which is normally the same as the renewal fee). In case I failed to mention it, one can initially register a domain for one, up to ten years, often with a slight discount per year for the longer terms. I have NEVER registered a domain for more than a year. It inspires me to flip my domains quickly!

There are many other valuable services a registrar can offer, *free* multiple e-mail addresses being an important one.

Now in the paragraphs above we are talking exclusively about new domain name registrations for names you thought of yourself.

The possibility of selling some for many hundreds of dollars, and a few for thousands, and hitting the occasional home run, makes it even more attractive. The sky is literally the limit!

Go to any registrar and see if your "domain word" is available in some form and with some top level domain extension (.com, .net, .org, .mobi, .us, .info, etc.) On most sites, just entering your word or words will immediately pop up a list showing what has already been registered and what is available. Once you get the hang of it it's a really fun exercise.

Some of the registrars will automatically list dozens of suggestions that relate in some way to what you were seeking in the first place. Remember, they are just trying to sell name registrations, as many and as fast as possible, and will provide all the help they can!

Need ideas for domain names as pure speculation? Think of a potential Presidential or Vice Presidential candidate for this election cycle or a future one, and list a number of URLs around that name: Snatorum.com; Newt.com; Romney.com; IloveHillary.com, etc.

In doing so you may get stuck for a time with the unsuccessful candidates (at $10/year) as in RudyForPresident.com or ILoveEdwards.com, but who knows if in 2016 or 2020 and beyond these could be worth a small fortune!

Olympics in 2020 or 2024?   Find the identity of potential city-candidates and register them all in some form. Sure it costs money, but all you have to do is hit ONE winner (ChinaOlympics.com for example) and the overall cost becomes of little consequence. But you've got to be fast on your feet......and sometimes a bit lucky. The pros are doing this every day.

There are hundreds of major cities worldwide. It is unlikely you could find any "majorcity.com" available, but what about that "majorcityshops.com" or "majorcityhotels.com". How about smaller cities?

There is one very clever way to decide on domain names to register. Follow closely the highest priced domain sales from various auctions. Once you see a domain name sell for thousands or even millions of dollars you at once (or someone out there will definitely beat you to it) begin looking for the identical name, or similar-meaning word combinations, but with lower level domain name extensions.

A good site to follow is bigspend.com. Look for synonyms expressing much the same message. Go for .net and .org first, then check out .biz, .us, .info, .mobi and continue through the ten most popular extensions. Any one of these, held over time for about $10/year each, could have major value in the future.

The way to do this is to key in words in search boxes at sites such as enom.com or godaddy.com. At no cost they will provide you with a list of available domain names that are similar and available. Whatever you end up registering will not be as attractive or as valuable as the biggie you are trying to closely copy, but in the future they could well be worth far more than your minimal cost.

The domain name "femalemale.com" sold for six figures. I immediately snagged "femalemale.net". We'll see the wisdom of that registration sometime in the future!

When you "bank" one or more of these domains you should either "park" them at a monitizer such as fabulous.com (the monitizer I use) or set up a simple Google AdSense site, and then just forget about it. They should bring it over time more than they are costing you to carry.

SO HOW ELSE DO I GET DOMAIN NAME IDEAS?

PURCHASE "USED" NAMES!
Everything we discussed above is based on your *original* ideas. This is by far the least expensive way to acquire domain names. But you can also buy quality domain names from other owners on-line from an on-line auction sites such as moniker.com.
There is another whole world of domain name buying, the world of the secondary market.

For starters, there is buying on eBay and Craig's list, but I have found these to mostly list overpriced domains offered by individuals who are looking for newbies who don't know domain values and tend to overpay.

You can bid on domains at any of the online auction sites. A word of advice on auctions....if you see something you want ALWAYS try to be the last bidder. Set a maximum price in your mind and never allow yourself to get into an emotional bidding war.

The most important place to buy secondary-market domains is from the drop-list brokers. These brokers publish daily lists of expiring domains. It is reported that upwards of thirty-thousand domains expire daily! That's a lot of potential inventory.

Many of these are domains where the owner may have spent a lot of time and money on a website or traffic and simply forgotten to renew it. I've been guilty of this myself I'm embarrassed to say. Some were simply registered and forgotten.

Different registrars have different policies on renewal grace periods after expiration. I have lost important domains in the past (I've learned the hard way to be more diligent) because I had them at a registrar that gave me no renewal notice at all and very little if any grace period....remember, all registrars are not created equal.

The key here is to analyze domains in which you have interest in terms of the criteria shown in Appendix II. Then backorder the same domain at EACH drop broker.

When the domain becomes available if you are the only one ordering it you pay $60.00 and it is yours. I have heard stories of individuals paying $60.00 and flipping it back to the person who let it expire for hundreds of dollars the very next day!

I've also heard stories of individuals who have paid $60.00 for domains with hundreds of links and high Alexi and Google rankings, and flipping these for thousands of dollars within a week.

If you are not the only one that has backordered a particular domain, then a bidding auction begins. I've seen $61.00 win because the other side doesn't bid at all for whatever reason, and I've seen $71.00 take a lot of good domains.

I've also seen bids go into the thousands. A friend of mine paid $20,000 for one of these domains and he tells me it was the best investment he ever made!

Remember one important truism, whether you are buying real estate (e.g., houses) or virtual real estate (domain names) you make your money when you **buy**, not when you sell. When you buy at the right price your ultimate profit is locked in and virtually assured.

To summarize, simple buying creatively from registrars and marketing creatively you can make a lot of money with a minimal investment of time and money. But if you want to have a much more time-intensive domain business with greater profit potential, then the secondary market drop brokers are your portal to potential riches.

WHO WANTS TO BUY MY DOMAIN NAME…AND WHY?

You must understand that the best domain name imaginable is absolutely worthless until someone (and preferably a number of some- ones) decides for whatever reason they simply *must* own it.

The significant fact is that today hundreds if not thousands of entrepreneurs have embraced the buying of domain names in the secondary market for a variety of reasons as a real viable business, and one that can be started on a shoestring and is limited only by the imagination.

It's the next best thing to having a legal money printing press! These days, Virtual Real Estate, domain names, may well be far more attractive than conventional real estate as a short and long term investment. Even though some foreclosed home prices are very tempting, it still takes cash and credit to play the house-flipping game.

And houses cost a lot more than ten bucks a year to carry!

Remember, the "U" in URL stands for "Unique". Much as an original oil painting is a one-of-a-kind, so is any domain name one of a kind. Supply and demand. Marketing 101. Is a unique Rembrandt oil painting inherently worth $50 million? Not to most. But it is to someone, somewhere, for whatever reason. Think "unique".

Is the dot com "SheMale" worth $400,000? It was to someone in January '08. Why? I'm certain the seller could not have cared less! I imagine the buyer had a very good reason. There are many different reasons why domain names are purchased.

The most obvious is pure speculation. You buy it for X$ and flip it to someone for 3X$, who expects to flip it later for 6X$, etc. That person (or you initially) may simply "bank" it, that is, just sit on it until it is flipped in the future. Simple flipping is the easiest way to earn money with domain names. It is an absolute "no brainer" business, which is why my wife and I focused on it!

Another reason one might buy a domain name is for "branding" some specific product or idea. We sold "BuffaloMilk.com" to a UK firm that wanted it for a product branding (I cared not at all *what* product, but I sure don't recall ever seeing a herd of buffalo in the UK!).

Yet another possible reason could be the development of a large commercial website somehow related to a particular domain name.

Still another reason to buy a domain name from you is "monetization" Any name can be "monetized", that is, submitted to any of a number of companies who place relevant advertising on a site they create for the domain owner and share with that owner any revenues generated. These ads can be created for them by Google in a program called "Adsense", or the ads can be created by the monetizing company themselves.

There have even sprung up a number of large conglomerates that exist solely for the purpose of buying up large quantities of domain names for future sale or monitization. Among these are companies reported to be controlled by H. Ross Perot, Richard Rosenblatt (former Chairman of MySpace.com before he sold it to News Corp. for a mere $570,000,000!) and Howard Schultz (Chairman of Starbucks, through his investing firm Maveron**). If these kinds of investors are involved you *know* it's a viable market.**

There is a very wealthy Chinese domain name speculator who has tried quite successfully to corner the market on domain names associated with weddings. He has become very wealthy.

Do you think you could dream up some combination of words that might not already have been conceived and registered that just might be flipable to someone for some multiple of your cost? No reason why you cannot. It's done every day.

SO WHERE DO I GO TO SELL MY DOMAIN NAMES?

A good place to start would be to list your domains on an on-line auction site such as moniker.com. There are other companies such as fabulous.com that not only will monetize your domain name with relevant ads but also list your domains for sale to the general public.

You might also consider trying eBay or Craig's List, but it is my experience that only bargain-hunting bottom-feeders shop for domains there. You would be much better off at one of the auction sites specifically geared to domain investing.

There are even specialty live auctions held worldwide for domains related specifically to a particular topic, such as "casinos and gambling" or "sexual content" or "weddings". And there are general auctions where anything at all might turn up.

These auctions often cost a thousand dollars or more just to attend, and are frequented by hundreds of wealthy domain-investment professionals eager to bid on premium domains! The owners of the domains themselves need not attend the actual auctions to have their domains sold there.

It is worthy of note that a large percentage of domains are sold *privately.* These transactions are seldom reported. This can occur in one of two ways.

It has been my experience that a buyer will contact a domain owner directly, finding the owner's name listed in the WhoIs Registry of domain owners. My wife sold VoiceTones.com and TopTenHawaii.com in this fashion. (Side note: Once you own a domain go in to the WhoIs Registry and after your name as owner add the words "Domain For Sale".)

A little creative marketing can go a long way. For example, if you owned the name "SanDiegoRealEstate.com" (or any other city, county, or state dot almost anything) you could send an email (or, God forbid, do a snail-mail broadcast letter mailing) to every licensed real estate agent in San Diego offering the name for sale at some price that you could state or leave open to negotiation. My guess is that one would snap it up in a heartbeat. Why wouldn't these real estate agents not just register the URL themselves? Because most people have not a clue how to go about registering a domain name!

The whole idea is to get your domain name, and the fact that it is for sale, in front of as many domain buyers as possible. This would include end users, small domain flippers, Wall Street players, and bulk portfolio buyers. My wife owns the domain MdUV.net, and she plans to someday offer it to every radiologist ("Doctor Ultraviolet") in the country for $50,000! Don't be surprised if she gets it!

Incidentally, the process of selling a domain name can be made vary safe for both buyer and seller through the use of domain name sale escrow company services. Escrow holds the money from the buyer. You do not get the money from escrow until the buyer gets the domain name.

The buyer does not get the domain name until escrow has the funds in their account. Escrow releases the funds to the seller once the buyer owns the domain name.

I highly recommend that all secondary market purchases from individuals, and all of your sales, go through an escrow service. Most every registrar offers this service. **_Never_** buy from or sell to any individual person in the secondary market without this protection. Always protect yourself with a third-party escrow service. The small cost is well worth it.

One <u>very</u> overlooked area is *barter*. There are some fine references on the subject of barter in general ...just Google "barter systems". This occurs when you have a domain name someone wants and they have something, anything, that you want.

I recently bartered the domain name PhotographWomen.com for a $6,000 internet training program run by a famous internet guru! The domain name might have been worth more, but I was very happy with the barter exchange because the domain name cost me ten bucks!

It is also possible to *swap* domain names. You might have a domain name that you are not overly fond of that someone who has a name you might want badly could want worse than you do. Swap time!

There is also the possibility of *renting out* your domain name. Perhaps a potential buyer might not have the ready cash to buy your domain name, but *could* afford a monthly rental cost of a few hundred dollars. This is exactly the same scenario as with real estate.

You could rent the domain name and give the renter the option to buy it at some pre-set price at some specified time in the future. You could also offer as an inducement the possibility of applying all timely rental payments against the ultimate selling price. It is a common real estate strategy that helps close many deals, and it applies equally well to virtual real estate.

The fact is there are many different avenues for making money with your domain names, and very often using a combination of them creatively can yield the greatest reward.

HOW MUCH MONEY CAN I MAKE?

Ah, the magic question! And the one for which attorneys are paid thousands to create disclaimers, like the one at the beginning of this book. Sorry, it just had to be there! Litigation is hell.

The fact is, there is no definitive answer. Somewhere between millions of dollars and nothing at all would be an honestly stated range.

Want to get your wealth juices flowing? Just go to any of the sites shown below (try dnjournal.com for starters) and take a look at prices that are being paid daily for domain names that cost someone $10 or so to register. Be sitting down!

There is virtually unlimited potential for wealth through various internet commerce pursuits. There are reported to be many thousands of internet millionaires, some of them in their early twenties and some in their teens. I have no doubt that some brilliant nine-year-old out there somewhere is showing his or her dad how he can retire next year!

I know one young gentleman quite well personally, Anthony Morrison (you can Google him, or click anthonymorrison.com).....totally self-made at 25. Amazing young man. True genius. Left med school to save his family from financial ruin through internet commerce. Great true story.

I have met, or have studied under, many other gurus of all ages.....the late, great Cory Rudl who died tragically in his 20's, not long after his wedding ceremony/conference which I attended. There's Dr. Jeffrey Lant; Robert Allen; Mark Joyner; Stone Evans; Sean Mize; Marlon Sanders; Yanik Silver; Armand Morin; Mike Filsame; Jay Abraham; John Reese and many others. Some if not most of these individuals say they started with nothing or next to nothing and attribute internet commerce for helping them generate their wealth within the past decade. They are the leaders, the "gurus" of net commerce. They are my idols.

But to the best of my knowledge, with the exception of Anthony Morrison, none of these ever focused their attention on domain names as their **initial** primary business.

I was fortunate to have been introduced to domain name acquisition quite by accident. I attended one of the very early internet commerce presentations on Long Island back in the mid-90s. It was focused on selling products on line. The seminar ended up costing me $2,000…and of course I brought the material home and never opened it.

As an aside, during the presentation the speaker casually mentioned what a cool idea it was to get a .com address containing one's "personal name.com." He said: "You never know, some day it might be worth something." He clearly did not have a clue that the program of selling products that he was pushing was puny in its potential compared to what could have been made buying .com names during those early years.

So I bought the "my name" dot com domain, and a few others that related to various interests of mine. As I recall they cost $35 each to register at that time. At the time very few persons were gobbling up .com domains, and virtually any short English language name .com could be had for a pittance.

A few very lucky souls bought names during that period that sold for up to $4,000,000 each! In fact, Diamonds.com reportedly sold for $7.5 million! That's quite a profit for a $35.00 investment!

Are such opportunities available today? Well, back in January 2008 at auction the dot com "SheMale", acquired rather recently, sold for $400,000!

If you want an extreme example of "the possible", consider the article in the June 2007 issue of *Business 2.0* Magazine. They ran a cover story titled: "The Man Who

Owns The Internet". That man, quite unknown to most, is Kevin Ham, dubbed "The Master Of Web Domains".

They claimed Mr. Ham has a net worth of $300,000,000.00 and earnes $70 million a year in revenue entirely by being a "Domainer", finding ways to make money through buying and selling and developing domain names. Now that is *serious* money!

How did Mr. Ham accomplish this in less than a decade? He did it starting in the late '90s by systematically buying up a massive portfolio of domain names....300,000 of them! Will you ever buy that many? Unlikely. But you could easily buy a few hundred over time, and earn a very good living from them.

There have been reported dozens of million-dollar-plus sales of individual domain names. One portfolio of domain names is reported to have fetched a mere hundred million dollars ($100,000,000)! That is **_serious_** money.

As mentioned elsewhere in this ebook there are many ways to make money by acquiring domain names, and many different ways to acquire them. The simplest and least work-intensive way to earn domain cash is by simply thinking up creative domain names, buying them, and selling them to others as quickly as possible, doing absolutely nothing else but that.

Can you expect to buy a domain name today and flip it for hundreds of thousands of dollars? Highly unlikely, though not entirely impossible. But it *is* possible to acquire domain names today that can be sold for hundreds, thousands, even tens of thousands of dollars. You just need to know how. A little luck doesn't hurt either!

Do only single-word domain names auction for big bucks? Can seemingly common phrase domain names sell for thousands? For example (and there are many thousands of examples) domains such as: artandframe.com, nextwavewireless.com, marinetechnology.com, marketingmix.com, and fashiongallery.com all sold for $4,000 or more.

Perfectworld.com sold for $30,000. Globalsearch.com sold for $67,000. Even some .net URLs sell well. Take freestuff.net which fetched $28,000 in a Moniker auction as proof.

Highly significant was the report of a recent sale of a domain name that had just been registered in a brand new domain name extension. The new extension is ".me", begun in late 2011. The domain name that was registered for ten bucks or so was "meet.me". Damn clever.

Beyond clever is the fact that this brand shiny new domain name was flipped quickly for $450,000.00!!!! That's a fast profit of $459,990.00. So are there possibilities today for instant riches? Apparently so.

 Don't expect to read this book and get rich overnight with little or no effort. You actually have to *do* something. It is an absolute fact......and I have personally been guilty of this myself many times......that buying an information product such as this book and not acting on the wisdom contained therein will be absolutely guaranteed to earn you zero dollars. Absolutely guaranteed! No disclaimer necessary.

Every individual has a different level of motivation, a different amount of time to devote to a new pursuit, and a different idea of what "a lot" of money might be. But with average intelligence, a real desire to earn money, and at least a few hours a week to devote initially, domain flipping can be very financially rewarding.

HOW CAN I ENHANCE THE VALUE OF MY DOMAIN NAMES WHILE I AM WAITING FOR THEM TO SELL?

As a general rule look to buy domain names that relate to your product in some ways. Ideally, you want to drive traffic to your website from visitors who search generically for your exact domain name.

Once you own a domain name there are two basic business models: develop a website and sell something, or park the domain it and earn advertising revenue.

For starters, you can just buy "original" domain names and do nothing more with them until they sell. It's very simple, straightforward, and, in fact, pretty much what my wife and I did for years.

I have heard of individuals who daily buy a number of domain names and quickly flip them the same day on eBay and other auction sites for $30.00 to $60.00. Small amounts daily can add up to a lot of profit yearly.

In fact, if this was all one did, day trade the same as commodity market day traders or stock market day traders, and all one's domain names sold for an average of $40.00, that's about $50,000 yearly for every five names registered daily.

You do *not* have to hit home runs to make money with domain names. An accumulation of bunt singles can make you rich!

One situation here is that the registrar holding your domain names is monitizing them themselves and pocketing 100% of the revenue (it's somewhere in the small print in their Agreements). I'm not sure they all do this, and some may share revenue with you, but don't count on it.

But there are a number of companies that will monitize your domains for you with little or no effort on your part. But all of these monetizing companies are not created equal.

It is a good idea at first to split your domains to be monetized among a number of these monitizers to see which perform best for you. You can always transfer them at a later date. It is a very simple matter to switch your domains between monitizers.

Simply go into your domain name account at your registrar of choice and go to the DNS (Domain Name Server) for your specific domain name and type in the DNS of any monetizer you want to point the name to.

Here again, getting back to the subject of registrars, some make this DNS change very simple, and some make it a royal pain. Choose your registrar wisely.

That all may sound complicated and time-consuming, but once you do it one time it takes less than a minute and a few mouse clicks to point a domain name to a monitizer.

Incidentally, most monitizers have a "sign up for a selling account" process. Some require a certain number of domain names be submitted. Some will only accept higher quality names. Some will accept any domain name at all. They will advise you which are acceptable to them

The ads the monitizers put on the sites for you are relevant to the domain names. Some are provided by Google in their "AdSense" program (go to Google.com and search "AdSense" for a full discussion). Other ads are provided by the monitizers themselves.

You won't earn much at first, but over time the domains gather momentum and attract more and more traffic.

The above discussion applies to those domain names you thought up and bought from a registrar (which accounts for about 95% of all the domains my wife and I have ever owned).

But for those better expired domain names that you buy in the secondary market at auction or from drop companies you can immediately begin to get revenue in many different ways.

One way is to solicit and sell advertising on your sites. Another is to sell site links. If a domain you buy has a high link rating, and gets or may get a lot of traffic, potential advertisers will do back-flips to pay you to run their ads.

The subject of selling links is beyond the scope of this chapter. It is a sophisticated endeavor, and there are many books on the subject. Suffice it to say that if you buy a domain name with a lot of existing backlinks and a lot of existing traffic, you own a cash-cow.

It would take many months and a lot of knowledge for you to duplicate the page rank and link popularity of the domain names that you buy from drop companies. Buy one of these and you take advantage of the hard work done by others over time.

In summary, there are three basic choices: flip immediately, park for ad revenue or develop a website. Buying domain names from a registrar or in the secondary market opens up a world of opportunities for creating wealth.

You must decide whether you will:

Flip domain names quickly with no enhancements;
Hold the name and develop a website, acquire links, get traffic;
Use your website to sell products or link to affiliate vendors;
Monitize your website with private ads or Google AdSense;
Use your developed website to sell links to others;
Use your domain name at a monitizer for them to run ads;
Rent your domain names;
Accumulate a portfolio of domain names for later use;
Sell entire developed websites.

Using a monitizer is almost the easiest business model of all. Domain parking at a monitizer is simply "set it and forget it" Once you own a domain name, set up and optimize the parking page with keywords, and move on. Then simply "rinse and repeat", domain after domain after domain, and let those puppies generate continuous income forever! This is the ultimate lazy marketer's business model, limited only by the number of domains you monetize.

Notice I said "almost" the easiest. There are many internet marketers who add no value at all to any domain name they buy. They simply buy creative names for ten bucks and turn around the same day and re-sell them to the apparently-limitless universe of eager, largely clueless buyers on eBay.
It's a great part time business.

It takes about a minute to buy a domain name, and ten more to list it on eBay. If you buy ten names a day and can sell them for $25 to $40 each, which is very commonly done, well, just do the math yourself. Some devote another ten minutes to listing the domain name with a monitizer and advertise it as an "ad optimized website" which, in fact, it is.

I suggest you watch domain auctions on eBay for a few weeks and decide whether you can make money this way in a few hours a day. You won't get rich with this business model, but you should be able to generate some extra cash. There is a basic blueprint you can follow step-wise that will help you decide a direction in which to proceed: Park with a monitizer and see what traffic you can get; If it shows some decent traffic, create a one-page website with three short relevant articles and your own AdSense ads through Google directly. The monitizer no longer gets his vig!

If that looks promising, take the next step and create a full-blown website, create products, gather email names, drive traffic, and get rich! **Welcome to the wonderful world of the Domainer!**

HOW CAN I TELL WHAT A DOMAIN NAME IS WORTH?

For starters, let's review the factors that make give value to a domain name. All of these factors are considered in the algorithms used by the appraisal services (see below) to determine value estimates.

First of all, the extension, .com, .net or .whatever, is a critical matter.

Because it is the oldest commercial dot something, and the most highly recognized, the entire domain and internet commerce industry has been dubbed "The Dot Com Revolution". You've heard of the "Dot Com Bubble" where stocks in highly inflated internet startups (which may have had nothing whatever to do with a .com domain name) dropped sharply in value almost overnight.

The revived current internet realm is often referred to generically as "dot com two" (.com2). "DotCom" has become the generic vernacular for the internet industry, "the dot com industry" as a whole.

And because of this name recognition, and the public perception that a company with a .com website has probably been around a longer time (which may or may not be the case, but perception is everything), the .com extensions for a given word or phrase command a premium price.

Next most recognized is .net, followed by .org, and the more recent .mobi, .info, .us, .biz and .tv. One only has to look at auction results (again, see Appendix I) to get a sense of the relative number of .com sales compared to any other extension.

This is not to say that the others cannot have value in the tens of thousands of dollars. They can and often do. It is just that if we compare apples to apples .com extensions are worth more than the others.

Equally important is the number of letters in the word before the dot something. One- and two-letter and most three-letter words (as well as all letters of the alphabet) were registered in most TLDs (the Top Level Domains, which includes all seventy or so ICANN dot somethings) many years ago, and are generally prohibitively expensive when they do appear for resale.

Occasionally one can snag a dropped four or five letter word domain name, but that is rare. In fact, finding any single-word .com that could relate to some product that has not already been registered is virtually impossible. If you want to waste an hour grab a dictionary and try to buy any three-letter or four-letter dot com domain name. You will quite quickly see what I mean.

You can even make up three and four letter acronyms, nonsense words, and you will still find them all gone bye bye. Single-word domains, the shorter the better, and .com, .net, .org, .mobi, .info, .us, .biz and .tv are worth the most, but are very hard to come by.

Then we have two-word domain names, again, the shorter the better. And the combination should make sense. "BestFood" would be worth vastly more than "FoodSand" if you get my drift. Here again, a good three-word domain name such as "BestOrganicFood" would be more valuable than a two-word nonsense phrase.

When we get beyond three words the domain name may be very useful to someone trying to brand something but is not as easy to sell. My wife a while ago acquired a very fine site for offering major credit cards: PremiumCardOffersOnLine.info. That domain name itself would have little value in the secondary market (which is not to say the entire website might not have value, but that is a different matter.)

It must be noted here that hyphenated words such as "Best-Organic-Foods" may be worth as much as the same domain name words without the hyphen. The thinking among those who feel this is true is that hyphenated domain names are easier to read. Those who do not believe in hyphenated names feel that buyers would tend to omit the hyphens and end up at a different website..

But abbreviations such as "4" for "four", "biz" for "business", etc. definitely diminish value. Certain numbers and number combinations of particular note, "666", "777",

"711", "911", or any single or two digit number dot com, would be extremely valuable, but these were registered years ago and have very high worth.

Many internet marketers have a sort of "gray hat" way of earning internet income. They register common misspellings of popular website domain names. The idea is to profit (usually through AdSense ads on their sites) from traffic they get because the misspelled search term is entered into a search engine's search box.

Just for kicks try misspelling the domain name of some popular site. Chances are quite good that you will land on an AdSense site. These sites do get traffic, but no self-respecting

For example: "weeding" instead of "wedding". "forevlosure" instead of "foreclosure" (note v is next to c on your QWERTY keyboard). My wife owns "noageing.com". I'm not sure we knew the correct spelling is "aging" when we registered it! I recently (intentionally) registered: "JamaicanIndependance.com". Sure looks right to me. It ain't!

The free download "Domain Name Analyzer" at domainpunch.com has a feature called "Traffic Finder" which can be used to research misspelled domain names.

I know another internet marketer who makes a very good living selling domain names on Craigslist. He takes advantage of their geographic-targeted feature. He chooses a city, registers names such as (city)hotels.com, or best(city)realestate.com.

Then he emails every hotel or real estate company in that city and asks them whether they would like to purchase this very special valuable domain name! He often gets a thousand dollars or more for his $10 investment and an hour's worth of emails. Awesome!

As a generality, the "memorableness" (I think I just made that word up!) of a word or phrase is counted highly in the valuation algorithm. (Memorability?)

Keep in mind, however, that simple domain buying and flipping has worked for my wife and me for years. Just good words and phrases and aggressive marketing can net tens of thousands of dollars for a minimal investment.

I have found a useful indicator of comparative value to be a limited-daily-use free site located at valuation.com. They come up with an "appraisal" that is of very little relevance to what one might be able to get for a particular domain name, but can be of some use in comparing similar domain names. Their algorithm for evaluation is based on "organic traffic" (a searcher typing in the exact domain name).

The fact is, there is absolutely no agreement on the value of a particular domain name amongst the various appraisal companies. For example, my wife owns EgyptianPapyrus.com. I have a written appraisal of $22,000. I also have five other appraisals of this name between $700 and $2,300.

All appraisals were obtained on the same day but from different appraisal services. The point is that a domain is worth what someone is willing to pay for it, and domain appraisals are, for the most part, **worthless.**

Some last thoughts on the value of domain names. My wife has used the value of her domain names, both estimated values and those values based on written domain name appraisals as valued assets stated on balance sheets in successful mortgage applications.

Domain names are legally real property, and showing a few million dollars of potential domain name sales value for an entire portfolio , especially with appraisal documentation, can go a very long way towards making an iffy personal balance sheet look fabulous!

A valuation that is an accepted generality in the industry is that a highly- developed multi-product website is worth twenty-four times (two years of monthly earnings) its median monthly earnings. Such a website that shows a $6,000/month median earnings over a long period of time would be valued at $144,000. This can make a balance sheet's assets really stand out!

A website selling only a few virtual products might be valued at just two times its median monthly sales. A twenty-four month time frame for sales statistics is generally desired by buyers, and required by lenders.

But it is also possible that a website might be worth far more than its earnings indicate, based on its double-opt-in visitor base which may not have been fully exploited. Email lists are pure gold. You can check out ebizvaluations.com for a FREE estimate of the value of a website based on an algorithm taking into account multiple factors.

You don't have to actually BUY a domain name to build yourself a profitable website. LeaseThis.com is the Hertz-Rent-A-Car of domain names! They provide you with the option to lease or rent a domain name for a flat monthly fee for a predetermined length of time, often with the option to buy. In so doing website owners can test the name for traffic and branding purposes without risking a large investment. Slick!

Believe it or not there is even a domain name pawn shop called DigiPawn. Go to digipawn.com and check it out. They loan money on their valuation of your domain names and websites!

KEY SITES TO VISIT:

General Domain Information: DNJournal.com; Icann.org; Bizbuysell.com; GenericDomainNames.com; UKreg.com; IwebTools.com (to check for a Google site-ban); DomainPunch.com ("Domain Name Analyzer");

DomainTools.com ($50/month intelligence);
Bizbuysell.com.

Domain Research: Alexa.com (Link Popularity);
Google.com (Page Rank and Link Popularity);
Yahoo.com (Link Popularity); MSN.com (Link
Popularity); AllTheWeb.com (Link Popularity);
AltaVista.com (Link Popularity); DomainProfiteer.com
(For DMOZ listing); WayBackMachine.com (History of
website content); Google.com (Google Cache for website
histories); Domaining.com (See historic sale prices);
DomainPunch.com (Many domain tools);
Domainstate.com (Valuable suite of FREE tools).

Where To Buy Domain Names (registrars/hosts):
thirdsphere.com; avahost.com; webwizzards.com;
bluehost.com; hostican.com; thinkhost.com;
liquidweb.com; arvize.com; hostexcellence.com;
lunarpages.com; webhostingpad.com; godaddy.com;
enom.com (bulkregister.com); namecheap.com;
moniker.com; dynadot.com; 1and1.com;
namesecure.com; networksolutions.com;
purchaseyour.com; sedo.com ("World's Largest Domain
Marketplace"); and premiumdomains.com.

Name Drops: exody.com; pool.com; snapnames.com
(recently merged with moniker.com); justdropped.com (my
favorite); domainersedge.com; expireddomains.com;
namespy.com; namejet.com; aftermarket.com; and
freshdrop.net.

Live Domainer Auctions: Moniker.com; NamePros.com;

Private Sales: Craigslist.org; EBay.com.

URL Appraisers: Afternic.com; Sedo.com; Estibot.com;
GoDaddy.com; Valuation.com; BulkRegister.com
(eNom.com); NamePros.com; DnScoop.com;
LeapFish.com.

On-line Auctions: Sedo.com (GreatDomains.com);
Afternic.com (BuyDomains.com); Moniker.com
(DomainSponsor.com); Pool.com; Domaining.com
TDnam.com; (GoDaddy.com) ; PremiumDomains.com
(Mocus.com); SnapNames.com; ENom.com
(BulkRegister.com); PremiumDomains.com.

Sell Websites: WebsiteBroker.com;
BuySellWebsites.com; Flippa.com (Excellent "Just Sold"
info).

Monitizers: Domainapps.com, (formerly whypark.com);
Fabulous.com; NameDrive.com; DomainSponsor.com
(Moniker); Sedo.com; Parked.com; Afternic.com;
Moniker.com.

Escrow Service: BulkRegister.com (eNom.com);
Moniker.com; eBay.com; Escrow.com.

Forums: DNforum.com; **NamePros.com (Also buy
and sell domains);** DomainState.com;
WebmasterWorld.com; WebHostingTalk.com;
DomainSalesMachine.com; AcornDomains.co.uk.

Pawn Services: DigiPawn.com.

Valuation: EbizValuations.com; WebsiteWorth.info;
Cubestat.com; EstimURL.com; Bizmp.com.

Blogs: DomainSalesMachine.com.

The above sites are listed in no particular order. They are
sites with which the author has had some experience. It is
not intended to be a complete list. You should definitely
spend a few days studying all of these sites to get a
thorough feel for the business of buying and selling
domain names.

CHAPTER 45

FLIPPING WEBSITES = FAST PROFITS

As explained above, you can make a lot of money buying and selling domain names without ever taking the step of creating or enhancing websites. But there is no question that with patience and a knowledge of website creation and optimization you can make far greater profits selling entire operating, proven money-making websites.

We talked about domain name auctions in the preceding chapter. Many of the domain names that are sold have never been developed into viable websites. But the ones that drew huge prices were almost always proven winners, with many backlinks and high PageRanks and demonstrated profits.

By developing a website and driving traffic to it, the domain name does not only have the potential or perceived value of a "raw" URL, but it has proven conclusively to have real market value.

This value can be established by showing Alexa rankings and Google analytics. You show me a website with an Alexa ranking of 50,000 or lower with tons of traffic and hundreds of relevant backlinks (other websites with links that point to it) and a Google PageRank of 5 or better and I'll show you a website that could easily fetch six figures at auction.

The individuals I know who make large sums of money flipping websites often do so by purchasing dropped domain names that already have some proven history. It can save a year or more of development of a domain name. There are countless domain names that come up for sale every week that have backlinks and a solid history of attracting traffic.

There are many dropped domain names associated with defunct web sites for sale every day. If you can locate a few of these every week that have some documented history, and find yourself to be the only bidder (rare) or one of very few bidders, and not pay a sum beyond your budget for such a domain name, you may have found the royal road to internet riches.

Frequently sites such as these can be purchased for $60. If there is a single other bidder for the domain they may drop out somewhere before the $100 level. Many eBay domain flippers stick to a single $60 bid as their business model.

Those who have a great deal of experience flipping websites are often willing to pay many thousands of dollars for a dropped domain name with a solid history. They know with some certainty from experience what profit they can expect after enhancement.

Searching the various auction sites can provide you with many historic full-website sales prices to give you some sense of the possible. Entire websites are often sold in eBay auctions. This is the "buy for $60, do minimal enhancement, and flip for a few hundred dollars above cost " business model crowd. Many individuals make a very good living in this manner with a minimum of effort.

Fast "cleaning up", i.e., enhancing a defunct site for eBay listing is generally just a matter of optimizing keywords and applying sound principals to make the site visually attractive. It is analogous to adding value to a beat-up house by making minor repairs such as applying a fresh coat of paint and "flipping" it ASAP. The added value is far greater than the cost of the enhancements.

Be CERTAIN to check whether a website you are planning to buy has not been banned by Google. I was burned once this way myself. I have learned to check this out on iwebtools.com. Always check out every advertised statistic for yourself. Many sellers puff up the numbers, or fabricate them out of thin air!

When selling a low-cost site on eBay advertise it as a "Premium Website". Offer "No Transfer Fees", "Best Deal",

"Free Push On (name of a registrar)". "Pushing" is the act of transferring ownership of a domain name/website held at a particular registrar where BOTH buyer and seller are registered with that registrar. It greatly facilitates the transaction.

Be certain to mention in your eBay ad all of the ways you can possibly imagine that the buyer could make money with it in the future. "Perfect for (blah, blah, blah)". Get the picture?

There are many ways to quickly add to a website's value. One quick way is to have the website dedicated to Google AdSense advertising. You will add some relevant keyword-rich articles, and develop as many "backlinks" from other websites as possible. Frequent blog posts to the site are also important. Then just leave the rest to Google. This is the best quick-flip eBay model.

The big bucks will not be achieved on eBay where the buyers are generally bargain hunters with a few hundred dollars to spend. To enhance websites with an eye on the big-time auction sites there are many factors to consider in turning a pig into a swan.

HOW DO I ENHANCE THE VALUE OF A WEBSITE?

Whether you have domain names currently parked or are actively engaged in the process of acquiring and selling website properties, it is possible to flip a domain name very quickly for profit. Domain-name marketplace Flippa, for example, has sold well over $50 million worth of websites and domains in its rather brief existence.

So let's say you have a some domain name attached to some sort of good, bad or otherwise website. What can you do to get it ready to flip?

First, focus on re-developing the content on the site. Look to optimize the site for **long-tail** keywords that can send more tightly targeted traffic to the site. Then look at analytics to see whether you can identify items that are lowering your conversions.

In this day of social media marketing be absolutely certain you at least have links to all of those social platforms. Ideally you should have some social media presence already established, but if not, at least show those cute link icons!

Make certain that all of the internal and external links on the website actually link to something. Broken links will greatly reduce a site's value. So will misspelled words,

Once all of that is out of the way, make an effort to add **new features** to the website. A blog, a forum, or anything customer- interactive, can be a big plus.

As with developing any website there are other important considerations. Is there an SSL Certificate? Are there any Better Business Bureau or other logos that apply? Is the visitor's purchase experience maximized? Are email boxes established? How about a squeeze page and an autoresponder? The presence of any of these can add value when flipping a site.

Creating a well-optimized website that can be flipped for multiples of what you paid for it will take some time and effort. Enhancing keyword use is one way. There are the five "keyword hotspots" for you to work on:

The description and keyword meta tags;
A well-written Title Tag;
The headline and sub-headline;
Within the text;
Behind the images.

There are also some additional "enhancements" you should definitely incorporate in the websites you will be upgrading, if these are not already present:

You MUST show **unique** content on the website. Try to have at least five, preferably ten pages of unique content; add a "Privacy Policy" page;
add an "About Us" page; and add a "Contact Us" page.

Have links to the above three pages at the bottom of the landing page.

Add an "Additional Useful Information" page with links to various other short articles.

Include a Site Map page, with links to every other page. This allows Google to easily spider the entire site. Very important.

The landing page content must be targeted and relevant to the keywords on which visitors might be bidding.

Consider including a Resource Page with a link at the bottom of the landing page. This should contain a list of any .edu or .org sites related to the website's niche. This scores big points with Google.

Try to make the site visually attractive.

Get listed in the DMOZ Directory.

Making all of the above enhancements will go a long way to adding massive value to any tired old pig of a dropped websites. Swans can be worth a fortune
Incidentally, all else being equal, when you buy a dropped website, look for the age (date of first registration) of the domain name, the older the better. It is one factor in Google's complex rating algorithm.

Your goal is to be able to document real earnings statistics, derived from product sales, ad revenue, affiliate programs, and AdSense ads. Once you achieve this you can price a website at large multiples of recent earnings.

Any potential buyer of your developed website can easily determine all of the analytical statistics about your site, so there is no way to "fake" value. The numbers tell the tale. Savvy buyers and sellers do a SWOT analysis: <u>s</u>trengths, <u>w</u>eaknesses, <u>o</u>pportunities, and <u>t</u>hreats.

At the end of the day the only valuation that matters at all is the one done by your prospective buyers who have both the desire and the liquid funds to buy your site. People are willing to pay high prices to avoid having to develop sites themselves, or perform search engine optimization, or identify profitable niches, or drive traffic to a website.

But value, as with beauty, is entirely in the eyes of the beholder. There simply is no exact valuation for any domain name or website. The most accurate valuation you can get online seems to come from ebizvaluations.com which employs not some vague math algorithm but uses prices for which hundreds of similar sites have historically sold.

A number of authors I know will create a website for a short book or report they have written, or had written for them. They create a nicely developed multi-page site and then offer to sell it **together with** all copyrights to the book. This can also work well for simple mini-sites, especially if it can be shown that the book sells reasonably well.

FOR WHAT IS A HIGH-STAKES BUYER ACTUALLY LOOKING?

A domain's value is most frequently based on the actual revenue it produces, averaged over time. That is something that is real and quite predictable. Essentially everything else, aside from verifiable traffic, is nothing more than hot air.

Revenue notwithstanding, the number of monthly visitors does factor significantly into the value of a site. A site receiving fewer than 2,000 visitors/month might be worth a thousand dollars, while one with 30,000 visitors a month might be worth $3,000. Hit 50,000 a month or more and six figures is possible. By creating verifiable traffic you have saved the buyer a great deal of trouble and time, and time to a wealthy website buyer is money. Many short but traffic-developed websites with high traffic have sold for six-figures

Blog sites are less attractive to buyers because they require a constant flow of content to keep traffic and revenues growing. The other side of the coin is that blogs may be easier for you to generate higher traffic figures than constant-contact sites. Static sites are reported to sell for 30% more than blog sites all else being equal.

The most profitable domains for resale are those that are NOT tightly niche-focused, but those with the broadest search parameters. Buyers want as many people as possible typing those terms into their browser bar.

A buyer willing to pay large sums for a domain takes many factors into consideration. Though it is highly unlikely that all of the following items would be present in any single website transaction, the more that are present the more a buyer is likely to pay.

A .com domain name, preferably one where the same name .net and .org and other extensions are part of the sale. This limits future competition.

An aged domain that has never been allowed to expire;

An aged site with a long earnings history;

A large number of backlinks from a wide range of relevant domains;

Links from .edu and .gov domains;

High Google PageRank

Low Alexa ranking, preferably under 100,000;

A very large database of double-opt-in subscribers;

A valuable demographic, e.g., adult professionals as opposed to pre-teenagers;

Opportunity for the buyer to **further** monetize the site;

High quality content, the more the better;

High cost to recreate the site from scratch;

Low expenses relative to gross profit;

Multiple sources of earnings;
A source of earnings that requires little regular work;

A loyal visitor base that makes repeat purchases;

Level of post-sale buyer involvement by the seller;

A built-up social community, forum, or blog, with wide participation;

A "beautiful" site can help, but a buyer can easily have any site re-designed as seen fit.

As you can see from the above list of enhancement factors, a six or seven figure website will take some considerable time to develop. But always keep these factors in mind as a goal in connection with any of your developing websites.

In negotiating a large sale there are other considerations that can help to seal the deal:

Will you as the seller accept partial payment with the balance contingent upon the buyer's achievement of some pre-determined goal?

Will you accept installment payments?

Will you offer to be a consultant for some period of time?

Will you sign a "no-compete clause" in the sale agreement?

If the site sells some unique products which you own, will you consider selling the exclusive rights to that product along with the website?

Are you interested in selling/retaining a part-ownership?

From your standpoint as seller a pure "cash & walk away" deal is preferable. This is not always possible. You may need to offer compromises, or walk away from the deal and seek the all cash/no contingency buyer you hope is out there somewhere. A bird in the hand, however, is often worth two (or more!) in the bush. Remember the old Wall Street adage: "Pigs get slaughtered".

Just as with a house for sale, a domain name or a website is **ONLY WORTH WHAT <u>SOMEONE</u> OUT THERE IS WILLING TO PAY FOR IT.** Not a penny more. Not what YOU think it's worth. This is a truism that one must accept, and then do everything possible to find the right "someone".

Also keep in mind that your sales pitch to the prospective buyers must be highly professional with details about the business and full disclosure of all available statistics. Stating a good believable reason why you are selling the website never hurts.

As pointed out in the preceding chapter, "Name Drops" such as exody.com, pool.com, snapnames.com and justdropped.com are a source of endless opportunities to find potentially profitable domain names both "virgin" unused, and semi-developed. Great places to flip your websites are eBay (for low end sales to inexperienced buyers), sitepoint.com, and digitalpoint.com.

What are the best places to list and sell your websites once you have optimized them for sale? There are many resale vendors for you to consider. Check out: GoDaddy at godaddy.com; Tucows at opensrs.com; ResellerClub at Directi; SRSplus at networksolutions.com; and eNom at bulkregister.com.

CONCLUSIONS

Flipping websites is a very profitable business model. Most seasoned internet marketers understand, however, that the flipping business model is NOT the most profitable for most of us. Developing websites and selling our own unique products and affiliate products to a huge universe of double-opt-in email subscribers trumps flipping.

The most consistently successful domainers employ the "develop, hold and market a product" business model. Simply flipping websites can leave too much potential earnings on the table.

In any event, I strongly recommend that you go to each of the above sites and study every aspect of them before you even think about flipping domain names or developed websites. Note in particular what final prices different sites sell for. Imagine yourself participating in the action.

There are many internet entrepreneurs who focus on this one business model alone and make a fortune doing it. There is no reason why you cannot become one of them. It takes time and patience but it can be one the most profitable of the many multiple streams of internet income, just not the easiest to execute.

From the looks of things today this Domain Flipping business is still in its infancy, and today's opportunities seem limitless. You have little to lose and potentially much to gain by getting involved at once.

The domain name you fail to register today will probably end up in someone else's portfolio tomorrow, and the profits from flipping that domain will end up in in someone else's bank account a year from now. It might just as well be in your account!

JUST DO IT!

CHAPTER 46

THE SUCCESS TOOLS

When buying domains in the secondary market, there are many factors to consider. The following research tools are invaluable in helping you decide which domain names to buy in the secondary market.

ALEXA: Alexa collects data on website traffic. To check the Alexa ranking of a domain name go to Alexa.com/siteinfo. Any ranking under 4,000,000 is actually considered quite good (remember, there are tens of millions of domain names registered). Any ranking around 1,000,000 is very, very good; under 500,000 is great. Anything under 100,000 is a super valuable gem!

In general, the lower the Alexa ranking the more it will be worth (and the more it will cost to buy). Of course, for any original domains you have bought with ideas from your own mind there will be no Alexa ranking at all, until the site is monitized or developed, and some time passes.

This does not mean "original" unranked domains have no value. Quite the opposite is true. In fact almost all of the domains we have sold over the years have been original-thought registrations, some for many thousands of dollars. And they had no Alexa or Google ratings.

In these cases the buyer wanted the "unused" domain name to brand some product or idea and did not care about existing traffic. Of course they would have preferred that the domain had lots of historic traffic, but if it did they would have had to pay lots more dollars to acquire it.

GOOGLE PAGE RANK: Go to Google.com. Type in: cache: (domain name).This is a highly industry-respected indicator of a domain name's importance compared to other domain names on the web. It is a single-integer 1 to 10 scale (1, 2, 3....), but it is not linear. That is to say a "2" is not twice as important as a "1". It is a logarithmic scale, like the Richter earthquake scale.

A "2" Google page rank is 10 to 100 times better than a "1". A Google page rank of 3 is good, 4 is very good, and 5 is excellent. Anything 6 and above is a rare gem! But to even attain a Google page rank of "1" is a fair achievement.

LINK POPULARITY: This statistic will tell you how many links from other websites the domain has acquired, the more the better. Go to:advertising.yahoo.com/article/yahoo-web-analytics.com. A site with under a hundred links is not extraordinary. A link total of 500 is very good, over 1,000 excellent. Some sites have tens of thousands of links!

SITE CONTENT: If you are buying a secondary market domain name for the purpose of a specific idea or product promotion, the relevance of the past and present content on that domain is important. Two ways to find this are: Google: google.com (type "cache"+domain name);

WAY BACK MACHINE: waybackmachine.com has cached historic content of millions of websites.

SPECIAL LISTING: dmoz.com. The "DMOZ Open Directory Project" is a manually-processed directory of domains. To be included DMOZ participants must show a domain to have valid relevant content. Being DMOZ listed makes a website and its associated domain name more valuable.

CONCLUSIONS

These three chapters are intended to provide a working overview of the domain name industry as my wife and I have participated in it for a decade. Spend some time learning from it, and you may be surprised at how much fun it can be to make money rather easily sitting at your computer. Along the way you might just get rich!

The myriad nuances and branches of the domain name business could fill many volumes such as this, and we surely do not "know it all". In fact, because of our focus on "flipping" to the exclusion of all else the domain name business has to offer, we have probably "left on the table" tens if not hundreds of thousands of dollars in the past. No longer. We try to learn from our past stupidity!

People reminisce about "the good old days" when they could have bought a stock or a piece of land dirt cheap that would have been worth a fortune today. Well guess what......in virtual real estate these *are* (almost) the good old days. Every year you own and hold a domain name is another year it can grow in value. Domain names get increasingly scarse as more and more are registered every day. Supply and demand. Marketing 101.

Profitable investing in Domain Names is one of the internet's most closely guarded secrets. It is impossible not to get excited when one realizes that the likes of Perot and Schultz and Rosenblatt are reported to have gotten into the domain-acquisition act!

But the fact is that the playing field is so huge, and the opportunities so varied, that literally anyone of average intelligence and a small budget can get started this very day on what could be a fun and extremely profitable lifelong adventure!

Don't be one of those people who look at this domaining opportunity and make the mistake that it is too late in the game to get started. The time is NOW to take advantage of one of the internet's best kept big-money-making secrets.

<u>JUST DO IT!</u>

MODULE TEN
OTHER WEALTH TECHNIQUES

CHAPTER 47: GET RICH SELLING TOP LOCAL POSITIONS
CHAPTER 48: HIGH-PROFIT MARKETING WITH POPOVERS
CHAPTER 49: HAVE FUN SELLING PICKS AND SHOVELS
CHAPTER 50: MULTI-LEVEL MARKETING (MLM)

CHAPTER 47
GET RICH SELLING TOP LOCAL POSITIONS

Here is a potential internet-related business that can make you a small fortune very quickly. I recently witnessed a live demonstration of this at an internet conference, and it was a real eye opener.

Most every brick-and-mortar merchant has a website of some sort. Most know that they waste a lot of money on Yellow Pages Advertising. Most know that customers search for vendors on the internet. They also know that their website gets very few visitors and generates very little revenue. They almost never know why this is so.

It can be a local restaurant, beauty parlor, electrical supply house, shoe store, pizza parlor, whatever. They all have the same problem. They spend a fortune on Yellow Page and other advertising, spend money on a website with poor payback, and haven't a clue how to improve the situation. What if you could offer them top positions in a search engine? What would that be worth to them? It has been found through experience that there is almost no resistance asking $1,000/month and getting it gladly, if you can produce results. You could try for more, or settle for less, but it is a good starting point.

At the conference three newbie students each called a few local businesses, made their offer, and closed $1,000/month deals! Each realistically expects to sign up twenty local vendors. How does a $20,000/month extra income stream sound? Beyond belief? It isn't.   Actually the basis for this program was taught to me many years ago at an internet conference I attended.   It was taught as a way for me to get top positions for my sites, and I can assure you it works. It never occurred to me to offer it locally to merchants in my town.

To make this happen it is necessary to understand that Yahoo! owns a rather obscure search engine. It is quite easy to buy a top position here at very reasonable prices for almost any long-tail keywords.

Go to https://securityservices.adcenter.microsoft.com/AdCenter.com. Sign up for a FREE account. Study the site, which works similar to Google AdWords.

Ever notice the websites shown in special boxes ABOVE the other search results? These are often derived from the above obscure search engine results! When you bid within this site, bid no more than $.05, or whatever minimum they allow, using obscure long-tail keywords that pertain to your local merchant..

Once you can show a local merchant that a search will put them above their competitors at the very top of the search pages you can negotiate your price. Try to determine how much they are paying annually for Yellow Page ads, and use this as a guide for your pricing. We have found that $1,000/month is a figure that most merchants will pay.

Of course there is a bit of "face to face" selling involved here, though I have seen sales actually made over the phone as mentioned above.   Most merchants realize that they get virtually no traffic from the Yellow Pages and other local advertising they do. You may not even need to convince them that the Yellow Pages are becoming obsolete, and that most people look on line for local merchants and any bargains they might be offering.

Explain that, as opposed to Yellow Page Ads which cannot be changed for a year, you can change their ad any time they want. They can offer specials and coupons whenever they choose!

You will need to maintain your bids to insure that you maintain their top position, and make whatever changes in their website that they want. Yes, there is some maintenance work to do, and some cost involved, but look at it this way. If you can get as few as three merchants on board you could be clearing over $1,000.00 each and every month. That's not a bad income for relatively little work. It certainly is worth a try.

CHAPTER 48
HIGH-PROFIT MARKETING WITH POPOVERS

When I first learned about this marketing technique I thought it might be illegal! Apparently it isn't. It is known as Cost Per View (CPV) marketing. Compared to other internet marketing methods, it is the newest and possibly the least used.

Have you not noticed an annoying number of advertisements appearing out of nowhere on top of some website you are trying to access? I know that when I visit Accuweather.com, an insurance ad would often appears. When I visit FoxSports.com, I often get an ad for some automobile or insurance product. They are easy to get rid of, just a bit of an annoyance because they have absolutely nothing to do with what I want to access in the first place.

Now had the Accuweather popover ad offered me a report on some weather phenomenon, or the FoxSports ad offered me the odds on next weekend's games, I might have at least clicked over to take a look. But to date I have not seen a single such ad that is directly relevant to the site I am trying to access.

Apparently the best kept secret on the internet is a company called **DirectCPV**. Here is what they can do for you:

For starters set up an account at directcpv.com. Choose a user name, password, and give your email address, and Presto! You have a free DirectCPV account of your very own. Take the hours necessary to "drill-down" through all of the links in the site.

After that I suggest you go to cpvden.com and download and print out the free "DirectCPV Campaign Launching Guide". It is very helpful.

Log in to your new account. To start a campaign you need to deposit $100.00. Create your URL campaign, hit "Save & Continue".

ONLY use "URL" campaigns for best targeting, rather than the "keywords" choice. Use a $5.00 daily limit, and 1/24 frequency. The "Destination URL" is your tracking link. Start with "minimum bid $0.01/maximum bid $0.01". See what your results are. Raise this in steps to at most "minimum bid $0.15/maximum bid $0.15". Always use "Fixed". Their system is not a bidding contest. Everything rotates evenly, so the bid prices are only relative.

You tell DirectCPV exactly where you want your popover ad to appear........ as in right over your favorite competitors website! Remember, these are RELEVANT popovers, so there is a **very** good shot at getting clicks. It is important to recognize that Google traffic from DirectCPV is much cheaper than traffic bought from Google AdWords directly.
For example, if you go to Google for any search term and find out who is on top, and what they pay per click, you may find they are paying many dollars per click. But at Direct CPV for a relative pittance you can pop-over that very site, creating a very cheap top position! If your popover ad is exactly what the visitor is seeking from the underlying site you have a great chance for a click-through.

If it is a fact that a number of major companies use DirectCPV (companies as shown on their website) it is a good bet that it is a profitable venture. Try it. You might be in for a very pleasant surprise.

The **content** of your popover is critical. You must present a RELEVANT message about which the viewer will want more information. In fact, you have to convince the visitor that the information you promise will be far better than the information on the site you just popped-over!

There is another company that is worth checking out as well. It is TrafficVance at trafficvance.com. They have virtually the same process to create narrowly focused relevant popovers. The drawback here is that they require a $1,000.00 deposit before you can start an ad campaign. This is obviously not for newbies, and in fact they only accept experienced marketers.

Using popovers won't make you any friends with your competition, but business is business. Besides, the other side of the coin is that your competitors could wise up and create popovers on top of **your** sites! All's fair in love and war.

Try it. You just might like it!

CHAPTER 49
HAVE FUN SELLING PICKS AND SHOVELS

In the great California Gold Rush many fortunes were made panning for gold. Many, if not most, toiled in vain. Some died trying. But there were many who got very rich who never searched for gold at all. These were the clever entrepreneurs who sold picks and shovels and slosh-pans to all of the miners!

How does that relate to your internet riches?

There are many different aspects to the background infrastructure of the internet and internet commerce. **It is possible for almost anyone to learn how to provide these services and make lots of money doing it.**

For starters there are Advertising Services. There is a huge demand throughout internet commerce for individuals who can create effective ad copy. Once you become proficient with your own advertising, don't be shy about offering your expertise for hire.

The same is true about writing all sorts of web-content copy, especially sales letters. You can advertise your services on your own, or join a network of copy writers such as Elance or RentACoder. I hesitate to suggest joining our friends at Fiverr here because I'll be damned if I would offer any valuable service for five bucks. Maybe if I lived in Burkina Faso, but I don't! You probably don't either.

Once you become a proficient infopreneur you can share your knowledge with others by writing profitable "How I Did It" reports that can be marketed on your own website or through Kindle Direct Publishing, Create Space or Smashwords (Chapters 28 through 34).

There are many other aspects of internet commerce that you can offer by becoming an affiliate of the providers of specialized services. There are affiliate programs out there for internet service providers (ISPs), web hosts, domain name providers, website designers, autoresponders, shopping carts, and credit card services.

Joining these various affiliate network companies provides you with affiliate programs covering these types of infrastructure providers. But you do not need to join a network at all to offer these products.

Most infrastructure provider websites have a link, either somewhere near the top of their home page or at the very bottom of all of their website's pages that reads something like: "Become An Affiliate"; "Join Us"; "Represent Us"; "Affiliate Program"; "Help Sell Our Products", etc. For example, if you want to represent a domain name provider, just do a Google search for "domain name providers" and check out some of these domain vendors. You will find most have affiliate programs.

One of the easiest and most profitable "picks and shovels" internet businesses is providing your own website hosting services. Check out ResellersPanel at: resellerspanel.com.

For FREE you can start your very own hosting company! You can even sell domain names! And aside from being FREE, you literally have to do nothing except drive traffic to your website offering these services.

These folks will host your hosting-services-business website, provide full customer support, do all of the billing and collecting. They pay you the difference between the wholesale price they offer you and the retail price they charge your visitors. Aside from the cost of acquiring a unique domain name for your new business, you do not put up a single penny ever! Sweet deal.

Another avenue of income is software. Creating software products is very profitable. You can create your own software products without any knowledge of programming by accessing: makeyourownsoftware.com. For $197 you can create almost any software you can imagine. I'd love these guys if it weren't for the uber-hokey "Answer 'yes' to the following questions and we will let you know if you qualify to buy and sell our product". And by the way, "what's your email address?"! Seriously?

In business, as in life, reputation is important. One of the newer "picks and shovels" ideas that I've seen focuses on "On-line Reputation Management". It is a sad fact of internet life that any anonymous moron out there in cyberspace can post negative messages about any person or company.

A disgruntled employee fired for theft can say untrue things in blogs and tweets about a fine company. They had every legitimate reason to fire the creep, but now see their reputation tainted and could well lose business because of it.

A great schoolteacher could have years of fine reputation destroyed by an ex-student who felt they were unfairly graded. It happened recently in Florida when a male student made totally untrue accusations of sexual exploits with his female teacher. There are training programs on line that apparently can teach you how to find the anonymous perpetrator and erase all of the negative postings. Google: "On Line Reputation Management Programs" and search for programs you can use to help others and earn a profit doing it.

There are a few additional ways to earn some money in rather offhand ways. Not exactly "picks and shovels", but not exactly internet commerce either!

The following programs can earn you some money. These offer virtually <u>certain</u> cash, but the time vs profit equation is a bit hard to justify. Check out the following sites: cashbackresearch.com "Take A Survey, Earn Cash Now"; surveymoneymachines.com "Earn An Extra $200-$500/Month";
clicksia.com "Get paid to do a handful of simple activities".

All you do on these sites is follow directions and get paid for doing it. This is for the really desperate or really lazy, but I thought it was worth mentioning. One can make **some** extra cash.

There are a number of companies that will pay you for getting people to download various software and toolbars. The payouts seem awfully small for the possible revenue, but you might find that there is something here for you to try. Check out: vombacash.com; zangocash.com (The Pinball Publisher Network). Personally I have never tried these sites, but I do know a few who have with modest results.

You can also look to eBay as a source of income beyond selling your own products. A number of individuals in my geographic area offer to sell any items someone delivers to them for a percentage of the final selling price. They are experienced eBayers who have found a way to profit from people who neither have the time nor care to learn eBay selling for themselves.

By overlooking the chance to provide ancillary internet services you are limiting your opportunities for earning internet cash. Ultimately you will find that it is the SUM of earnings from <u>multiple streams of internet income</u> that is the key to internet riches.

Virtual products, affiliate marketing, self-publishing, social site marketing, email marketing, ezine marketing, newsletter marketing, membership sites,

domain marketing, eBay commerce, and "picks and shovels" all combine together to represent your blueprint for ultimate internet success.

Remember, you have to get started somewhere, the sooner the better. JUST DO IT!

Why anyone would ever consider participating in a multi-level-marketing program is beyond me, but vast numbers do. Sadly almost all fail. I have studied dozens of different programs, and personally participated in some of the best known. I know many others who have done the same.

Many MLM programs are run by large reputable companies with excellent product lines and good training and support. And yes, a **very** few people make large sums of money participating in them. The process is also known as "Network Marketing".

Many MLM programs are run by small and start-up companies with poor products and very little support. Even fewer people succeed with these.

But there are two unalienable facts that are true regardless of the company behind the program:

You generally have an up-front cost, and often an on-going cost, to participate;

YOU ARE TAKING ON THE JOB OF A <u>RECRUITER</u>, NOT A MARKETING PERSON. You become the networkmeister!

No matter how attractive the commission scale might appear, no matter how many "levels deep" you can earn commissions, no matter how many incentives you are offered, you are still a **RECRUITER**. And you are at the mercy of your recruits. "INCOME AT HOME" correctly translates to "RECRUIT FROM HOME".

And if you can somehow successfully fulfill your role as a recruiter, you then become a **<u>TEACHER</u>**, because every other sap you recruit has to be taught to recruit as well.

Ask yourself this: Do I want to be an internet entrepreneur, an infopreneur if you will, free to market anything you want to whomever you want, whenever you want, with your financial destiny in your own hands, **or** do you want to be a RECRUITER and TEACHER with virtually no control over your income which is largely in the hands of your army of recruits? Duh!

Much of the MLM TV and radio advertisements are misleading. They are very cleverly scripted to avoid Federal Truth In Advertsing Laws, but the manner in which they are delivered, the vocal emphasis, can leave a listener with a totally false impression.

Case in point: One very often heard radio commercial carried on major talk-radio shows begins with the words, spoken forcefully: "Many work at home advertisers will tell you that you can earn a hundred thousand dollars a year income at home". Long pause, while this very attractive incoime figure sinks in. This certainly catches your attention, so you now actually listen to the ad. The ad does **not** then follow with any sort of disclaimer such as: "But of course we are not telling you that you could actually earn this amount with us because it is extremely unlikely anyone will **ever** earn anything even close to that amount using our program." No indeed.

The ad now goes on to extoll the many virtues of **their** way to earn income at home by joining **their** incredible offer backed by some multi- billion dollar company. And of course with "$100,000 a year" already implanted in your brain you cannot help but believe that they are at least suggesting that you can earn that figure with **their** program.

And when you then hear the paid actors excitedly tell you how both spouses were able to quit their regular jobs and focus on this magical income from home program and earn more money than their combined salaries ever produced in the past, well, how could you **not** get excited! So you go to their very attractive website and read sales copy that is REALLY compelling. You simply MUST join these folks. And many do.

Then it occurs to you that maybe, just for the heck of it, you should read the "fine print". After all, you are about to quit your job and start a new life of luxury! And there, quite effectively buried in the website, and to keep the government from putting them out of business and sending the executives to prison is **THE TRUTH!** Even once you discover it, the disclosure is so cloaked in math that it is not easy to interpret.

But when you finally do figure it all out you discover to your surprise and horror that most all of people who join lose both money and far more important, lose valuable time! This is precious time they could be applying to affiliate marketing or any of the other multiple streams of internet income described in this book that can work well for anyone. The number of people who actually make a living with their program, compared to the number who sign up, is **laughably small by their own written admission.**

And I defy them to provide the names and addresses of any newbies who joined, quit two jobs, and aren't living in a cardboard box under a bridge somewhere! Don't hold your breath.

There is not just one single company guilty of this sort of deceptive-yet-legal advertising. On late night TV there are dozens of ads nightly that stretch credulity. And there are many prison cells occupied by once-famous "make money with my perfect system" gurus who went a bit too far posing in front of huge yachts and Ferraris they didn't own, and 20,000 square foot mansions they could only dream about. They'd finish filming the commercial and then slink back to their hovels, and eventually jail!

I even watched one ad recently by a very famous old-line mail-order-guru turned internet-guru where a succession of ten or more seriously "average" dumb-looking individuals (clearly from Central Casting) gave verbal testimonies of earnings of hundreds of thousands of dollars **a month**! I hope the IRS was listening! I do not believe in the tooth fairy! Santa Claus maybe.

The few who do succeed in MLM, in all likelihood, are individuals who already have huge customer lists from either the mail-order days or other similar programs that they spent years working on to make a living. They can pick up a new program and run with it. I do not believe that **ANY** of the few top earners actually started as a total work-at-home newbie and achieved a great living wage through participation in any such program.

As I mentioned earlier in this book, most "warehouse delivery direct to your buyer" programs will have you competing against everyone else who was dumb enough to buy in to the program. Worse yet, no one can compete with Walmart and Costco and expect to get rich working from their kitchen table.

And I have yet to see a single program that did not require some sort of investment of real money. Remember, even a seemingly nominal "$19.99 one-time opportunity" , called a "processing fee" or some other innocuous euphemism multiplied by a million or so fools who buy in to one or another of these programs equates to a very sizeable profit for the purveyor of the program. Sure, they may profit more if you are successful on some level, because they get a piece of the action somewhere along the line, but that "nominal amount" up front has made untold millionaires who couldn't care a damn if **you** ever make a dime!

Have some programs actually been successful for at least a fair number of people? Unquestionably they have. There is a special skill set that very few possess that seems to inspire a few individuals to put in the work necessary to make a living in MLM. For those who insist on giving MLM a shot over the dozens of other ways to make a living on line I suggest you obtain a copy of a short book written some years ago by Daren Falter (you can Google his name) titled: "*How To Select a Network Marketing Company*". It is as good a read on MLM as I have seen.

My advice very simply is: "DON'T BE TEMPTED BY MLM HYPE". There are simply too many other possible streams of internet income that are proven every day to offer anyone a real chance to earn a decent living.

CONCLUSIONS TO PONDER

You have in front of you a book, physically in your hands or on an e-reader, that can change your life if you choose to read it and follow one or more of the success paths presented.

If you are unemployed or under-employed this information could be salvation. If you are in a job that you know will never bring you the goodies that only money can buy, starting to supplement your income with an on-line adventure could set you on a path you never thought possible. **But you must take action.**

The internet is extremely dynamic. It literally changes month to month. New ideas and new techniques are published in monthly magazines such as *Websites.* Google, which is responsible directly and indirectly for the bulk of our internet income, adds new tweaks at a rapid clip. They also constantly evolve their rankings algorithm.

The social media sites Facebook , MySpace, YouTube, Twitter and Pinterest are regularly adding features and enhancing the social-interaction experience. Almost anything that matters to us as internet marketers changes often. Too often.

Because of the dynamic nature of the internet, virtually anything written before 3Q- 2012 will contain outdated, harmful to follow, information. Do not be misled by all of the wonderful "FREE" publications you will be offered as bonuses or "Private Label Rights" material or incentives to purchase various internet courses.

Just look at the copyright dates. Most will be around 2003-2004! Some I've seen are as old as the late '90s. Rarely will one be as recent as 2010, and even that is probably mostly outdated.

Certain of the popular best-selling "National Best Seller" hard-cover books on earning internet income have **never** been updated. One in particular has so many link-references in it that no longer exist that it's laughable! Amazingly, it still sells, to the peril of its readers who will end up more confused than helped. The majority of this old stuff is potential fish wrappings!

There's a lot of excellent **current** training out there. I buy and learn from it continuously. If you don't stay on top of new developments your competition will bury you. At the very least you will waste a lot of time and occasionally make a damn fool of yourself. Just be careful to stay away from the worthless outdated material.

Anyone who <u>purchases</u> this book, if they wish, can be placed on a special email list to receive FREE reports of new developments and techniques as I learn, apply, or react to them. I will also point out anything in this book that is no longer valid if I find such to be the case. I'm not aware of anyone else offering to do this. Just send your email address to: author@askburt.com. INCIDENTALLY: **<u>We never sell or *SHARE* your email address in any way.</u>** (Note that many will promise not to "sell" your email address, but they freely share (swap) with other marketers).

No one can argue that the internet has changed the world. It has, and in ways so profound that only someone who has celebrated many decades of life can truly appreciate the changes. No one under twenty-five can begin to appreciate, even imagine, life before computers, cell phones, Ipods and Ipads, Kindles and Nooks and Xboxes and flat screen TVs.

Just as these new technologies have evolved over the past decade and a half, internet marketing has evolved rapidly as well. All internet entrepreneurs need to evolve with it, and to <u>never</u> stop learning. New ideas and techniques literally appear almost weekly. And it all began less than two decades ago. Quite amazing.

There are certain absolutely timeless principals that can be applied to internet marketing today. If you have never read "Think And Grow Rich" by Napoleon Hill, written in the 1930s, do so, and then re-read it a few times. I strongly recommend that you study its wisdom. I read it once a year. It can change your life. In my opinion it is the most profound book on marketing and on life itself ever written.

Our jobs as internet marketers is quite straight forward: _Maximize the number of customers; Maximize the amount of the average order; and Increase the frequency of those orders._ That's the whole enchilada. Master those basic principles and you have the key to boundless wealth. Reread and memorize this paragraph, because it is fundamental to your success.

Remember: _**IF YOU WANT YOUR CUP TO RUNNETH OVER BE THE PERSON POURING THE PITCHER!**_ You have that opportunity in internet commerce.

You possess one asset that no one else in the universe can claim...... **YOU!** You are the only "you" on the planet. You are totally unique, with your own personality, quirks, and perspectives. When dealing with your customers always be honest and **be yourself.**

Your level of motivation will be key to your success. Some people need to be between a rock and a hard place before taking action. Some see the handwriting on the wall and act early. Some will take action out of pure curiosity over what might happen if they don't!

The internet is **huge**, with millions of websites and billions of visitors. The internet marketing pie is immense. As I've said before, you don't need even a small slice of the internet pie. You just need to lick the knife! I'm not a greedy person. Heck, I'd be satisfied with just a dollar a month from every person on line in the USA!

Abe Lincoln is credited with saying, as a young man, **"I will study and get ready and someday my chance will come".** You have the material here in this book for you to study. Especially if you are unemployed or underemployed there is no better time to start getting ready than **now**. You "chance" **HAS** come. It is credibly reported that countless individuals earn a substantial income sitting in front of a computer screen from the comfort of their homes. I do. You can too.

Traffic to your internet-offers can be free or costly to obtain. Cost in terms of dollars is optional. Cost in terms of time is not. If you are not ready to invest a lot of time in your pursuit of internet riches you should not even start, because you are sure to fail. It is real work.

Despite what a lot of internet guru's ads would have you believe this is not a "few hours a week" project. Far from it. Just deciding on your niche areas of focus takes time. The simple act of deciding which of many possible profit paths, the multiple streams of internet income to follow, is time consuming in itself. Just reading and starting to absorb the material in this book is time consuming.

Everything you will be doing takes time, more at the beginning, but time is always a consideration. Finding relevant keywords, writing titles, writing ads, and writing website copy takes time. Programming your autoresponder takes time. The good news is that once you have set everything up and going it all pretty much runs itself! Eventually your "job" is reduced to updating details, monitoring to make certain your links are functional, and checking your statistics. And counting your money!

I have found that most internet training sold today is vastly "puffed up" to make its perceived value appear greater. I could expand every Chapter in this book and make it into a

$997 course many thousands of pages long. <u>And people would buy it</u>.

I know this is true because I have bought multi-thousand page training that could easily have been condensed to a few hundred pages. The <u>perceived</u> value of a huge course is greater. Its <u>true</u> value in helping you make lots of internet cash is not.

Any single Chapter in this book could be expanded into a long, drawn out course. I could provide endless "screen shots" with details of which button to push to make something happen. I think these types of courses, filled with superfluous fluff, are always overpriced and are an insult to anyone who buys them. A button that says "click here" doesn't need a video shot of a finger pressing the button!

If my reader cannot go to a suggested website and figure out how to navigate it without seeing screen-shots on a page telling you to "click on this, go to that", with pages of idiotic illustrated instructions, then they probably could never make a living on line.

I leave it to my readers to have the initiative to search the internet for any highly-advanced training aids they might believe to be of value. Please be assured that this book gives you all of the knowledge you need to become a very successful internet entrepreneur, but you can never acquire too much knowledge. The problem that can occur is called the "paralysis of analysis". You cannot permit yourself to spend ALL of your time learning. Again, as Yoda said to Luke: "There is no try, there is just do or not do". **You simply must "do".**

I've done my best to share the ideas I have learned over many years that relate to making money with a computer. No doubt there are many techniques out there in cyberland that some young genius is using today to get rich and has not yet shared with the unwashed masses. If and when such information becomes available I will undoubtedly purchase it! And if I have your email address, I'll share my experiences with you.

I have learned over a lifetime not to even think of trying to reinvent the internet-commerce wheel. Let others spend years of trial and error making some technique work. Everything I know about making money on line I have learned from others, as I hope you can learn from me.

I cannot assure you that you will make a single dime applying my ideas. Everyone has a unique skill set, and some are simply resistant to learning anything new. Many lack the requisite persistence to succeed in an endeavor such as this. Being an internet entrepreneur requires study, practice, and patience, and "persistence, persistence and persistence".

Many people never see the pattern of their own self-destructive actions. They incorrectly assume that the reason things did not work out as planned must have been **due to someone else**. This is true among the ignorant and the brilliant alike, among business leaders and politicians, and us regular folk. And surely true among many aspiring internet marketers.

If you try, or have tried internet commerce and are unhappy with your results you simply have not taken the time and effort needed to get it right. Sorry folks, it ain't nobody's fault but your own.

I promise you that if you read and follow the information in this book that it is very possible for you to begin making money within the next few days. I want you to succeed and make money. Just believe in me and that what I am sharing with you works. If you become confused or don't believe you know enough just do it and learn by doing. **Action is the critical step.**

The great motivational speaker Anthony Robbins said it best: "You see, in life, lots of people know what to do, but few people actually do what they know. Knowing is not enough! You must take action." Even a poorly set up plan of action that is actually acted upon is far better than a perfectly structured plan that just sits there unused and untried. Do whatever you can **NOW.**

At any time just do what you can and skip what you cannot, and later do those other things when you gain experience and knowledge. I want you to go from zero to hero! **Start selling something somewhere.** Ask yourself: "How many 'Buy Now!' buttons do I have on the internet this very moment?" The answer should **never** be: "None".

In biblical terms, I am trying to teach you to fish. I have no control over what you do with this fishing guide, where you fish, and what fish you seek, and how good you become at setting the hook.

I offer you this traditional Gaelic blessing: "May the roads rise up *to* meet you. May the wind be always at your back. May the sun shine warm upon your face, the rains fall soft upon your fields, and until we meet again, may God hold you in the palm of His hand."

GOOD LUCK AND GOD BLESS!

ABOUT THE AUTHOR

There is one very logical question you should ask: "Who are you and why should I listen to what you have to say?" It is a very valid question.

I'm going to resist the urge to show you copies of my bank statements, as many "internet gurus" are so fond of doing. These are just too easy to fake or embellish or show out of context to have any credibility. Suffice it to say I have been rather successful at internet commerce far longer than most, since 1995 in fact. During that time I have made it a point to learn as much as I can from all of the biggest names in internet marketing, and to apply that knowledge. I share all I can in this book.

I didn't invent the e-commerce wheel, nor did I try to re-invent it along the way. I simply made it my job to learn as much as I could as often as possible from those rare pioneers who blazed the trail to internet riches.

I was born in a slum called Bedford-Stuyvesant (known affectionately as "Bed-Sty") in Brooklyn, New York. (Go Dodgers!) The "hood" was an interesting mixture of immigrant Catholic Italians and Irish, Protestants, Blacks, and Hassidic Jews, about in equal proportions. Both of my parents worked two menial jobs just to put food on the table. I had no siblings, and no educated role models. My birth year was 1938. Yep, I'm an old poop in his mid-seventies! Surprised? My plan: Live to 110! Maybe 111.

I was a typical "street kid", frequent truant, hustler, shop-lifter, and a survivor in a neighborhood where survival was both an art-form and a not-always reality. My best and only real skills were staying alive and shooting pool, the latter providing sustenance cash. Back in those days today's recreational drugs were almost unheard of. Had I been born in the modern era I might well have ended up a junkie, in prison, or dead.

My first job, at age ten, was delivering staggering shoulder-hung loads of dry-cleaned clothes for a local cleaner. My first "real" job was packing and shipping bottles of arthritis pills for a company called Dolcin, under the ever-watchful eye of the meanest lady that ever lived, my wretched first boss the evil Sheila! She was the direct descendant of a long line of slave drivers!

What happened between then and a decade or so ago I won't bore you with. I had the usual nine-to-fives, learned a lot from the school of hard knocks, suffered through two divorces, and served in the Army as a grunt during Vietnam. I flew search and rescue for the Civil Air Patrol. I almost died in a SCUBA accident! I more or less raised three kids. I never quite made the "big time". During a "religious period" I even became an ordained minister! But after a succession of failed business attempts, in 1994 I found myself in Chapter 7 bankruptcy and absolutely penniless.

Fortunately I had by then married my third wife, an exceptional and beautiful very young lady who certainly didn't marry me for my money! She always believed in me, often more than I believed in myself. I'm thrilled to say we are soon to celebrate our 30th Anniversary! She is one of a kind. Post-bankruptcy, from reaching up to touch bottom, today we live in absolute paradise on a twenty-acre ranch bordering millions of acres of State lands in the High Sonoran Desert in sunny southern Arizona. We have a beautiful 5,572 square foot stone home, have travelled the world, and have every creature comfort we could ever want.

THE LOVELY MELANIE, WITH OUR VIPs COCOA AND CAPPY

What could conceivably have happened between a 1994 bankruptcy and today? From Chapter 7 and reaching up to touch bottom to total creature comfort? *THE INTERNET HAPPENED!*__

Back in the mid-90s, quite by accident, a buddy of mine mentioned that he heard about a local seminar being held on Long Island. It had something to do with computers and making money on the internet. Neither of us knew diddly-squat about either one! At that time very few individuals did. It cost a thousand dollars to attend the seminar, but you could bring a friend for free. So we both scraped up five-hundred bucks and attended.

I have no recollection of who ran that two-day seminar. The focus was on buying up "dot com Domain Names" and somehow or other reselling them at a profit. Our first homework assignment was to go home and register "(OurOwnName).com". Next we were instructed to think up a lot of possibly useful words and phrases and to buy the corresponding dot com domain names. These could be bought at that time for $35 each for a year. Almost any word or phrase you could think of was available.

My friend Paul thought it was a scam and a waste of money and never bought any domains at all. For whatever reason I found it fascinating, and over the next year I bought a few every time I had an extra hundred bucks. I never tried to sell any of them. I eventually accumulated a few dozen dot coms.

One day out of the blue I got a phone call from someone who had tracked me down as the owner of one of my dot com domain names. He asked me if I would take five thousand dollars for it. I almost fainted! After a milli-second of contemplation I agreed. Score a really big one for me, $35 to $5,000.00, right? Not quite!

A few weeks later I learned to my horror and chagrin that the buyer re-sold my domain name the day after he bought it from me, for $125,000! Lesson learned. Seller beware. Make no emotional decisions **ever**. Sleep on everything. Knowledge is power. A very painful and costly learning experience to say the least.

Suffice it to say that over the next few years my focus was on learning the true value of my domain names and selling them at the then-going market prices. It is a documented fact that some domain names (unfortunately none of mine) have sold for millions of dollars each! To this day sales in the hundred-thousand-dollar-plus range are not uncommon. Domain Name auctions occur almost monthly worldwide.

These early domain experiences got me very interested in the internet overall. If dot com domain names actually had value, why was this true? Apparently there was some way to make money with .com websites. Some internet visionaries began to emerge, and some were willing to share the money-making knowledge they had learned through long and tedious trial and error.

Internet "wealth seminars" proliferated. In the late '90s I made it a point to attend every seminar I could, all around the country. I always made certain to meet the "guru" running the classes and try to pick their brains clean. Some were late teenagers, half the age of my kids! Some were clearly geniuses. Some were obviously out to make a fast buck. But all had useful lessons to be absorbed, and I was a willing sponge.
Early motivational seminars from which I learned a great deal were run by some famous individuals (Tom Hopkins, Zig Ziegler and Art Linkletter among them). Others were hosted by some younger geniuses who were lesser known by the general public. A few of the best, who were getting top grades from the internet community, were Jeff Paul (of '70s mail-order fame), Jay Abraham, Dr. Jeffrey Lant, Charles Carboneau, Darren Falter, Ken Varga, Robert Allen, and a very young man named Cory Rudl.

Cory Rudl was in my opinion the Steve Jobs of internet marketing. Cory was a young visionary who was so far ahead of his time that much of what he taught seemed far beyond the possible. Some thought he was a scam artist. He was, in fact, the real deal. I made it a point to attend all of his many seminars, and got to know him very well. Shortly after I attended his wedding reception conference he was killed in a tragic race car training accident. I believe he was 28. He left an indelible mark on internet training, and on me.

The following are a few of the photos I have accumulated over the years. These are among the individuals to whom I owe a debt of gratitude for guiding my internet and business career :

THE AUTHOR WITH INSPIRING LECTURER THE LATE GREAT ART LINKLETTER

THE AUTHOR WITH WORLD FAMOUS WRITER AND INTERNET GURU ROBERT G. ALLEN (ROBERTGALLEN.COM)

THE AUTHOR WITH FAMOUS INDUSTRIALIST, AUTHOR AND LECTURER KEN VARGA (KENVARGA.COM)

**THE AUTHOR WITH HIS WRITING MENTOR DAN POYNTER
(PARAPUBLISHING.COM)**

**THE AUTHOR WITH THE INCOMPERABLE WRITER AND
INTERNET GURU DR. JEFFREY LANT (WORLDPROFIT.COM)**

THE AUTHOR WITH THE GIFTED INTERNET GURU CHARLES CARBONEAU (CASHCONNECTION.COM)

THE AUTHOR WITH THE INTERNET GURU JONATHAN MIZEL IN THE "EARLY DAYS" (MARKETINGLETTER.COM)

**THE AUTHOR WITH THE LATE CORY RUDL AT ONE OF CORY'S
FIRST SEMINARS IN THE 1990s**

I learned all of the internet basics from Cory. Much of his
original material is still valid today. But the internet is very
dynamic, and changes happen almost weekly. For
example, the entire idea of marketing on social sites such
as Facebook and Twitter was unknown only a few years
ago, because neither social site even existed! And Google
and other search engines are continuously tweaking their
ranking algorithms, often with surprise dramatic and
occasionally detrimental effects on internet marketers.

Over the ensuing years I was privileged to meet, and in
many cases get to know well, a number of other internet
marketing geniuses. Names that come to mind are John
Reese, Marlon Sanders, Armand Morin, Alex Mandossian,
and Jim Edwards, but there were many others. I not only
learned what they taught but have profitably applied each
and every concept of theirs at one time or the other.
I have purchased internet training material from literally
dozens of individuals. My belief is that if I can learn one
single new idea that I can convert into internet cash then
the training was well worth whatever its cost. I calculate
that I have spent over $97,436 on such material. And it
was all well worth it.

I have courses from Yanik Silver, Gabor Olah, John Thornhill, Kim Enders, Brad Callen, Avril Harper, Matt Garrett, Socrates Socratos, and literally dozens more. I study them all, test the techniques they share, and incorporate many of them in my overall internet marketing strategy. **I never stop learning.**

Within the past three years another young marketing genius has appeared on the internet marketing scene. His name is Anthony Morrison. I met Anthony at a seminar he was running at a hotel conference center in Tucson. He was promoting an interesting new Domain Name marketing program which brought me back to my Long Island domain-seminar roots of a decade earlier! Of course Anthony had greatly refined the Domain Flipping concept to mesh with modern day realities.

I made it a point to meet Anthony in person. Because of my early experience with domain names Anthony invited me to do an infomercial with him at CBS studios in Orlando. It was really fun to do, and of course seeing oneself on late-night TV is a pretty amazing ego trip!

Anthony has gone on to become yet another self-made internet multi-millionaire still in his twenties!

He is a living testimony to what can be achieved in internet marketing in a relatively short time starting from ground zero with little or no operating capital.

If a young man in his early twenties with very limited capital can achieve this sort of success, don't you think there is just the slightest possibility that you could make a decent living learning internet commerce techniques?

THE AUTHOR WITH INTERNET GENIUS ANTHONY MORRISON (ANTHONYMORRISON.COM) AT CBS STUDIOS IN ORLANDO

This young man has progressed far beyond the domain-selling business. He has written three great training books, and conducts internet training seminars that are second to none. I thought I "knew it all" from my fifteen years in the business, but I have learned a great deal more from Anthony and apply it profitably on a daily basis.

I have no pressing need to continue my daily internet work. I believe it was Samuel Clemens (Mark Twain) who first said: "Make your vocation your vacation", and I really do enjoy doing the tasks that are needed to earn money on the internet. I plan to do it forever. With an occasional trip to Paris thrown in!

If I can help others, especially the unemployed and under-employed to improve their lives, so much the better. If I can interest seniors such as myself in supplementing their retirement incomes that would be wonderful. Can I make life easier for stay-at-home moms and dads? I sure hope so. If I can show college students how they can reduce their loan debt I'd feel quite good about that as well.

Personally, regardless of how much money I earn on the internet it will never be enough. My dreams of creating an enduring charitable foundation to fund a worthy cause will require as much as I can ever earn. I need quite a few internet millions to make a real dent in this project. It's a five-year plan. And it will happen. The aforementioned Anthony Morrison is very philanthropic, and I'd like to copy his example.

To summarize, I have over the past decade-plus participated in every phase of internet commerce I could find. I know that **any** of it can be profitable, but I have also learned which methods are most cost effective for me, and which I found could be implemented the fastest. <u>**I can save you years of time and and of thousands of dollars by sharing with you what I have learned through my years of study, and trial and error, and sweat and tears.**</u>

I am certain that this book can provide you with the knowledge you need to begin your quest for internet wealth. There is absolutely no reason for you not to give this wonderful journey a try. <u>**JUST DO IT!**</u>

There are so many different paths to internet wealth that I cannot imagine anyone not being able to find some aspect of the endeavor within their abilities and to their liking, and within their budget. And you might just get very rich in the process!

Good luck, and GOD bless.

Rev. Dr. James Burton "Burt" Anderson, SOB*, BChE, MBA, GRI, LLO, LIB, RFP
P.O. Box 2100
Green Valley, Arizona 85622
DRJBA@askburt.com

*<u>S</u>weet <u>O</u>ld <u>B</u>urt!

GLOSSARY OF INTERNET, AFFILIATE & PUBLISHING TERMS

As you become involved in internet commerce you will encounter a vast number of unfamiliar terms that are unique to the internet.

The following is some of the more commonly used internet terminology with which you should become familiar. If you come across a term not defined here, Wikipedia.com is always my first choice for a definition.

3-WAY MATCHING: A way of blending ads into a web page taking into account the ads background color, font color, and font size.

404 ERROR: A message that appears on a computer screen when you arrive at a web page that does not exist.

ABOVE THE FOLD: The area of a website that appears immdediately when someone arrives at your website and does no scrolling down.

ACCEPTANCE RATE: The percentage of email accepted by a mail server. This is not necessarily the amount of email actually arriving at desired inboxes.

ACPA (ANTI-CYBERSQUATTING CONSUMER PROTECTION ACT): A Federal law that prevents domainers from registering copyrighted or trademarked names or the names of private individuals for the purpose of profit. Fines can be as high as $100,000.

ACTIVE CHANNEL: A channel hosted on a Web server that features frequently updated information

ACTIVE SERVER PAGES: Special pages that allow Web developers to create dynamic by using database-driven content. Content is generally produced on th server-side.

AD RANK: The order in which Google AdSense ads appear on your site, as determined by Google.

ADSENSE: One side of Google's AdWords cost per click ad platform. Google pays you for these ads on your website.

ADSENSE CODE: The HTML instructions for your web page that places a Google AdSense ad on that webpage.

AD UNIT: A group of AdSense ads presented as a set. A maximum of three ad units are permitted per web page.

ADVERTISER: Also known as the "Merchant", pays affiliates for sending traffic to the merchant's website to either provide information or buy something.

ADWORDS: The advertiser side of Google's ad program.

AFFILIATE: Also called "Associate". Any website owner who earns a commission (i.e., a finder's fee) for sending traffic to a merchant's website. An individual who markets another's book for a percentage of the proceeds. Certain platforms, such as Smashwords, have an available affiliate program within their platform. You can always register with clickbank.com and offer your book at a percentage split upon which you decide; you become the merchant, those who promote your product are your affiliates.

AFFILIATE AGREEMENT: All of the terms that define the relationship between an affiliate and a merchant.

AFFILIATE LINK: Unique identity links that identify the affiliate to the merchant.

AFFILIATE MANAGER: The person responsible for running the vendor's affiliate program. Many vendor's will assign you a personal affiliate manager.

AFFILIATE PROGRAM: Also known as a referral program, revenue-sharing program, partnering program, and associate program. A vendor rewards his affiliates based on number of visits, leads, or sales.

AFFILIATE PROGRAM DIRECTORY: A listing of affiliate programs categorized according to niches.

AFFILIATE SOFTWARE: The software that runs and manages an affiliate program. It includes analytics, commission calculation, and making payments.

APACHE: A popular open source public-domain Web server that provides users with CGI, SSL and virtual domains. Apache's open source code allows users to adapt the server to suit their unique needs, which provides them with strong performance, security and reliability. This is the most widely used Web server on the Internet.

APPLET: A small Java-based program that runs in a sandbox and is embedded into a website to allow users to create virtual objects that can move or interact with the site.

ARCHIVE: Large files that contain valuable data.

ASCII (AMERICAN STANDARD CODE FOR INFORMATION INTERCHANGE: The worldwide standard for the code numbers used by computers to represent all letters, numbers and symbols.

AUTHENTICATION: An ISP's technical standards by which email gateway administrators establish sender identity.

AUTHOR PAGE: The various publishing platforms provide you with adequate space to tell about yourself, and to list other books you have published.

AUTO-APPROVE: Affiliate application process whereby anyone applying to be an affiliate member is accepted.

AUTO VETTER: AutoVetter is Smashwords' proprietary technology that automatically scans your uploaded ebook and reports back to you about potential formatting problems.

AUTO RESPONDER: A computer program that detects the receipt of an email and automatically replies to the sender with a pre-programmed response.

AVAILABILITY: See Uptime.

BACK ORDER: A domainer's order to register a URL if the current registrant allows it to expire.

BACKUPS: Data from you that your Web hosts copy (typically once a day) in case of a loss of data situation. Backups allow hosts to easily restore lost data. Be certain your host offers backup.

BANDWIDTH: The amount of information transferred both to and from a website or server during a prescribed period of time. This is usually measured in "bytes". Hosting companies generally offer packages that come with different bandwidth transfer limits per month.

BANNER AD: An ad promoting a product by means of a rectangular box (the Banner) containing an image, text, gif, .jpg, or video.

BISAC: "Book Industry Standards and Communications" is the standard book category coding system. You will find drop-down menus in the publishing platforms that offer you these choices.

BIT RATE: The speed that bits, the smallest units of digital information, are transferred over a communication link.

BITS PER SECOND (BPS): It is a measurement of how fast data flows from one place to another. A 56K modem can move about 56,000 bits per second.

BLACKLIST: A list of email sender addresses believed to be sending SPAM.

BLOCK PARAGRAPH: When paragraphs are not indented, but are stretched from one side of the page to the other, that's a block paragraph. It is generally accepted that "right justified" is more readable for the viewer.

BLOG HOSTING: These are special scripts that let users automatically post new information to a website.

BLOGOSPHERE: The sum of all information available on blogs.

BLUE SCREEN OF DEATH: When a computer crashes your monitor displays a blank blue screen.

BROADBAND: Refers to internet connections with much greater bandwidth than possible with a dial-up modem.

BROWSER: (or "Web Browser"): A computer program used to view and interact with the content of Web pages on the internet.

C+/C++: Programming languages used to created server-side programs that run after compilation. C++ includes objects.

CASCADING STYLE SHEETS – CSS: Rules that determine how an HTML document is displayed by a browser and adds functionality to and controls all design elements of simple HTML pages.

CHALLENGE RESPONSE: An automated message that identifies a sender of an email as a trusted source.

CHARGE BACK: A forfeited commission due to a cancelled sale.

CLICK FRAUD: The practice of sending traffic to a merchant using automated "huitbots" where the merchant pays a commission to a scammer and not to the legal affiliate.

CLICK THROUGH: The action of a visitor to your website clicking on a link that takes them to the merchant you represent.

CLICK THROUGH RATE (CTR): Ratio of the visitors who click a link and visit the merchant's site.

CLIENT: A software program designed to contact and obtain data from a server. For example, a Web Browser is a kind of client.

CO-BRANDING: This occurs where you as an affiliate can add your logo and branding on the pages to which you send visitors.

CO-LOCATION: When a user owns his/her own Web server, but houses it in the hosting provider's facilities for easy management, a high-speed connection, security, backup power and technical support, said user is "co-locating".

COMMISSION: This is the income you earn by sending a visitor to your website to your merchants website.

COMMON GATEQWAY INTERFACE (CGI): A program that helps servers and scripts communicate, enabling interaction between HTML documents and applications.

CONTEXUAL ADVERTISING: Ads that relate to the content on a web page.

CONTEXUAL LINK: A link within the text in an article or on a website which is a highlighted word or words within the text.

CONTROL PANEL (C-Panel): A Web-based application that allows you to manage various aspects of your hosting account. This includes uploading data and files, adding email accounts, changing contact information, installing shopping carts and/or databases and viewing statistics.

CONVERSION: When your visitor clicks over to your merchant and performs some positive action that is a conversion.

CONVERSION RATE: Percentage of clicks by visitors to you website that result in you earning a commission.

COOKIE: A piece of information sent by a Web Server to a Web Browser that forces the Browser to save the information and alert the Server whenever the Browser makes additional requests from the Server! It is used by vendors to keep track of a computer user's surfing history.

COPYRIGHT: (Not "copywrite".) A copyright is the exclusive legal right, normally held by the author of a book, to copy, adapt or distribute their creation. Often a publisher will control the copyright. Wikipedia has good technical descriptions found under "Copyright" and "Authors' Rights".

CPA (COST PER ACTION): A method by which you earn a commission as an affiliate when your visitor clicks over to your merchant and takes some positive action.

CPC (COST PER CLICK): Also known as PPC (Pay Per Click). Cost when paying on a per-click basis for an individual click to your website.

CPM (COST PER THOUSAND): (M = Roman numeral for 1,000). This is the cost for every thousand page views.

CPO (COST PER ORDER): Same as PCA except a sale must result.

CRON: The ability to run programs based on a server's clock

CTR (CLICK THROUGH RATE): The percentage of your visitors who click through to the merchant's website.

DATABASE: Data stored on a Web server in a structured format.

DATA FEEDS: Product-sales information provided by a merchant to an affiliate to aid in promotion of the merchant's products.

DATA TRANSFER: See bandwidth.

DEDICATED HOSTING: When you rent or lease your own Web server that is housed at a hosting provider's facilities for easy management, a high-speed connection, security, backup power and technical support, you are buying dedicated hosting.

DEDICATED IP: See static IP.

DIAL-UP: A method of connecting to the internet using telephone lines. It is very slow compared with other "high-speed-internet" and "wireless" connections.

DIRECT NAVIGATION: This is also known as "type-in traffic". This occurs when a visitor reaches your website through their address bar.

DISCOVERY: This is an important term used in ebook publishing. It describes how "findable" your book is by a prospective buyer. The key is **proper categorization.** You want people to find your book whether or not they are specifically looking for it! This is why it is so important to publish across as <u>many different publishing platforms as possible.</u>

DISK SPACE: The amount of space available for you to house your website files on your host's server.

DOMAIN NAME: An address assigned to a website for identification purposes that can be translated by a domain name server into a server's IP address that includes a top-level domain.

DOMAIN NAME SYSTEM (DNS): Keeps a database of domain names and their corresponding IP addresses, so that when a user searches for a domain name, the request can be routed to the server where the desired website resides.

DOMAIN PARKING: The ability to hold a domain name on a hosting server without the service provider requiring that users have the corresponding website up and running.

DOMAIN REGISTRAR: A company responsible for managing your domain names and helping you secure the rights to a specific domain name you wish to purchase.

DOWNLOAD/UPLOAD: This refers to electronically getting a file from an internet location "down" to your computer, or sending a file from your computer "up" to an internet site. You "upload" your files to your publishing platforms.

DOWNTIME: That period of time whae a server or browser is unavailable.

DOUBLE OPT-IN: This is a verification process used in email marketing. The individual receiving your first email must click on a link confirming that they actually wanted the email in the first place.

DRM: This stands for Digital Rights Management, and is offered as an option by some publishing platforms. On the surface it sounds like a good idea. It is "copy protection" technology designed to prevent piracy of your work. It makes it harder for someone who has bought your book to print or duplicate it. The problem with DRM is two-fold. First of all, a dedicated book pirate can easily bypass DRM. But more important it restricts your reader from enjoying your book on different devices. Although I have never "split tested" to see whether DRM helps or hurts my bottom line, conventional wisdom is to never employ it.

EBOOK: This is a generic term for any book offered electronically, intended to be read on portable devices or downloaded from a website.

EMAIL FORWARDER: A program that will automatically forward a received email message to a specified remote email address.

ENCRYPTION: Encoding data with a cryptographic cipher so that only authorized entities can view it

EPC (EARNINGS PER CLICK): A mathematical expression of total earnings divided by each click on the merchant's link.

EPUB: This is an open industry standard ebook format It is the format used almost universally, with the major exception of Amazon Kindle which does not support it.

EPUBCHECK: This is an EPUB validation tool designed to automatically determine if an EPUB file is compliant with the EPUB standard. Many ebook platforms require its application to your book's manuscript to insure that your book will appear on customers' devices correctly. You can learn more about it at: code.google.com/p/epubcheck/.

ESCROW: A third party service that acts to protect both buyer and seller in an internet transaction.

EVERCOOKIE: A persistent cookie created with JaveScript that remains on a site even after other cookies have been deleted.

EXCLUSIVITY: A merchant's requirement that an affiliate promote no competing products on their website.

EXTENSIBLE MARKUP LANGUAGE – XML: A meta-programming language used to specify other document types being used on the Web.

EXTENSIONS: The "dot something" that follows a domain name.

FACEBOOK APPLICATIONS: These are programs within Facebook that let users share content with other users.

FACEBOOK CONTENT: Items posted on a Wall, such as status updates and recent actions. Becoming a Fan would be an action.

FACEBOOK EDGERANK: Facebook's algorithm that determines what content gets shown in users' News Feeds.

FACEBOOK FAN: Users who choose to "Like" your business page.

FACEBOOK FRIEND: As a noun, a personal connection. As a verb, to add a Facebook member as a friend.

FACEBOOK FRIEND LIST: An organized group of friends.

FACEBOOK GROUP: This is an aggregation of users having a common interest. You can create and/or join a Group.

FACEBOOK LIKE/LIKES: AS a verb, to "like" your business page means someone became a fan of that page. As a verb, to like others' comments on their Wall or News Feed. As a noun, "Likes" are the number of users who have liked your business page.

FACEBOOK NETWORK: An associated group of users based at a school or workplace.

FACEBOOK NEWSFEED: A collection of your friends' Wall posts published on your homepage.

FACEBOOK PAGE: The official Facebook presence from which your business shares information and interact s with Fans.

FACEBOOK PROFILE: Your personally stated information about yourself or your business.
FACEBOOK WALL: This is the core of a Facebook Page or Profile that collects new content.

FALSE POSITIVES: The almost one in five of the valid permission-based emails that are blocked erroneously by SPAM filters.

FAQ: Stands for "Frequently Asked Questions." All publishing platforms offer this collection of questions that have been asked by publishers in the past. Studying the entire set of FAQs will often answer every question you might have about a particular publishing platform.

FEEDER SITE: A website set up only to redirect traffic to another site.

FILE TRANSFER PROTOCOL (FTP): A commonly used method for exchanging files over the Internet by uploading or downloading files to a server. (An example would be "cuteFTP".)

FILENAME EXTENSION: A tag that appears at the end of each file name. It consists of a dot and then three or four letters that signify the type of file and format.

FIRE WALL: A software/hardware security program that splits elements of a network into various parts.

FIRST LINE INDENT: This is a style of printing your manuscript in a word processing program such as Microsoft Word. It refers to indenting the opening line of every paragraph a few spaces to differentiate it from the next paragraph. Personally I never use it.

FORMAT (noun): This is a reference to a particular electronic program. There are many different ebook formats specific to particular reading devices.

FORMAT (verb): It is used in the context of how you prepare your file in a particular way before uploading it to a publishing platform.

FORMMAIL: An application that lets users create interactive forms and include them on their websites to let visitors submit information

FRONTPAGE: A server-side, HTML editor for website creation from Microsoft

FRONTPAGE EXTENSIONS: Scripts and programs installed on a server that allow sites, or features of sites, created with Microsoft FrontPage to operate smoothly

FTP CLIENT: A software that lets two computers transfer files over the Inte

FTP (FILE TRANSFER PROTOCOL): The method of moving information files between two internet sites.

GIF: Stands for Graphic Interchange Format. It is a format used for image files, especially those with large areas of the same color.

HONEY POT: A planted email address designed to identify and trap spammers.

HARD BOUNCE: A failed email delivery due to a non-existent address.

HIT: A single request from a web browser for a single item from a server. A web page with four graphics would require five hits, one for the page and one for each graphic.

HOME PAGE: The first page of your website that a visitor sees.

HOST: A computer on a computer network that is the repository for services available to other computers on that network.

HTML (HYPERTEXT MARKUP LANGUAGE): This is the programming language commonly used to build websites, It is read and processed by web browsers (as opposed to PHP which is read by servers).

HYPERLINK: This is a clickable line of text that takes a reader elsewhere. It can be an internal hyperlink taking the reader somewhere within the book itself, as with the "clickable" table of contents. An external hyperlink takes the reader to a site outside of the book, such as your website. To create a hyperlink highlight the text, right mouse click, and select hyperlink. From the Word panel that appears on the left side chose internal or external.

HYPERTEXT MARKUP LANGUAGE (HTML): The cross-platform language in which the majority of Web pages today are written. Codes are interpreted by Browsers to be properly formatted for visitors. It is relatively easy and helpful to learn, but not entirely necessary.

HYPERTEXT TRANSFER PROTOCOL (HTTP): This is the primary protocol for transferring and receiving data on the Web. It involves a browser connecting to a server, sending a request that specifies its capabilities and then receiving the appropriate data from the server in return. (In general you do not need to type http:// in to your browser before typing in the domain name.)

IMPRESSION: Also known as a "page impression". It is recorded every time a web page is viewed.

INBOUND LINKS: Links from a remote website to your website.

INDIE AUTHOR/INDIE PUBLISHER: "Indie" is an abbreviation for "Independent", and is synonymous with "Self-Published. These are the many writers, publishers, and writer-publishers today who have come to recognize that they need neither an agent nor a traditional publishing house to successfully market their books.

INTERNET: This is the huge collection of interconnected networks that are connected using the TCP/IP protocols. It connects tens of thousands of independent networks.

INTERNET MESSAGE ACCESS PROTOCOL (IMAP): The means by which an email provider offers their interactive services.

INTERNET PROTOCOL (IP): Sets of rules and regulations agreed upon internationally for all internet functions.

INITIAL CAPS: (as opposed to ALL CAPS): "Caps" is short for "capitals". Initial caps is where the first letter of every word is capitalized. Generally articles of speech such as "the" "this" or "and", and prepositions such as "over" or "on" are only capitalized if they are the first word.

IP ADDRESS: A numerical address that domain names piggy-back. The nameserver resolves the domain name to the IP address.

ISBN: Is the acronym for International Standard Book Number.
It does NOT convey copyright. It is a digital identifier that helps second-parties (publishers, retailers and distributors) to identify your particular book to track it or communicate with others about it. It is 100% unique to each specific version of your book.

JAVA: A programming language that produces dynamic pages for websites.

JOINT VENTURE (JV): A business venture designed to take advantage of a synergy of two products or services, the sum of the venture being greater than the sum of its parts.

KEYWORDS: A single word or a word-phrase (known as a long-tail keyword) of any length which is the word or words used by a visitor to a search engine to find the information for which they are looking.

LANDING PAGE: The first page seen by a visitor to a website. (See "portal").

LINK CLOAKING: A way to hide the real destination of a hyperlink.

LINK FARM: A website set up solely to create links to other sites in an effort to improve search engine ranking. These are not looked on favorably by search engines.

LOG FILES: These are text documents that document activity on a website or server.

MAILBOX: An individualize account where email messages are received.

MAILING LIST: A list of email addresses that facilitates sending a single message to a group of email addresses simultaneously.

MALWARE: A generic term to describe programs that are placed on your computer without your knowledge, designed to extract all manner of personal information.

MANAGED HOSTING: A system whereby you own or lease a server that is located with a service provider. All of its management needs are taken care of by on-site personnel beyond your need to input or control anything.

MEATGRINDER: This term is proprietary to Smashwords. It refers to their software that takes your .doc file once it is properly formatted and converts it to all of the other formats required by the various ebook readers.

METADATA: This is every piece of information that pertains to your particular book. It facilitates your customer finding your book. It includes everything from your title and cover, the ISBN, your book description, your biography, the category classifications, and your price.

META TAG: A specific piece of HTML coding that contains information not normally displayed to the visitor. They are typically used to help search engines categorize a web page.

MOBI: This is the format used by Amazon Kindle, as opposed to EPUB. It is also called a .prc file. (This has nothing to do with the .mobi top-level URL extension.)

MODEM (*MO*DULATOR / *DE*MODULATOR): A device that connects a phone line to a computer.

MULTI-LEVEL MARKETING (MLM): Also called "network marketing". It involves buying products wholesale, selling them at retail, and sponsoring other people to do the same.

MySQL: A relational database encountered in the building of websites.

NAMESERVER: These are the servers that issue an IP address for a given domain name.

NCX: This is short for "**N**avigation **C**ontrol File for **X**ML". It is the Table of Contents summary that accompanies a book presented in EPUB format.
]
NETIQUETTE: Internet etiquette.

NETIZEN: Someone who uses internet resources.

NEWBIE (NOOB): A new or inexperienced internet commerce or self-publishing person.

NUCLEAR METHOD/OPTION: This is a term coined by Smashwords for a system by which an author can strip out Microsoft Word's various unintended glitches. It creates a "virgin" copy of your text from which to begin proper formatting.

OPERATING SYSTEM (OS): A program that can manage computer or server hardware so that it provides the desired operations.

OUTBOUND LINKS: These are links on your webpage that lead to web pages on another domain.

PARASITEWARE: Programs that are placed on your computer without your knowledge that attach themselves to programs you commonly use (such as your browser) and force you to use their program in lieu of your chosen program.

PDF: This is short "Portable Document Format". It is a .pdf format created a decade ago by Adobe Systems. It is a fixed-layout format that freezes the layout of a book and its word positions. It is the standard for books sold on websites and downloaded by purchasers to their computers. It is not compatible with ebook readers.

PERFORMANCE BASED AMRKETING: A generic term for affiliate marketing.

PERFORMANCE INCENTIVE: A "bribe" from a merchant to an affiliate designed to encourage better results.

PHP: Technically "hypertext preprocessor". This is the programming in a website that is read by the web server, as opposed to HTML which is read by the web browser.

PIN: An item put onto a Pinterest pinboard.

PINTEREST PINBOARD: The electronic bulletin board where Pinterest users post pictures and any theme-based material.

PLUG-IN: A small item of software that adds some feature to the software on a website.

POINT OF PRESENCE (POP): "POP" has dual meanings. It is a physical geo-location to where a network can be connected. Or:

POST OFFICE PROTOCOL (POP): The email retrieval standard by which email messages are downloaded and manipulated on a computer.

PORTAL: This is the main point of entry to a website, synonymous with "Landing Page".

POSTING: A single message "posted" (entered) into a netword communication.

PREMIUM CATALOG: This is unique terminology used by Smashwords. It refers to the set of publishing platforms outside of Smashword's own store. To be included in the "catalog" you must upload very specialized file formatting in accordance with their massive "Style Guide". (Think Fiverr!)

PROTOCOL: Rules governing the sharing of information between two parties.

REDIRECT: This is where one URL sends visitors directly to a different URL.

REFLOWABLE TEXT: Electronically delivered books, ebooks, are formatted very differently from printed books. While print book text is rigidly fixed, reflowable text can shape-shift across any size reading device screen. This can be anything from a huge computer screen to the smallest iPhone. Readers can alter the font size and spacing to suit their personal needs.

REGISTRAR: A company offering domain registration services.

REGISTRY: The central URL authority for domain name extensions.

RESIDUAL EARNINGS: Affiliate programs where the merchant pays the affiliate commissions for all present and future customer purchases.

RETAILER: This is the company that sells your ebook directly on its websites, such as Amazon or the Smashwords store.

ROAS (RETURN ON ADVERTISING SPENDING): The revenue generated per dollar of advertising spent. An ROAS of "4" means you earned four dollars revenue for each dollar spent on advertising.

ROI (RETURN ON INVESTMENT): What you earn equated to everything you spent to earn it.

ROOT SERVER: Servers containing software and data necessary for locating name servers containing authoritative data for top level domains.

ROUTER: A hardware device that communicates with your computer to the network sending you the electronic internet information.

RTF: This is shot for Rich Text Format. It is a format that permits any word processor to open your book, and allows manipulation of the fonts before printing (something that a .pdf file does not permit).

SALES LETTER: The text on a website designed to entice a visitor to make a purchase.

SEARCH ENGINE: A system for looking up information on the web. (Google is the best-known search engine.)

SEARCH ENGINE OPTIMIZATION (SEO): This is the practice of designing websites so that they rank as high as possible in search results made on search engines.

SECURE HTTP (SHTTP): An HTTP protocol that uses encryption to protect the traffic between the Server and Browser.

SECURE SOCKETS LAYER (SSL): A website encryption (evidenced by a "Certificate") that can be purchased that enables absolutely data-secure transactions between browsers and servers.

SENDER SCORE: A 0 – 100 rating of how easy it is to get email to a particular in-box.

SERVERS: These are specially- networked computers that handle client requests including Web pages, data, email, file transfers and more.

SERVER SIDE INCLUDES (SSI): Special files that instruct servers to add dynamic information (e.g., time countdown) to a webpage before it is sent to a viewer.

SHARED HOSTING: A system in which multiple clients and websites share a single server. Each account has specific limits on how much space they get and how much data they can transfer. This is the most basic and affordable type of hosting. The downside is if one client manages to crash the servers you go down with them!

SHOPPING CART: Software that lets website visitors select, add and remove products and pay for them online. This software can automatically calculate extra price considerations, such as tax and shipping. It then sends all of the information to the merchant once the transaction is complete.

SIDELOAD: This refers to copying a file directly from your desktop or laptop computer hard drive, or a flash drive, directly to an electronic reading device.

SIMPLE MAIL TRANSFER PROTOCOL (STMP): A way to transfer email messages from server to server.

SITE BUILDER: An application offered by most hosting service providers. It allows you to create a website from scratch based on predesigned templates without requiring knowledge of HTML. The finished sites then run on the host's servers and can be accessed and used through any Web browser.

SITE MAP: A file on a website page that has links to everywhere else on the website.

SMASHWORDS SATELLITES: This is a series of narrowly focused ebook sites operated by Smashwords. They are intended to facilitate buyer search by narrowing their search parameters.

SOFT BOUNCE: A failed email delivery due to a temporary matter such as a full in-box or busy server.

SPAM: Unsolicited email, generally containing advertising. **SPYWARE:** Software secretly installed on your computer that is used to provide a third party with your personal information.

SQUEEZE PAGE: The first page of a website a visitor sees if the intent is to gather an email address before the visitor reads the Sales Letter.

STATIC IP: A unique and unchanging IP address given to a website by the hosting provider.

STREAMING: The playing of audio or video files without executing a full download.

STRUCTURED QUERY LANGUAGE (SQL): A programming lannnguage cooommonly employed to update and perform queries on databases.

SUBDOMAINS: These are third-level domains, addresses that replace the typical "www". This sends visitors to special URL (i.e. subdomain.website.com) that requests data from a different directory within the original website.

SUPER AFFILIATE: The best performing affiliates. It is reported that 1% of all affiliates are responsible for 90% of all affiliate commissions.

SUPPORT: Technical help provided by Web hosting companies, usually via phone or email, to correct any problems that customers may encounter.

SURFING: The act of looking for information on the web.

TABLE OF CONTENTS: Often referred to as the "TOC" it provides the reader with a summary of your chapter headings. In ebooks this TOC must be formatted in such a way that a reader can click on a chapter name in the TOC and be taken directly to the start of that chapter.

TARGETED MARKETING: Offering the right product to the right buyer at the right moment.

TCP/IP: Stands for Transmission Control Protocol/Internet Protocol. This is a suite of software protocols universally used by every kind of computing system.

TELNET: Standard internet protocol for accessing remote systems.

TERMINAL: Generic for a hardware device (e.g., your Personal Computer) that allows you to send commands to a remote computer.

TEXT LINK: A link with no graphical image.

TOP-LEVEL DOMAIN (TLD): The domain name element to the far right of the address (i.e. .com, .net or .org).

TRACKING CODE: Refers to the hidden tracking code to track sales conversions.

TROJAN HORSE: A form of malware or virus designed to obtain your personal information.

TRAFFIC: The data being transferred over a network, typically between the Browser and Server

TWITTER TWEET: A short message sent from one Twitter account to another.

TWITTER RETWEET: A tweet that is forwarded to another Twitter member.

UNIFORM RESOURCE LOCATOR (URL): This is your "domain name". It is the standard for giving the address of a resource on the World Wide Web that makes up your Web page's full unique address using alphanumeric characters.

UNIQUE CLICK: A click from a visitor counted only on the first visit by means of recording the visitor's IP address.

UNIX: The most popular operating system used for servers on the World Wide Web.

UNMANAGED HOSTING: This is a system whereby you own or lease your own server and are fully responsible for the management of it. This includes troubleshooting, maintenance, applications and security, and is not recommended for anyone who is not an industry professional.

UPTIME: The amount of time in a 24-hour period in which a system is active and able to service requests. Most hosts claim 99%+.

VIRALITY: This is a term with its roots in biology (i.e., viruses). It describes the spread of any data across the internet. This can be through word of mouth, or word of **mouse**! All of the social networking platforms, Facebook,

Twitter, MySpace, Pinterest, YouTube or whichever can, " as a virus can spread across the population", spread the word (both good and bad) about your book across the internet. Forums also do this as well. Many substitute the words "Auto-Effective Marketing" for "Viral Marketing" because of the negative implication of a virus!

VIRUS: A malicious program that infects your computer for the purpose of mining your data or corrupting your files.

WEB HOSTING: This is the service that provides a physical location, space and storage, connectivity and services for websites that allow your files to be accessed and viewed by internet users. Sites are created and then uploaded to a Web hosting service provider's server. Some services provided include email addresses, free site builders and databases, among many other things.

WEB MAIL: A service that facilitates sending, receiving and storing email messages.

WHITELIST: Opposite of "blacklist". A list of sender addresses that a recipient manually approves for delivery into their email in-box bypassing SPAM filters for those addresses.

WIKI: This is a kind of website within which the content can be edited and altered from the web browser in which it is being viewed.

WILDCARD DNS SETTING: When your domain name server setting points the following to your website: www.yourdomain.com; yourdomain.com; www.yoursubdomain.yourdomain.com, and yoursubdomain.yourdomain.com.

WORLD WIDE WEB (WWW): Often incorrectly used as a synonym for "the internet". It is the universe of all web servers that serve web pages to web browsers.

WORM: A self-replicating virus that alters or destroys specific programs.

XML (EXTENSIBLE MARKUP LANGUAGE): A general purpose code that differs from HTML in that it allows the user to define the mark-up elements. It is used in applications such as site maps and RSS feeds.

###

www.ingramcontent.com/pod-product-compliance
Lightning Source LLC
LaVergne TN
LVHW022300060326
832902LV00020B/3193